PENGUIN BOOKS

THE MAKING OF AN AFRICAN LEGEND:
THE BIAFRA STORY

Frederick Forsyth was born in 1938 in Ashford, Kent. He was educated at Tonbridge School and Granada University, Spain, before serving in the R.A.F. as a pilot from 1956 to 1958. For three and a half years he worked as a reporter on the Eastern Daily Press in Norfolk, then in 1961 he joined Reuters and was posted the following year, at the age of twenty-three, to Paris as foreign correspondent. He was subsequently sole correspondent in East Germany and Czechoslovakia and, after another period in Paris, he returned to London in 1965 to join the B.B.C. as a radio and television reporter. As assistant diplomatic correspondent he covered the Biafran side of the Biafra–Nigeria war from July until September in 1967, and in February 1968 he left the B.B.C. to return to Biafra; he reported on the war first as a freelance and later for the *Daily Express* and *Time* magazine. Frederick Forsyth, who speaks fluent French, German and Spanish, has travelled widely in Europe, the Middle East and Africa. He has also written *The Day of the Jackal*, *The Odessa File*, *The Dogs of War* and a novella, *The Shepherd*.

FREDERICK FORSYTH

THE MAKING OF
AN AFRICAN LEGEND:
THE BIAFRA STORY

PENGUIN BOOKS

Penguin Books Ltd, Harmondsworth, Middlesex, England
Penguin Books, 625 Madison Avenue, New York, New York 10022, U.S.A.
Penguin Books Australia Ltd, Ringwood, Victoria, Australia
Penguin Books Canada Ltd, 2801 John Street, Markham, Ontario, Canada L3R 1B4
Penguin Books (N.Z.) Ltd, 182–190 Wairau Road, Auckland 10, New Zealand

—

First published as *The Biafra Story* 1969
This edition, with new material, published under the present title 1977

—

—

Made and printed in Great Britain
by Richard Clay (The Chaucer Press) Ltd,
Bungay, Suffolk
Set in Linotype Times

Contents

Prologue

ONLY this prologue, and the epilogue at the very end of the book, are contemporary, being written specifically for the present edition in the early spring of 1976. Everything between the prologue and the epilogue dates from the year 1969, while the Nigeria–Biafra war was still in progress.

The great bulk of the manuscript was written during January 1969 in a small caravan parked by a roadside in the town of Umuahia, which was then the Biafran capital. It was written in conditions of intense, sweaty heat, and the writing was frequently interrupted by air raids as Russian-supplied MiG fighters, flown by Egyptians on behalf of Nigeria, screamed across the township strafing and rocketing whatever they could. During these raids one had to dive into a slit trench and wait until they went away.

This first manuscript was finished, apart from two chapters, in the last days of January, and I returned with it to London. By then I had spent two extended periods inside Biafra as a war correspondent; the first for the B.B.C., from 10 July 1967 to 10 September; the second, as a freelance, from 18 February 1968 until the end of January 1969. During these two periods I had personally witnessed most of what is narrated in Part Two of this book.

On returning to London I dug into contemporary archives to finish the two unfinished chapters, 'The Role of the British Government', and 'Refugees, Hunger and Help'. There were facts and figures for these two chapters that could not be obtained inside the Biafran enclave.

By early March 1969 I had finished the manuscript, which in those days brought the narrative up to the end of January 1969; obviously no further, since one could not see into the future. Accompanied by my agent, Bryan Hunt, I sought a publisher, and found him in Rob Hutchinson of Penguin Books.

The slim paperback was published on 26 June 1969 as a Penguin Special, with a print of 30,000 copies. In the interim I had returned to Biafra and made further notes which brought the narrative up to June 1969.

To my surprise, the book quickly sold out until copies were being unavailingly sought by those who wished to read it. Thus it was that in September Mr Hutchinson urged me to return again to Biafra and prepare for an addendum to the book, bringing the narrative even further up to date, to the end of 1969. The idea was for a reprint in the spring of 1970, or so I understood.

I returned therefore in October and stayed until the latter half of December, finally coming back to London in time for Christmas. Over the period up to 31 December I prepared an addendum to each of the chapters of the second part of the book, bringing the narrative to the end of 1969. In the interim, however, Mr Hutchinson had left Penguin to take up an academic post, a new man had taken his place, and in early January I was informed that a reprint was no longer intended.

Thus, for the present reissue, the narrative dealing with events between 1 February and 31 December 1969 was researched and written during that year, but never published before. From New Year 1970 until now it has lain in a drawer.

In fact, Biafra finally collapsed, or was bludgeoned into submission by a tidal wave of military hardware, mainly supplied by Britain, on 10 January 1970. The Biafran leader, General Ojukwu, departed into exile in the Republic of the Ivory Coast, whose President Houphouet-Boigny gave him asylum. Being by then an out-of-work reporter, I tried my hand at novel-writing and jotted down a tale called *The Day of the Jackal*.

When it was proposed to me in the last days of 1975 to reissue *The Biafra Story*, I read the book again. There were temptations to revise, re-edit and modernize the text; to temper the polemic, to mute the anger of the opinions.

I have not tampered with the script at all, simply adding this prologue and the epilogue for explanatory purposes. The book was controversial at the time of publication; the issue of Biafra was emotive, public concern was widespread. As regards the facts one may say this: although on original publication the book was examined by experts on West Africa at the behest of those who disagreed with the book's contents and wished to demolish it, the facts were never seriously contested. There are two errors of fact: one concerns a date which was wrong by twenty-four hours, the other an ambush at Abagana village where a typing error added an extra nought to the Nigerian casualties.

As for the opinions, on reflection I'll stick with them. The passage of time may mellow viewpoints, or expediency may change them. But nothing can or ever will minimize the injustice and brutality perpetrated on the Biafran people, nor diminish the shamefulness of a British government's frantic, albeit indirect, participation.

For better or worse, the story is the way I wrote it then. It does not say everything because one could not know everything. Other books have been written on the subject since 1970, which included more and better statistics, but they also include recollections by participants in the events, which I know to be different from what happened or what the participants said and thought at the time. Victors write history, and the Biafrans lost. Convenience changes opinions, and the memory of Biafra and what was done there remains inconvenient for many.

The following book therefore has this at least to recommend it: it remains the only contemporary narrative of Biafra from start to finish, written at the time and inside the Biafran enclave by a European eye-witness.

When I was a cub reporter on an English provincial newspaper, I came under the tutelage of a wonderful teacher, the chief reporter of the office. He impressed on me two maxims, 'Get the facts right', and 'Tell it the way it was'. In the following pages I have tried to tell it the way it was.

On its original appearance it was roundly condemned in certain areas and by certain circles. All those who condemned it had one thing in common: they were all in positions of power and authority, to wit, the establishment, or firmly on the side of the establishment. That, to me, is its own commendation.

Ireland, February 1976   FREDERICK FORSYTH

Preface

THIS book is not a detached account; it seeks to explain what Biafra is, why its people decided to separate themselves from Nigeria, how they have reacted to what has been inflicted on them. I may be accused of presenting the Biafran case; this would not be without justification. It is the Biafra story, and it is told from the Biafran standpoint. Nevertheless wherever possible I have sought to find corroborative evidence from other sources, notably those foreigners (largely British) who were in Biafra at the start of the war, and from those who stayed on like the magnificent group of Irish priests of the Holy Ghost Order in Dublin, or who came later, such as journalists, volunteers and relief workers.

Where views are expressed either the source is quoted or they are my own, and I will not attempt to hide the subjectivity of them. So far as I am concerned the disintegration of the Federation of Nigeria is not an accident of history but an inevitable consequence of it; the war that presently pits 14 million Biafrans against 34 million Nigerians is not a noble struggle but an exercise in futility; and the policy of the British Labour Government in supporting a military power clique in Lagos is not the expression of all those standards Britain is supposed to stand for, but the repudiation of them.

The Biafra Story is not a history in full detail of the present war; there is still too much that is not known, too many things that cannot yet be revealed, for any attempt to write the story of the war to be other than a patchy fabric.

Because it would be unreal to suppose that Biafra simply came into existence out of a vacuum on 30 May 1967, I begin by briefly recounting the history of Nigeria before the break-away. It is necessary to understand how Nigeria was formed by Britain out of irreconcilable peoples, how these peoples came to find that, following British rule, the differences among them, far from shrinking, became accentuated, and how the structure

9

left behind by the British was finally unable to contain the explosive forces confined within it.

Umuahia, Biafra, January 1969   FREDERICK FORSYTH

Part One: The Road to Partition

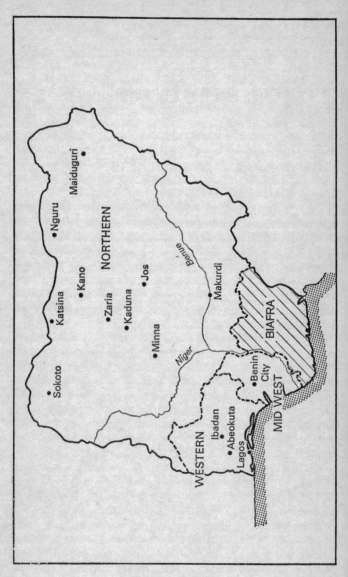

Nigeria and Biafra

1. The Background

ONE of the main complaints made against the policy of the Biafrans, and in support of the Nigerian war policy to crush them, is that the breakaway of Biafra wrecked the unity of a happy and harmonious state, which General Gowon of Nigeria is now trying to restore. In fact through all the years of the pre-colonial period Nigeria never was united, and during the sixty years of colonialism and the sixty-three months of the First Republic only a thin veneer hid the basic disunity.

By 30 May 1967, when Biafra seceded, not only was Nigeria neither happy nor harmonious, but it had for the five previous years stumbled from crisis to crisis, and had three times already come to the verge of disintegration. In each case, although the immediate spark had been political, the fundamental cause had been the tribal hostility embedded in this enormous and artificial nation. For Nigeria had never been more than an amalgam of peoples welded together in the interests and for the benefit of a European Power.

The first Europeans to make their appearance in today's Nigeria were travellers and explorers, whose tales brought slave-traders in their wake. Starting around 1450 with the Portuguese, this motley collection of freebooters bought healthy young slaves from the native kings of the coast for resale. At first they were exchanged for gold in the Gold Coast, later shipped to the New World at a handsome profit. After the Portuguese came the French, Dutch, Danes, Swedes, Germans, Spaniards and the British.

While the European slavers made private fortunes, several dynasties were founded on the African side and flourished on the profits from the role of middleman, notably at Lagos Island and Bonny Island. Penetration by the Europeans into the interior was discouraged by the coastal kings. Gradually other commodities were added to the slave trade, mostly palm oil, timber and ivory. In 1807 the British outlawed slaving and for the rest of the first half of that century British naval com-

13

manders supervised the coastal trading to ensure that the ban was effective.

Faced with the Hobson's choice of concentrating on other commodities, the traders saw little reason in continuing to pay money to the native potentates, and urged for permission to press inland and deal directly with the producers. This caused great friction with the coastal kings. By 1850 a series of British consuls held office along the coast, and penetration had already started to the north of Lagos, in what is today Western Nigeria.

The most notable of these traders was Sir George Goldie. This colourful pioneer had, by 1879, succeeded in uniting the British merchants along the coast into a fighting front, not against the Africans but against the French who were their more natural rivals.

He and the local consul, Hewett, wanted the British Government to step in and declare the area of the Oil Rivers and the Lower Niger a British colony. The Liberal British Government, however, demurred, believing colonies in such places to be an expensive waste of time. Although this government had rejected the recommendation of the 1875 Royal Commission on West Africa which called for withdrawal from existing colonies, it did not seem willing to set up any more. So for five years Goldie waged a two-front struggle – on the one hand against the French traders whom he had finally bought out under pressure by 1884, and on the other against apathy in Whitehall.

But the mood in Europe changed in 1884. Germany's Chancellor Bismarck, having previously been as lukewarm as Gladstone to the idea of West African colonies, called the Berlin Conference. In the same year Germany annexed the Cameroons, lying to the east of present-day Biafra. The point of the conference was ostensibly to enable Bismarck to back French and Belgian demands for a cessation of British activities in the Congo basin – activities being carried out by Baptist missionaries and merchants from Manchester and Liverpool. In this he got his way; the conference declared the Belgians' Congo Free State to be the authority administering the Congo. Not wishing to push Franco-German collaboration too far, the conference had little hesitation in permitting Britain to be responsible for the Niger River. Goldie attended the conference as an observer.

The result of all this was the Berlin Act, which provided that any European country which could show that it had a predominant interest in any African region would be accepted as the administering power in that region, *providing it could show that its administration was a reality*.

But the British were still unwilling to saddle themselves with another colony. Accordingly Goldie's company was in 1886 granted a 'charter of administration'. For the next ten years Goldie pushed north, establishing a monopoly of trade in his wake, flanked by the Germans in the Cameroons on his right hand and the French in Dahomey on his left. Of the two Goldie feared the French more, the latter being led by the energetic Faidherbe whom Goldie suspected of wanting to cut across from Dahomey to Lake Chad and link up with other French interests moving north from Gabon. In 1893, largely by his own efforts, Goldie managed to persuade the Germans in the Cameroons to extend northwards to Lake Chad, foiling the French link-up and buffering his eastern flank. But by this time the French under Faidherbe had conquered all Dahomey and were pushing eastwards into present-day Nigeria.

Goldie had neither the men nor the resources to keep them out, and sent heartfelt appeals to London. In 1897 the British Government sent out Sir Frederick Lugard, a soldier and administrator who had seen service in Uganda and Nyasaland. Within a year Lugard had pushed the French out of Nigeria and war with France threatened. The Niger crisis was settled by the Anglo-French agreement of June 1898, which established the basis for the new country's borders.

Britain had gained a colony. It had not been conquered, it had not really been explored. It had no name, so later Lady Lugard gave it one – Nigeria.

It was a land of great climatic, territorial and ethnic variety. From the four-hundred-mile-long coast of tangled swamp and mangrove a belt of dense rain-forest ran inland to a depth of between a hundred and a hundred and fifty miles. This land, later to become Southern Nigeria, was split into an eastern and a western portion by the Niger River flowing south from its confluence with the Benue River at Lokoja. In the western part of the south the predominant group was the Yoruba, a people with a long history of highly developed kingdoms. Because of the British penetration through Lagos, Western culture first reached the Yoruba and the other tribes of the West.

In the eastern part of the south lived a variety of peoples, predominant among them the Ibos, who lived on both banks of the Niger, but mainly east of it. Ironically, in view of their later speedy development and progress which finally enabled them to overtake the other ethnic groups of Nigeria in terms of European-style development, the Ibos and the other peoples of the East were regarded as being more backward than the rest in 1900.

North of the forest line was the woodland, verging into savannah grass and prairie, and finally to semi-desert and scrub. Along the southern fringe of this enormous area runs the Middle Belt, inhabited by numerous non-Hausa peoples, mainly pagan and animist in religion, who were nevertheless vassals of the Hausa/Fulani Empire. The North proper was the land of the Hausa, the Kanuri and the Fulani, the latter having originally come south from the Sahara in conquest, bringing with them their Muslim religion.

Lugard spent three years subduing the North, conquering with his tiny force one emirate after another. The stiffest opposition was provided by the sultanate of. Sokoto. Despite the greater numbers of the Fulani armies Lugard was able to depend on superior firepower, as expressed by Belloc in the couplet: 'Whatever happens we have got/The Maxim gun, and they have not.' Lugard's repeating-guns cut the Sultan's cavalry to pieces, and the last bastion of the Fulani empire in Hausa-land fell.

Lugard forms the bridge between the haphazard trail-breaking of the merchants and missionaries and bona fide imperialism. Yet his was not the first empire in Northern Nigeria. Between 1804 and 1810 Usman Dan Fodio, a Muslim scholar and reformer, had led a *jihad* (holy war) against the Hausa kingdoms, and had subjected them to his Fulani kinsmen. What started as a crusade to clean up irreligious practices in Islam turned into a move for land and power. The Fulani

Empire swept southwards into the land of the Yoruba. The movement of the *jihad* was stopped between 1837 and 1840 by the northward move of the British up from Lagos and came to rest at Ilorin and along the Kabba Line. Everything north of this line became Northern Nigeria, occupying three fifths of the land area of all Nigeria and having over fifty per cent of the population. The enormous preponderance of the North became one of the factors that later condemned the viability of a truly balanced Federation.

During Lugard's wars against the Emirs, the latter were largely unsupported by their Hausa subjects who comprised, and still do, the great majority of the people of the North. Yet when he had won, Lugard opted to keep the Emirs in power and rule through them, rather than to sweep them away and rule directly. It may be that he had no choice; his forces were small, the attitude of London indifferent, the area to be ruled was vast and would have required hundreds of administrators. By contrast, the Emirs had a nation-wide administrative, judicial and fiscal structure already in place. Lugard chose to permit the Emirs to continue to rule as before (subject to certain reforms) and maintained for himself only a remote overlordship.

Indirect rule had its advantages. It was cheap in terms of British manpower and investment; it was peaceful. But it also fossilized the feudal structure, confirmed the repression by the privileged Emirs and their appointees, prolonged the inability of the North to graduate into the modern world, and stultified future efforts to introduce parliamentary democracy.

Lugard's idea seems to have been that local government would start at the village council level, graduate to the tribal council, from there to the regional level, and finally produce a representative national government. It was a neat theory and it failed.

For one thing the concern of the Emirs and their courts, like that of most feudal potentates, was to remain in power in conditions as unchanging as possible. To this end they set themselves against the biggest challenge to their own conservatism – change and progress. The obvious forerunner of these two is mass-education. It was no accident that in Independence Year

17

1960 the North with over half of Nigeria's 50-million population had 41 secondary schools against the South's 842; that the North's first university graduate qualified just nine years before independence. Western education to the Emirs was dangerous, and they did their utmost to confine it to their own offspring or those of the aristocracy.

By contrast the South, invaded by missionaries, the precursors of mass-education, soon developed an avid thirst for education in all its forms. By 1967 when the Eastern Region pulled out of Nigeria it alone had more doctors, lawyers and engineers than any other country in Negro Africa. Missionary work in the North which might have eased that area into the twentieth century was effectively stopped by Lugard at the request of the Emirs when he pledged to discourage Christian apostolic work north of the Kabba Line.

In the sixty years from Lugard to Independence the differences in religious, social, historical and moral attitudes and values between North and South, and the educational and technological gap, became not steadily narrower but wider, until the viability of a united country which would be dominated by either area became impracticable.

In 1914 Lord Lugard amalgamated the North and the South as an act of administrative convenience – on paper at least. 'To cause the minimum of administrative disturbance' (his own phrase) he kept the enormous North intact, and the two administrations separate. Yet he also imposed the indirect-rule theory that he had found worked so well in the North on the South, where it failed, notably in the eastern half of the South, the land of the Ibos.

The British were so concerned with the idea of regional chiefs that where there were not any they tried to impose them. The Aba Riots of 1929 (Aba is in the heartland of the Ibo) were partly caused by resentment against the 'warrant chiefs', men imposed as chiefs by the British but whom the people refused to accept. It was not difficult to impose measures on the Northerners, accustomed to implicit obedience, but it did not work in the East. The whole traditional structure of the East makes it virtually immune to dictatorship, one of the reasons for the present war. Easterners insist on being consulted in

18

everything that concerns them. This assertiveness was hardly likely to endear itself to the colonial administrators and is one of the reasons why the Easterners came to be referred to as 'uppity'. By contrast the English loved the North; the climate is hot and dry as opposed to the steamy and malarial south; life is slow and graceful, if you happen to be an Englishman or an Emir; the pageantry is quaint and picturesque; the people obedient and undemanding. Unable to run the newly installed offices and factories, the Northerners were content to import numerous British officials and technicians – one of the reasons why today there is a vigorous and vociferous pro-Nigeria lobby of ex-colonial civil servants, soldiers, and administrators in London for whom Nigeria is their beloved Northern Region.

But the gaps in society caused by Northern apathy towards modernization could not be filled by the British alone. There were posts for clerks, junior executives, accountants, switchboard operators, engineers, train drivers, waterworks superintendents, bank tellers, factory and shop staff, which the Northerners could not fill. A few, but only a very few, Yorubas from the Western Region of the South went north to the new jobs. Most were filled by the more enterprising Easterners. By 1966 there were an estimated 1,300,000 Easterners, mostly Ibos, in the Northern Region, and about another 500,000 had taken up jobs and residence in the West. The difference in the degree of assimilation of each group was enormous and gives an insight into the 'oneness' of Nigeria under the public-relations veil.

In the West the Easterners' assimilation was total; they lived in the same streets as the Yoruba, mixed with them on all social occasions, and their children shared the same schools. In the North, at the behest of the local rulers, to which the British made no demur, all Southerners, whether from East or West, were herded into *Sabon Garis,* or Strangers' Quarters, a sort of ghetto outside the walled towns. Inside the *Sabon Garis* ghetto life was lively and spirited, but their contact with their Hausa compatriots was kept at the wish of the latter to a minimum. Schooling was segregated, and two radically different societies coexisted without any attempt by the British to urge gradual integration.

The period from 1914 to 1944 can be passed over briefly, for British interests during those years had little to do with Nigeria. First there was the Great War, then ten years of British reconstruction, then the Slump. Nigeria got out of this a brief period of prosperity when her raw materials sold well in the arms race before the Second World War. During this period Britain's colonial policy remained traditional and orthodox: maintain law and order, stimulate the production of raw materials, create demand for British exports, and raise taxes to pay for colonial rule. It was only in the fifteen years between 1945 and 1960, and notably in the last ten years of that period, that a serious attempt was made to find a formula for post-independence. This attempt got off to a disastrously bad start and never quite recovered. The bad start was called the Richards Constitution.

In 1944–5 the Governor Sir Arthur Richards, now Lord Milverton, a man who (according to contemporary descriptions), despite his deep love of the North, managed to make himself unpopular, made a tour of the country sounding out local opinion about constitutional reform. It was the North that made it quite clear, and has maintained this attitude ever since, that it did not want amalgamation with the South. The North agreed to go along only on the basis that (1) the principle of separate regional development should be enshrined in the new constitution, and that (2) the North should have nearly fifty per cent of the seats in the legislature (North 9, West 6, East 5).

The opposition of the North to amalgamation with the South, given voice in numerous statements by their leaders ever since, was in 1947 (the year of the inauguration of the Richards Constitution) expressed by one of the Northern members, Mallam Abubakar Tafawa Balewa, later to become Prime Minister of Nigeria. He said, 'We do not want, Sir, our Southern neighbours to interfere in our development. ... I should like to make it clear to you that if the British quitted Nigeria now at this stage the Northern people would continue their interrupted conquest to the sea.'

From a unitary state, ruled by a central legislative authority, Nigeria became a three-region federal state in 1947. Since the war started between Nigeria and Biafra, Lord Milverton in the Lords has been an advocate of Nigerian unity, apparently oblivious of the fact that it was his constitution which watered the seeds of regionalism, the disease which killed Nigeria. The three-regional state was the worst of all possible worlds once the attitude of the North had been ascertained; an attempted marriage of the irreconcilables.

It was the North which in a sense was the most realistic. Northern leaders made no secret of their separatist wish. After Richards came Sir John Macpherson who introduced a new virtually unitary constitution. But the damage had been done. The North had learned that it could get its way by threatening to pull out of Nigeria (thus sending shivers down the British spine), and the Macpherson Constitution yielded to a fresh one in 1954.

During the various regional conferences summoned by Macpherson during 1949, the Northern delegates claimed fifty per cent representation for the North at the Central Government, and at the General Conference at Ibadan in January 1950 the Emirs of Zaria and Katsina announced that 'unless the Northern Region is allotted fifty per cent of the seats in the Central legislature, it will ask for separation from the rest of Nigeria on the arrangements existing before 1914'. They got their wish, and Northern domination of the centre became an inbuilt feature of Nigerian politics.

The North also demanded and obtained the loosest possible form of Federation, and made no secret of their deep conviction that the amalgamation of North and South in 1914 was an error. The expression of that conviction runs right through Northern political thinking from the end of the Second World War to Independence. In March 1953 the Northern political leader Sir Ahmadu Bello told the House in Lagos: 'The mistake of 1914 has come to light, and I should like it to go no further.'

In his autobiography *My Life* Bello recalled the strong agitation for secession by the North and added that 'it looked very tempting'. He admits he decided against it on two grounds, neither having any connexion with the ideal of Nigerian Unity that possessed the British. One factor was the difficulty of collecting customs-duties along a land border, the other the unreliability of access to the sea through a neighbouring independent country.

By the time of the 1953 conferences which yielded the fourth constitution, the North had modified its views on separatism to 'a structure which would give the regions the greatest possible freedom of movement and action; a structure which would reduce the powers of the Centre to the absolute minimum'.

About these ideas the London *Times* commented on 6 August 1953: 'The Northerners have declared that they want a simple agency at the centre, and are apparently thinking on the lines of some organization like the East African High Commission. But even the High Commission is linked to a Central Assembly, whereas the Northern Nigerians have declared that there shall be no central legislative body.'

What the Northerners were demanding, and apparently with the will of the overwhelming body of Northern opinion behind them, was a Confederation of Nigerian States. This was what Colonel Ojukwu, Military Governor of the Eastern Region, asked for at Aburi, Ghana, on 4 January 1967, after 30,000 of the Eastern people had been killed and 1,800,000 driven back to the East as refugees. Even then, he only asked for it as a temporary measure while tempers cooled. If the Northerners had got their wish in 1953, or the Easterners in 1967, it is likely that the three Regions would today be living in peace.

Again the British gave way to Northern isolationist demands, but failed to see the danger in the North's unwillingness to integrate. So a British compromise prevailed. It was the Southerners who wanted a state with several regions in it to give the forthcoming federation a political equilibrium. The British Government argued for three – North, West and East, the most unstable option of them all, but also the wish of the North. Two other phenomena during the last decade of pre-independence are worth looking at, inasmuch as they indicate Britain's refusal to take note of warnings about Nigeria's future stability, even when those warnings came from their own civil servants. Throughout the decade Northern speeches and writings revealed a steadily growing dislike of the Easterners in their midst. Time and again speakers in the Northern House

22

voiced their deep conviction that 'the North was for the Northerners' and that the Southerners should go home. (Most of these Southerners were from the East.) Sporadic violence against Easterners had occurred in the past, notably during the bloody Jos Riots of 1945.

In May 1953 a delegation from the Action Group, the leading Yoruba political party, was due to visit Kano, the largest city of the North. Intense fomentation of public opinion against the visit was undertaken by Mallam Inua Wada, Kano Branch Secretary of the Northern People's Congress. In a speech two days before their scheduled arrival Wada told a meeting of section heads of the Native Administration: 'Having abused us in the South these very Southerners have decided to come over to the North to abuse us. . . . We have therefore organized about a thousand men ready in the city to meet force with force. . . .' The Action Group's visit was cancelled, but on 16 May a series of massacres began. Failing to find Yorubas the Hausas set about the Easterners with what the official report compiled by a British civil servant termed 'a universally unexpected degree of violence'.

In his autobiography Sir Ahmadu recalls that 'Here in Kano, as things fell out, the fighting took place between the Hausas . . . and the Ibos; the Yorubas were oddly enough out of it.'

The official report was a conscientious effort. The rapporteur condemned Wada's speech as 'very ill-advised and provocative'. Of the conservative estimates of 52 killed and 245 wounded, he comments that 'there is still a possibility that more were killed than have been recorded, in view of conflicting statements by ambulance- and lorry-drivers [who carted away the living and the dead]'. Of the whole affair he observed that 'no amount of provocation, short-term or long-term can in any sense justify their [Hausas] behaviour'. But perhaps his most notable utterance was in the conclusion: 'The seeds of the trouble which broke out in Kano on 16 May 1953 have their counterparts still in the ground. *It could happen again,* and only a realization and acceptance of the underlying causes can remove the danger of recurrence.' There was no realization, nor any attempt at one.

In 1958 the British, while studying the question of the minority tribes – that is, the people who are not members of the 'Big Three', the Hausa, the Ibo and the Yoruba – asked Sir Henry Willinck to conduct a survey and make his recommendations. Of the Eastern Region, now divided into three by Lagos' unilateral decision in 1967, Sir Henry found that the difference between the Ibo and the non-Ibo minorities was sufficiently slight to be soon expunged by the growing nationalism. Oddly, it *has* largely been expunged, not by Nigerian nationalism but by common suffering at the hands of Nigerians, and by Biafran nationalism.

Another observation of Sir Henry Willinck concerning the East was that Port Harcourt, the Region's biggest city, was largely an Ibo city. In the pre-colonial period it had been a small town inhabited by the Rivers peoples, but in the intervening time it had grown to a flourishing city and port, mainly on the strength of Ibo trading enterprise and initiative. Inside the city Ibos and non-Ibos lived peacefully side by side. In May 1967 when the Government of General Gowon in Lagos decided unilaterally to divide Nigeria into twelve new states, three of these were carved out of the East, and Port Harcourt was named to be the capital of the Rivers State, which caused an even greater sense of outrage east of the Niger.

After the 1954 constitution, there were a further five years of negotiations about the future form of Nigeria, and a fifth constitution. On 1 October 1960 Nigeria stumbled into independence, loudly hailed from within and without as a model to Africa, but regrettably as stable behind the gloss as a house of cards. None of the basic differences between North and South had been erased, nor the doubts and fears assuaged, nor the centrifugal tendencies curbed. The hopes, aspirations and ambitions of the three Regions were still largely divergent, and the structure that had been devised to encourage a belated sense of unity was unable to stand the stresses later imposed upon it.

Mr Walter Schwarz, in his book *Nigeria*, commented: 'The product which emerged from a decade of negotiations between government and governed was far from satisfactory. Nigeria became independent with a federal structure which, within two years, was shaken by an emergency and, within five, had broken down in disorder, to be finally overthrown by two military coups and a civil war.'*

The new constitution was a highly intricate assemblage of checks and balances, rights and guarantees, too Utopian to withstand the ruthless power struggle that soon after independence began to seethe inside Nigeria.

In Africa as elsewhere political power means success and prosperity, not only for the man who holds it but for his family, his birthplace and even his whole region of origin. As a result there are many who will go to any lengths to get it and, having got it, will surpass themselves in order to keep it. The pre-independence 1959 election gave a taste of things to come, with Southern candidates in the North being intimidated in their election campaigns. This election was the last in which the electoral and returning officers were mainly British civil servants, who did the best they could. In subsequent elections ballot-rigging and thuggery became more or less the order of the day.

Nevertheless the 1959 election gave Nigeria a government. The pattern of the power struggle that was to follow was already established, and followed very closely the lines of regionalism laid down by the ill-fated Richards Constitution twelve years earlier. The East was dominated by the National Council of Nigerian Citizens (NCNC) party, headed by Dr Nnamdi Azikiwe, pioneer of West African nationalism and a long-time struggler (albeit a peaceful one) for Nigerian independence. In its early days the NCNC had had the makings of a truly national party, but the rise of other parties with a wholly regional rather than political appeal following the Richards Constitution had driven it more and more into the East. Nevertheless Azikiwe himself still preferred the more pan-Nigerian atmosphere of Lagos, although he had been by independence already five years Prime Minister of the East.

The West was dominated by Chief Awolowo's Action Group party, whose appeal was strongly and almost exclusively Yoruba. He had been for five years Premier of the West.

The North was the bailiwick of the Northern People's Con-

* Walter Schwarz, *Nigeria*, London, 1968, p. 86.

25

gress (NPC) whose leader was the Sardauna of Sokoto, Sir Ahmadu Bello. This triangular balance of power had already existed for five years since the 1954 election in which the NPC and the NCNC in a coalition with 140 out of 184 seats had put Awolowo's Action Group into opposition.

The 1959 election repeated the process; in an expanded Chamber, the NPC held the North with 148 seats, the NCNC held the East and a chunk of the West (mostly those non-Yoruba parts now called the Midwest) gaining 89 seats, and the Action Group took most of the Yoruba-speaking West but gained only 75 seats. Although none of the parties held a clear majority, any coalition of two could put the third into opposition. After some behind-the-scenes wheeling and dealing the NPC clinched the deal with the NCNC and continued as before, with Awolowo consigned to another five years of helpless opposition.

Already in 1957 after the last of the constitutional conferences a Federal Prime Minister had been appointed. He was Alhaji Sir Abubakar Tafawa Balewa, a Hausa, deputy leader of the NPC and up till that time Minister of Transport. There was no surprise that Sir Ahmadu, leader of the majority NPC, who could have had the post for himself, refused to come south and head the country. As he himself said he was quite content to send his 'lieutenant' to do the job. The phraseology indicates the future relationship between the Federal Prime Minister and the Premier of the North, and where the real seat of power lay.

It was in this form that Nigeria entered into a shaky independence. Shortly afterwards Dr Azikiwe was appointed the first Nigerian Governor-General, and the premiership of the East passed to his Number Two, Dr Michael Okpara. In the West Chief Akintola had already taken over from Awolowo as Premier while the latter headed the Opposition in the Federal Chamber. The Sardauna stayed on as lord of the North.

The brief history of Nigeria under parliamentary rule has already been well documented. What seems to emerge from all the accounts, although it is seldom so expressed, is that the traditional form of parliamentary democracy worked out in Whitehall proved to be unsuitable to the existing ethnic group

26

structure, incomprehensible even to its local practitioners, inapposite to African civilization and impracticable in an artificially created nation where group rivalries, far from being expunged by the colonial power, had been exacerbated on occasion as a useful expedient to indirect rule.

Within twelve months of independence a split developed in the Action Group, as may only be expected in a party already six years in opposition and destined to another four years. Part of the Group supported Awolowo and the others Akintola. In February 1962 the party's convention supported Awolowo and the parliamentary party declared Akintola guilty of maladministration, asking that he be removed from the premiership.

In response to this request the Governor of the West dismissed Akintola and appointed an Awolowo supporter called Adegbenro to form a new government for the Western Region. Akintola replied by appealing to the Federal Premier in a rather roundabout way. In the Western House of Assembly he and his supporters started a riot which police finally had to clear with tear gas. Premier Balewa in Lagos was able with his majority to push through a motion declaring a state of emergency in the West, despite the protests of Awolowo. Balewa then appointed an Administrator for the West, with powers to detain persons, and suspended the Governor. As luck would have it the Administrator was a friend of Balewa. Restriction orders were placed on Awolowo, Adegbenro and Akintola, who promptly formed a new party, the United Peoples Party (UPP).

The next step of Awolowo's opponents was to institute an inquiry into corruption in the West. It was a useful weapon, and not difficult to prove, either in the West or anywhere else.

Corruption in public life was no new thing; it had been present under the British and had flowered alarmingly after independence. The 'ten per cent' that Ministers habitually required of foreign firms before granting them lucrative contracts, the holding of stock in businesses subsequently singled out for preferential fiscal treatment, down to the open bribing of Native Court officials and policemen, was the order of the day. Few ministers held power who did not make a profitable thing out of it, partly no doubt from simple cupidity, partly also because any man of power was expected to maintain a large retinue, fix his forthcoming re-election, and shower benefits on his home town. Along with simple financial corruption went nepotism, thuggery and ballot-rigging.

The Coker Commission had little trouble showing vast channelling of public money, largely through the government-controlled Marketing Board and the National Investment and Properties Company, into party funds and subsequently to private use. Chief Awolowo and one of his lieutenants Chief Anthony Enahoro came in for publicity during this inquiry that gave an indication of their attitude towards the responsibilities of public life. Both men now occupy high positions in the Nigerian Government once again.

Between the date of regional self-government in 1956 and the inquiry in 1962 the Coker Commission disclosed that £10 million had found their way into the Action Group's coffers, the sum representing thirty per cent of revenue over that period. Oddly, Chief Akintola, who had been premier since 1959 when Awolowo went to the Federal Chamber in Lagos, was found to have had no part in these defalcations.

Whether any court procedure against the leading members of the Awolowo faction would have taken place in the wake of the Commission is open to conjecture. At any rate the affair was overtaken by events. Towards the end of 1962 Awolowo and Enahoro were charged among others with treason.

The trial was a tortuous affair lasting eight months. The prosecution claimed Awolowo and Enahoro had imported arms and trained volunteers for a coup scheduled for 23 September 1962, when the Governor-General, the Prime Minister and other leading figures were to have been arrested while Awolowo took over and announced himself Prime Minister of Nigeria. The defence was that the atmosphere of violence and fear which had prevailed in the West since independence made such precautions advisable. Awolowo was sentenced to ten years in prison, reduced on appeal to seven, and Enahoro, after repatriation from Britain and a subsequent separate trial, to fifteen years, reduced on appeal to ten. The Judge of Appeal who reduced Enahoro's sentence was

Sir Louis Mbanefo, later Chief Justice of Biafra. Judge and jailbird met again when they faced each other at the Kampala peace talks in May 1968, each heading his country's delegation.

The affair enabled Akintola to consolidate his hold on the West despite a Privy Council ruling from London in May 1963 that his dismissal from the premiership by the Governor had been valid. Akintola's protector, the Federal premier Balewa, described the findings of the Judicial Committee of the Privy Council as 'unsound and out of touch with reality'. The same year appeals to the Privy Council were abolished and another safeguard passed into history.

The Awolowo trial in its latter stages had to vie as a scandal with the rigging of the national census. The previous census in 1953–4 had somehow been stigmatized by a presumption that it had to do with taxation purposes, and so many people managed to avoid being counted, particularly in the East, that the overall figure at that time of 30.4 million for the Federation was probably on average ten per cent low. The 1962 census was widely presumed to have something to do with representation at a political level, and the figures were consequently enlarged in all regions, notably in the East. The 1962 census cost £1.5 million and the figures were never published. Actually they purported to show that the population of the North had gone up thirty-three per cent in eight years to 22.5 million, while the South had gone up over seventy per cent to 23 million. This gave the whole of Nigeria a population of 45.5 million. Mr J. J. Warren, the British leader of the 45,000 enumerators who had done the head-count rejected the Southern figures as 'false and inflated'. This decision did not displease the Sardauna of Sokoto who was not amused to find the population of the South apparently dominating by half a million that of the North. He is reputed to have torn up the figures in disgust when they were shown to him, and to have ordered Balewa to try again. Another census was held in 1963, this time without the help of the sceptical Mr Warren.

Perhaps that was just as well, for he might well have had a fit if he had seen the preparation of the next set of figures under the personal supervision of Balewa. One morning in

February 1964 the Nigerians awoke to find that there were now 55.6 million of them, of which a fraction under 30 million were in the Northern Region.

Mr Warren had refused to accept the figures for the South the previous year for several reasons: among others because they showed at that time between three and four times more adult males than appeared on the tax register, and more children under five than all the women of childbearing age would have been able to produce if they had all been pregnant continuously for five years. He had accepted the figures for the North in that year because they seemed reasonable, showing a two per cent per annum growth rate over the previous census.

If the North was caught napping in 1962 it was wide awake in 1963. Boosting its population from 22.5 million to just under 30 million in one year, it managed a birthrate of twenty-four per cent per annum. The South, whose figures in 1962 had been for Mr Warren unbelievable, had gone up again, from 23 million to 25.8 million. Expatriate wits asked themselves if these figures included the sheep and goats, while Nigerian politicians hurled recriminations at each other, each refusing to accept the figures of the other half of the country. The population came to the view that the whole thing was another 'fix' and was probably right. More sober and realistic assessments put the total Nigerian population at about 47 million by the end of May 1967, of which Biafra (including the enormous reflux of refugees) detached about 13.5 million at the end of that month by declaring its own independence.

The census scandal gradually yielded to the general strike of 1964. All this time, and right up to the first military coup in January 1966, the Tiv Riots had been seething in that area of the Middle Belt where the Tivs had their traditional homeland. These tough, independent but largely backward tribesmen had long clamoured for a Middle Belt State, and were represented by the United Middle Belt Congress. But while NPC leaders made little objection to the carving of the Midwest Region out of the West in 1963 as a home for the non-Yoruba minorities they felt there was no need at all to perform the same service for the Tivs, seeing that the latter could politically be counted as Northerners. In consequence the army was sent in to crush

30

the Tiv revolts that occurred soon after independence, and stayed there until the military coup of 1966. Most of these army units were from the predominantly Northern-recruited First Brigade. Some army officers objected to the use of the army for putting down civil disturbances, but others sought to curry favour with their Northern politicians by being more royalist than the king in crushing the dissidents. However, the harder the Tivs were treated the harder they fought back, and by 1966 independent observers estimated that close to 3,000 people had died in these disturbances, over which a modest veil was drawn before the world.

Soon after the general strike came the 1964 general election. The ten-year alliance between the NPC and the NCNC was broken by Sir Ahmadu Bello, who announced baldly that 'the Ibos have never been true friends of the North and never will be'. With that he announced an alliance with Akintola, now firmly in the saddle in the West. It appears more likely that, knowing yet another alliance with one of the southern parties would be necessary to keep his lieutenant in power in Lagos, Bello found the heavily indebted Akintola a more pliable ally than Okpara. Thus Akintola merged his party with the Sardauna's NPC to form the Nigerian National Alliance (NNA), leaving the NCNC with no option but to make common cause with the rump of the Action Group, those of the party who had remained loyal to the imprisoned Awolowo. Between them they became the United Progressive Grand Alliance (UPGA)

The campaign was as dirty as it could possibly be (or so it was thought at the time, that is, until Akintola surpassed himself the following year during the Western Region elections). In the West the NNA electoral appeal was strongly racist in tone, pitched hard against alleged 'Ibo domination', and some of the campaign literature was reminiscent of the anti-Semitic exhortations of pre-war Germany. Dr Azikiwe, President of the Federation since Nigeria became a republic in 1963, appealed in vain for a fair election and warned of the dangers of tribal discrimination. In the North UPGA candidates were molested and beaten by NPC party thugs when they tried to campaign. In both North and West UPGA candidates complained they were either prevented from registering or that even after registration their NNA opponents were returned 'unopposed'. Up till the last minute it was in doubt whether there would be any election at all. In the end it went ahead, but the UPGA boycotted it. Not unnaturally the result was a win for the NNA.

President Azikiwe, unhappy about the constitutional position, nevertheless asked Balewa to form a broad-based national government, and a crisis was averted that might have broken the Federation in 1964. Eventually in February 1965 the Federal elections were belatedly held in the East and Midwest, where there was heavy voting for UPGA. The final figures were 197 for the National Alliance, and 108 for the UPGA.

This scandal had hardly abated when the preparations went ahead for the November 1965 elections in the Western Region. Here Akintola was defending his premiership and an appalling record of government. There seems little doubt that the general unpopularity of Akintola could well have led to a victory by the opposition UPGA if the elections had been fair. This would have given the UPGA control of the East, the Midwest (which they had already), the West and Lagos, a feat which would have entailed UPGA superiority in the Senate, even though the Northern/Western alliance would have continued to control the Lower House.

In all probability Akintola was aware of this, as he was also of the unalloyed support of the powerful and ruthless Ahmadu Bello in the North and of Balewa in the Federal premiership. Confident of impunity he went ahead with an election procedure that showed considerable ingenuity in failing to omit a single opportunity for scurrilous behaviour.

The UPGA, warned by the Federal election, got all their candidates' nominations accepted well in advance, and backed by sworn affidavits that all ninety-four intended to stand for election. Nevertheless sixteen Akintola men, including the premier himself, were declared as returned unopposed. Electoral officers disappeared, ballot papers vanished from police custody, candidates were detained, polling agents were murdered, new regulations were introduced at the last minute but only mentioned to Akintola candidates. While counting was going on UPGA agents and candidates were kept out of the counting houses by a number of means, the mildest of which was a curfew selectively applied by the Government-employed police. Almost miraculously a number of UPGA candidates were declared elected by the returning officers still at their posts. Instructions were given that all returns were to be routed through Akintola's office, and bemused listeners to the radio heard the Western radio under Akintola's orders giving out one set of figures, while the Eastern Region radio gave out another set, the latter figures coming from UPGA headquarters which had obtained them from the returning officers.

According to the Western government the result was seventy-one seats for Akintola and seventeen for the UPGA and Akintola was asked to form a government. The UPGA claimed it had actually won sixty-eight seats and that the election had been rigged, a contention observers had little difficulty in believing. Adegbenro, leader of the UPGA in the West, said he would go ahead and form his own Government. He and his supporters were arrested.

It was the signal for a complete breakdown of law and order, even if it could truly be said to have existed before. Rioting broke out across the length and breadth of the Western Region. Murder, looting, arson, mayhem were rife. On the roads gangs of rival thugs cut down trees, stopping motorists to ask for their political affiliations. The wrong answers brought robbery or death. Within a few weeks estimated deaths were between 1,000 and 2,000.

In the face of this, Balewa, who had been so fast to declare a state of emergency in 1962 because of an uproar in the Western House of Assembly, remained quiescent. Despite repeated appeals to him to declare an emergency, dissolve the Akintola government and order fresh elections, he declared he had 'no power'.

The mighty Federation of Nigeria was crumbling into ruin before the eyes of foreign observers who had only a few years before hailed Nigeria as the great hope of Africa. Yet to the outside world hardly a word of this penetrated. Indeed, anxious to keep up appearances Balewa's Government invited a Commonwealth Prime Ministers' conference to meet in Lagos in the first week of January 1966 to discuss the question of restoring law and order in rebellious Rhodesia. Mr Harold Wilson was pleased to attend. While Commonwealth premiers shook hands and beamed at each other on the apron of Ikeja International Airport, a few miles away Nigerians were dying in scores as the army moved in on the UPGA supporters.

The army could not restore order either, and at the insistence of the General Officer Commanding, Major-General Johnson Ironsi, the troops were withdrawn. The majority of the ordinary infantrymen at that time serving in the Federal Army were drawn from the Middle Belt, that is, the minority tribes of the North. These troops, particularly the Tivs who formed the highest percentage among them, could not be used to quell the Tiv riots still raging, for they would probably not have turned their guns on their own fellows. Thus most of the army units available outside Tiv-land were heavily salted with Tivs.

For the same reason that they could not be used in Tiv-land, they were not much use in the West either. Their sympathies lay not with the Akintola régime, for was not Akintola the ally and vassal of the Sardauna of Sokoto, persecutor of their own homeland? They tended to sympathize more with the rioters, being themselves in much the same position *vis-à-vis* the Sokoto/Akintola power group.

By the second week of January 1966 it had become clear that something had got to give. Subsequent painting by the present Nigerian military régime of what followed as an all-Ibo affair fails to take into account the inevitability of either a *démarche* from the army or complete anarchy.

On the night of 14 January, in the North, the West and the Federal capital of Lagos, a group of young officers struck. Within a few hours Sokoto, Akintola and Balewa were dead, and with them the First Republic.

At the time of Nigeria's independence, Britain was pleased to claim much of the credit for the seeming early success of the experiment; Britain cannot now avoid much of the responsibility for the failure, for Nigeria was essentially a British and not a Nigerian experiment. For years Whitehall's political thinking on Nigeria had been based on a resolute refusal to face the realities, an obstinate conviction that with enough pulling and shoving the facts can be made to fit the theory, and a determination to brush under the carpet all those manifestations which tend to discredit the dream. It is an attitude that continues to this day.

2. The Coup that Failed

Two coups were probably brewing during the first fortnight of 1966. The evidence for the one that did not occur is largely circumstantial; but subsequent assertions that the coup of 15 January baulked another coup scheduled for 17 January are certainly very plausible.

The other coup which was planned would have begun with a brief reign of terror in the Niger Delta of the Eastern Region, headed by a student at Nsukka University, Isaac Boro, who was supplied with funds for the purpose. This would have offered Prime Minister Balewa the chance of declaring a state of emergency in the East. Simultaneously, according to the charges later made in the West, units officered by Northerners were to carry out a 'ruthless blitz' against opposition (that is UPGA) elements in that region. The two-pronged action would have broken the UPGA opposition party, again reinforced Akintola in the premiership of a region which by now hated him, and left the Sardauna of Sokoto's NNA party in supreme control of Nigeria.

A number of moves were made which seem to give credence to this. On 13 January Sir Ahmadu Bello, who had been on a pilgrimage to Mecca, returned to his Northern capital Kaduna. The following day there was a secret meeting between him, Akintola who flew north for the day, and the Commanding Officer of the First Brigade, a pro-Akintola Western officer Brigadier Ademolegun. Previously the Federal Defence Minister, a NPC Northerner, had ordered the Army Commander Major-General Ironsi to take his accumulated leave; the Inspector-General of Police, Mr Louis Edet, another Easterner, was also ordered on leave; the Deputy Inspector-General, Mr M. Roberts, a Westerner, was sent into premature retirement to be replaced by the Hausa Alhaji Kam Salem, who would thus have been in control of the Federal Police by 17 January. The President, Dr Azikiwe, was in England on a health cure. If that was the plot, it failed because it was preceded by the other coup, plotted in equal secrecy by a small group of junior officers, led mainly though certainly not exclusively by men of Eastern origin.

In Kaduna the group leader was the left-leaning and highly idealistic Major Chukwuma Nzeogwu, an Ibo from the Mid-west Region who had lived all his life in the North and spoke Hausa better than Ibo. On the evening of the 14th this brilliant but erratic chief instructor at the Nigerian Defence Academy of Kaduna led a small detachment of soldiers, mostly Hausas, out of town ostensibly on routine exercises. When they arrived at Sir Ahmadu's splendid residence Nzeogwu told the soldiers they had come to kill the Sardauna. They made no demur. 'They had bullets. ... If they had disagreed, they could have shot me,' he said later.* They stormed the gate killing three of the Sardauna's guards and losing one of their own number in the process. Inside the compound they shelled the palace with mortars; then Nzeogwu tossed a hand grenade at the main door, coming too close in the process and injuring his hand. Once inside the Sardauna was shot along with two or three house servants. Elsewhere in Kaduna another group entered the house of Brigadier Ademolegun and shot him and his wife while in bed. A third group killed Colonel Shodeinde, the Yoruba second-in-command at the Defence Academy. With that the bloodshed in the North was over.

In the afternoon of 15 January Nzeogwu broadcast from Kaduna Radio, telling his listeners, 'Our enemies are the political profiteers, swindlers, men in high and low places that seek bribes and demand ten per cent, those that seek to keep the country permanently divided so that they can remain in office as Ministers and VIPs of waste, the tribalists, the nepotists, those that make the country look big for nothing before international circles.' Later he said privately: 'Our purpose was to change our country and make it a place we could be proud to call our home, not to wage war. ... Tribal considerations were completely out of our minds at this stage.'

In Lagos the coup was in the hands of Major Emmanuel Ifeajuana, a young Ibo who had had a taste of fame for his earlier performances as an athlete. Some hours after dark he

* *West Africa*, 29 January 1966.

drove into Lagos with several truckloads of troops from Abeokuta barracks. Small detachments went off all over Lagos seeking their objectives. Three senior army officers of Northern origin, Brigadier Maimalari, commanding the Second Brigade, Lieutenant-Colonel Pam, the Adjutant-General, and Lieutenant-Colonel Largema, commanding the Fourth Battalion, were killed, the first two at their homes and the third at the Ikoyi Hotel where he was staying. Major Ifeajuana himself went after the politicians. The Prime Minister, Balewa, was arrested at his home and bundled into the back of a Mercedes where he was made to lie on the floor. The Finance Minister, Chief Festus Okotie-Eboh, a Mid-Westerner who had made himself a byword for corruption and venality even in Nigerian politics, was shot at his home and his body dumped in the boot of the Mercedes. The troops also went after Dr Kingley Mbadiwe, the Ibo Minister of Trade, who escaped across open gardens and hid in the empty State House, home of the absent President Azikiwe. It was the one place the soldiers never thought of searching.

The last casualty in Lagos that night was another Ibo, Major Arthur Unegbu. He was in charge of the ammunition store at Ikeja Barracks, and was shot dead for refusing to hand over the keys of the armoury to the dissidents.

At Ibadan, capital of the West, the obvious target was the hated Akintola. Soldiers surrounding his house were met by a volley of automatic rifle fire. The Premier kept his own private arsenal. After storming the house, during which three soldiers were killed, Akintola was dragged out badly wounded and finished off. Elsewhere in Ibadan his Deputy Premier Chief Fani Kayode was arrested. As the soldiers dragged him away he cried, 'I knew that the army was going to come, but I did not know that was the way they would come'.

So far the coup had gone roughly according to plan. By the small hours the insurgent officers, if they had consolidated, could have claimed to control the capitals of the North, West, and Lagos, the Federal capital. Benin City, the capital of the tiny Midwest Region, seems to have been left out of their plan; not without reason, for the Midwest could have been taken later.

Even from eye-witnesses and participants, versions of what

exactly went wrong vary considerably; one can only try to draw some kind of coherent account from the varying impressions. Major Ifeajuana and his co-plotters in Lagos seem to have headed back towards Abeokuta in the Mercedes, dumping the bodies of Balewa and Okotie-Eboh on the way. It is still largely presumed that Balewa was shot, although one eye-witness has sworn he died of a heart-attack. The bodies were found on the Abeokuta road a week later.

Ifeajuana and his collaborator in Lagos, Major David Okafor, Commander of the Federal Guard, seem to have made the crass error of not leaving anyone of calibre in the Federal capital when they left. This was largely why the plot failed, coupled with the brisk action of the G.O.C., Major-General Ironsi.

The result was that when the Ibadan group swept into Lagos shortly after dawn with the body of Akintola and the trussed but living form of Fani-Kayode in the back of the car, the city had changed hands. The Ibadan group were arrested by soldiers loyal to Ironsi, and Fani-Kayode was freed.

Meanwhile Ifeajuana and Okafor realized there was no officer to take charge of Enugu, capital of the East and the last of the four cities they aimed to control. They then set off in the Mercedes, followed by a Volkswagen with some soldiers, for the 400-mile cross-country drive to Enugu.

One of the props for the idea that the coup of 15 January was an all-Ibo affair aimed at bringing about Ibo domination of Nigeria has always been that there was no coup in Enugu. The evidence does not support this theory. Troops of the First Battalion, garrisoning Enugu, moved against the Premier's Lodge at 2 a.m.; they surrounded it, but waited for orders before attacking the house and its occupants. The Commanding Officer, Lieutenant-Colonel Adekunle Fajuyi, a Yoruba, was away on a course; the second-in-command, Major David Ejoor, a Midwesterner, was in Lagos. The troops, not predominantly Ibo as has been suggested but largely Middle-Belt infantrymen from the Northern Region, crouched round the house as dawn rose and waited for orders. Meanwhile Ifeajuana and Okafor were speeding across country to give those orders.

No man did more to foil the coup than the Army G.O.C. Major-General Ironsi. Himself an Ibo from Umuahia, he had joined the army as a boy soldier and come up through the ranks. He was a big bull of a man, a thorough-going professional soldier who knew where his duty lay and stood no nonsense.

It seems he too was destined for death that night. Earlier he had been at a party given by Brigadier Maimalari and had gone on to another party on the mailboat Aureol, moored at Lagos docks. When he returned home after midnight his telephone was ringing. It was Colonel Pam, to say there was something afoot. Minutes later Pam was dead. Ironsi put down the phone as his driver, a young Hausa soldier, came in to say there were troops driving through the streets. Ironsi moved fast.

He jumped into his car and ordered the driver to take him straight to Ikeja barracks, the biggest barracks in the area and home of the Army Headquarters. He was stopped by a roadblock of Ifeajuana's soldiers who pointed their guns at him. Ironsi climbed out, stood up straight and roared 'GET OUT OF MY WAY'. They moved.

At Ikeja he headed for the regimental sergeant-major's quarters and rallied the garrison. From Ikeja he sent out a stream of orders throughout the morning. Troops loyal to him and the Government took over. Major Ejoor, reporting to him just before dawn, was ordered to get back to Enugu and resume command as fast as he could. Ejoor went to nearby Ikeja airport, took a light plane, and headed for Enugu airport. On the way he overtook Ifeajuana's Mercedes driving along the road below.

Ejoor, arriving first in Enugu, took over the garrison and withdrew the troops around Dr Okpara's home. At 10 a.m. the same troops stood guard of honour as a fearful Premier said good-bye at the airport to President Makarios of Cyprus who had been finishing a tour of Nigeria in Enugu. Later Dr Okpara was allowed to leave for his hometown of Umuahia.

In the Midwest dissident troops arrived at the Premier's Lodge at 10 a.m., but were withdrawn on orders from General Ironsi at 2 p.m. The coup had failed. Ifeajuana and Okafor

40

arrived in Enugu to find Ejoor in the saddle. They hid in the house of a local chemist, whence Okafor was arrested; Ifeajuana fled to Ghana, later to return and join the other plotters in prison.

It was not a bloodless coup, but it was far from a bloodbath. The Premiers of the North, the West and the Federation were dead, as was one Federal Minister. Among senior army officers three Northerners, two Westerners and two Easterners were dead. (Another Ibo major had been killed, this time by loyal troops who thought wrongly that he was among the plotters.) Apart from that a handful of civilians including the wife of one of the officers and some houseboys from Sir Ahmadu Bello's household, together with less than a dozen soldiers, had died. Nzeogwu maintained later that there should have been no deaths at all, but that some of his colleagues became over-enthusiastic.

In Lagos General Ironsi had taken command of the army and had restored order, but it was not that which put him later in power. It was the reaction of the population as much as anything else that made quite plain to all that the reign of the politicians was at an end. This public reaction, often forgotten today, gives the lie most firmly of all to the idea that the January coup was a factional affair.

In Kaduna a throng of cheering Hausas sacked the palace of the dead autocrat. A smiling Major Hassan Usman Katsina, son of the Fulani Emir of Katsina, sat beside Nzeogwu at a press conference prior to which the latter had named Hassan Military Governor of the North. Alhaji Ali Akilu, Head of the Northern Civil Service offered his support to Nzeogwu. But the Ibo major's star was falling.

In Lagos and the rest of the South, Ironsi held the reins and would have no truck with the plotters. But he had the sense to realize that, although what the plotters had done went against all his own training and inclinations, they had still performed a popular service and had a lot of mass support. On Saturday afternoon, 15 January, he asked the Acting President to appoint a Deputy Premier from whom, according to the Constitution, Ironsi could take valid orders. But the politicians procrastinated through into the Sunday morning, and when

41

the Cabinet finally met he had to tell them that he could not ensure the loyalty of his officers and prevent civil war unless he himself took over. In this he was almost certainly right, as numerous officers have made known since. Even those who had not taken part in the coup would not have accepted a return to the rule of the now thoroughly discredited politicians.

The situation had deteriorated, too. Nzeogwu, realizing his colleagues in the South had muffed their job, took a column of troops and drove south, and reached Jebba on the Niger River. If the garrisons of the South had split into warring factions for or against Nzeogwu, civil war could have been the only outcome. Fifteen minutes before midnight Ironsi broadcast from Lagos that since the Government had ceased to function, the armed forces had been asked to form an interim military government and that he, General Ironsi, had been invested with authority as head of the Federal Military Government.

The crisis swung in his favour. The army obeyed his orders. Nzeogwu withdrew to Kaduna Barracks whence he too later emerged to go into custody.

It may be that the Nigerian Cabinet (meeting under the chairmanship of Alhaji Dipcharima, Transport Minister, a Hausa, and senior NPC minister after Balewa) had no option but to accede to General Ironsi's request for authority to take over. But it is equally true that Ironsi had no choice but to make the request, if civil war was to be averted between rival units of the army.

This was important for three reasons; it explains why the accusation that the whole affair was an Ibo plot to overthrow constitutional rule and install Ibo domination of Nigeria was an invention adduced long after the coup and at variance with the facts; it belies the later suggestion that subsequent massacres of Easterners living in the North were excusable or at any rate explicable on the grounds that 'they started it all'; and it throws light on the conviction to this day of Lieutenant-Colonel Ojukwu that Ironsi's accession to power was both constitutional and legal while that of Lieutenant-Colonel Gowon six months later after Ironsi's murder was illegal and therefore invalid.

3. The Man Called Ironside

JOHNSON THOMAS UMUNAKWE AGUIYI-IRONSI was born near Umuahia, a pretty hill town in the centre of the Eastern Region, in March 1924. He was educated partly at Umuahia and partly at Kano in the North, enlisting in the army as a private at the age of eighteen. He spent the rest of the Second World War along the West African coast and returned in 1946 as a twenty-two-year-old Company Sergeant-Major. Two years later he went to Camberley Staff College for officer training and returned in 1949 as a Second Lieutenant to West Africa Command Headquarters, Accra, and thence to Ordnance Depot, Lagos. Here he transferred to an Infantry regiment. As a Lieutenant he was A.D.C. to the Governor, Sir John Macpherson, and, a newly promoted Captain, attended the Coronation in London in June 1953. Becoming a Major in 1955 he was named equerry to the Queen on her tour of Nigeria in 1956. In September 1960 he was promoted to the rank of Lieutenant-Colonel and got his first command, the Fifth Battalion at Kano. The same year he commanded the Nigerian contingent of the United Nations force in the Congo against the Katangese and showed he was more than a staff officer. When the Austrian medical team and the relieving Nigerian soldiers were besieged by the rebels, he flew in alone, in a light plane, and personally negotiated their release. The Austrian Government decorated him with the Ritter Kreuz First Class.

In 1961 and 1962 he was Military Adviser to the Nigerian High Commission in London and while there was promoted to the rank of Brigadier. He then did a course at the Imperial Defence College. In 1964 he returned to the Congo as Commander of the entire U.N. Peace-Keeping Force with the rank of Major-General, Africa's first officer to hold that command. During operations there he confronted single-handed an enraged mob in Leopoldville and persuaded them to disband. These and similar exploits earned him the affectionate nickname of 'Johnny Ironside'.

On his return to Nigeria he reverted to Brigadier and took over the First Brigade, but soon succeeded Major-General Welby-Everard, the last British G.O.C. of the Nigerian Army, and again became a Major-General. He was, said a British civil servant speaking later and choosing his words carefully, 'a very upright man'.

The new régime started well. It was backed by enormous popular support. All over Nigeria, including the North, people rejoiced at the end of the rule of the corrupt politicians and hoped for a new dawn. The last of the plotters of January had been brought peacefully out of their hiding places and were detained in their various regions of origin. Loyalty to the new régime was pledged by the NPC of the North, the Action Group of the West and the NCNC of the East and Midwest, even though the politicians of these parties were out of power and some were detained. Support also came from the trade unions, the students' union and the Emirs of the North. Foreign correspondents noted the popularity. A columnist in the *African World* noted in March: 'The favourable reception accorded to these constitutional changes by different sections of the Nigerian population clearly shows that the army movement was in fact a popular revolt by the masses.'* A month earlier the Nigeria correspondent for the *Economist* of London had visited Sokoto, the city in the far north of Nigeria from which Sir Ahmadu Bello had taken his title, and reported: 'Sokoto was the spoilt darling of the Sardauna of Sokoto's régime, yet even here his passing was accepted quietly. If there are any misgivings about what has happened, the death of the Sardauna has left nobody to express them.'† It was later to prove a rather too sanguine view.

General Ironsi was an honest man and he tried to run an honest régime. Although an Ibo himself, he bent over backwards to show no favouritism towards his own people or his region of birth, and sometimes went far enough to excite criticisms from his own fellow-Easterners. Among his first acts was to appoint Military Governors to all four regions; for the North Lieutenant-Colonel (ex-Major) Hassan Katsina, who

* 'The Nigerian Revolution', *African World*, March 1966.
† 12 February 1966.

44

had actually been appointed to that post by the now imprisoned Nzeogwu; for the West Lieutenant-Colonel Fajuyi, formerly of Enugu garrison; for the Midwest Lieutenant-Colonel (ex-Major) Ejoor, also of the Enugu garrison; and for the East Lieutenant-Colonel Chukwuemeka Odumegwu Ojukwu, former commander of the Fifth Battalion at Kano, a convinced Federalist who had played no part in the January coup other than to join with local Hausa authorities in Kano in keeping that city peaceful and loyal to constituted authority.

Ironsi's advent to power also put an end to the warring in the Western Region, the violence in Tiv-land, and the insurrection of Isaac Boro in the Niger Delta. The latter was put in prison. All parties seemed to have enough confidence in the General to give his régime a try.

Despite his honesty, General Ironsi was not a politician; he was totally devoid of cunning and showed little aptitude for the intricacies of diplomacy necessary inside a highly complex society. He was also on occasion ill-advised, a common fate of military men in government. Nevertheless he did nothing to merit what happened to him.

In the South he ordered the detention of former politicians who might be likely to cause unrest and foment trouble. But the Northern politicians were permitted their liberty, and within a short time they were making use of it. Ironsi formed a Supreme Military Council and a Federal Executive Council to help him govern. In view of later suggestions that his régime was pro-Eastern, the composition of these bodies is interesting. Apart from himself there was in the nine-man Supreme Military Council one other Ibo, Colonel Ojukwu who had an *ex officio* membership as one of the four Regional Military Governors, and one non-Ibo Easterner, Lieutenant-Colonel Kurubo, the head of the Air Force and a Rivers man. The Executive Council comprised the Military Council and six others, of which only two were from the East, the Attorney-General, Mr Onyiuke, an Ibo, and the Inspector-General of Police, Mr Edet, an Efik. Both had held their respective offices before the January coup. When naming permanent secretaries in the Federal Public Service (the permanent secretaryships are powerful posts) Ironsi distributed the twenty-three jobs thus: Northerners, eight; Midwesterners, seven; Westerners, five; Easterners, three.

The political appointees in public corporations were swept away and Tribunals of Inquiry were set up to examine the activities of the dismissed men while in office. The first three Tribunals – examining the Nigerian Railway Corporation, the Electricity Corporation of Nigeria, and the Lagos City Council – were headed respectively by a Westerner, a Northerner and an Englishman. Later the twenty-five General Managers, Chairmen and Secretaries of the Federal Corporations were appointed thus: Westerners, twelve; Northerners, six; Easterners, three; Midwesterners, one; Foreigners, three.

General Ironsi made several other appointments which give a clue to his attitude towards the concept of One Nigeria. He named Lieutenant-Colonel Yakubu Gowon, a Sho-Sho from the North, as his Army Chief of Staff and right-hand man; Mallam Hamsad Amadu, a young relative of the Sardauna of Sokoto, became his private secretary; his personal escort were composed mostly of Hausa soldiers commanded by another young Hausa, Lieutenant W. G. Walbe, a fact which may later have cost the General his life.

His brisk attitude towards corruption in high and public places had its effect, and within a short time international confidence in Nigeria had been largely restored. The Six-Year development plan was continued.

But the main problem had still to be solved. It concerned the future constitution of Nigeria, which was largely synonymous with the question of Nigerian unity. Once again the inherent disunity of Nigeria made itself manifest. Despite enormous support in the South and the Army for the abolition of regionalism and the inauguration of a unitary state, the very mention of amalgamation with the South other than on the basis of Northern control was enough to send the North on the warpath, which was exactly what happened.

General Ironsi had promised in his earliest hours in power that a return to civilian rule would be preceded by a series of studies of outstanding problems, the establishment of a Constituent Assembly and a referendum on a new constitution. Chief Rotimi Williams and the former Attorney-General Dr

T. O. Elias, both Westerners, were asked to draw up outlines for the latter. Another commission, under Mr Francis Nwokedi, an Ibo, was to inquire into the unification of the public services. After protests that such an important issue should be entrusted to one man, and an Ibo to boot – protests notably from the North where the separation of the civil service was venerated as their main safeguard against domination by the South – a Midwesterner was added to the Nwokedi Commission. Another commission was to explore ways of bringing unity to the judiciary. Yet another, on economic planning, was entrusted to Chief Simeon Adebo, a Yoruba, and Dr Pius Okigbo, an Ibo. The commissions reported, and their reports all pointed one way – to unification.

Unification had been mooted from the earliest days of the Ironsi régime. At the end of January Colonel Ejoor in the Midwest called for 'a unitary form of government'. At a press conference in February General Ironsi said: 'It has become apparent to all Nigerians that rigid adherence to "regionalism" was the bane of the last régime and one of the main factors which contributed to its downfall. No doubt the country would welcome a clean break with the deficiencies of the system.'

The General was being over-optimistic. The South would undoubtedly have welcomed such a break. In fact it did. But the North was a different entity altogether. It was their representatives – the Northern House and the Emirs – who years before had seen in regionalism under the Richards Constitution an undying protection of their own society, with all its lethargy and inertia, from incursions by more vigorous and educated Southerners.

Unification was particularly popular among the Ibos of the East. They were the most travelled and best qualified of the major ethnic groups, and amply confident of their ability to compete on equal terms with anybody. For them regionalism had always meant treatment as second class citizens in the North, and a double system in the making of public appointments outside the Eastern Region.

Thus what was for the South a glorious opportunity was for the North an almost deadly threat. Nearly two years later in Enugu the American Consul James Barnard nicely summed up the innate conflict of interests that has bedevilled Nigeria all these years. He said: 'It's no good ducking under or hedging round the single immutable political reality of this country, which is: in any race for the material benefits of life, starting from the same point and on the basis of equal opportunity, the Easterners are going to win by a mile. This is intolerable to the North. The only way to prevent it happening is to impose artificial shackles to progress on the East. This is intolerable to the Easterners.'*

Discontent in the North started to seethe shortly after the commissions inquiring into various aspects of unification went to work. This discontent was later to be portrayed as entirely spontaneous and to involve the supposedly widespread grief over the death of the beloved Sardauna of Sokoto at the hands of an Ibo in January. That is a false picture.

Firstly the Sardauna, to judge from the immediate reaction of his subjects after his death, was regarded not as a benevolent father but an unscrupulous old despot, which he was. Secondly the violence that broke out in the North in May 1966 was not spontaneous. It took a lot of hard work.

When the politicians fell, it was not just the downfall of a small handful of men. Thousands more lost an easy meal-ticket when the politicians were separated from access to public funds. Enormous families found themselves without support and the prospect of work loomed before them; hangers-on, party hirelings, agents, canvassers, contractors who had made plump profits through their connexions in high places, administrators who could not have held down their jobs without political protection, found themselves on the breadline. When a few souls started to agitate against the Ironsi régime the accoutrements were easily to hand: an army of willing voices to spread the rumours, inflame the passions and fire the hearts; the spectre of the all-dominating Ibo; the apparent stripping from the North of its traditional protective isolationism; lastly the revenge motive could be easily played upon, and it was. Thus the dead Sardauna was built up again into a saint, and the jailed officers who had led the January coup into devils.

Colonel Fajuyi in the West, an able and energetic man, had

* Conversation with the author at Enugu, July 1967.

rigorously purged public life of its former parasites, dismissing all local government officials appointed by the hated Akintola régime and eleven ministers of his party. In the Midwest and East similar measures went through. These were, however, less draconian because the NCNC, which controlled both regions prior to January 1966, had been voted into office (latterly under the UPGA banner) by the great majority of the electors without any jiggery-pokery.

In the North it was different. Here political power and the emirate aristocracy had been almost synonymous from time immemorial. Colonel Hassan, the new Military Governor, was the son of the Emir of Katsina. There was not exactly a choice of competent men to run the Native Administration, and those in power were in any case often the appointees of the Emirs. Thus the aristocratic and the administrative Establishments stayed in power. The politicians, although not in power, were not in detention either, nor even for long out of favour. It was from these that the whispering campaign started, and it soon flowered in fertile soil.

Particular exception was taken at once to Mr Nwokedi, whose inquiry into the possibility of unifying the civil service took him on a tour of the North. Though he listened to the Northerners' views, his final report to General Ironsi contained conclusions that did not coincide with those views.

In Lagos General Ironsi was being pulled both ways. He knew of the discontent of the North towards the idea of unification, but there were powerful advocates of it in his immediate entourage. On 24 May he came off the fence. In a radio broadcast he announced the Constitution (Suspension and Modification) Decree. The provisions involved the abolition of the Regions and their conversion into groups of provinces, although with the same boundaries, Governors and administrations. Nigeria would cease to be a federation, and become simply the Republic of Nigeria. The public services were to be united under a single Public Services Commission, but regional (or now provincial) commissions would continue to appoint all but the most senior staff. He then added that these measures were entirely transitional and should be seen as such, and that they were made 'without prejudice' to the findings of the Rotimi Williams Commission. Unhappily that commission was working precisely on the problem of the relative merits of the federal and unitary systems.

It may well be that General Ironsi was seeking to placate the radical firebrands of the South who wanted reform quickly, while at the same time trying not to provoke the North by going too far. An examination of the Unification Decree (as it became known) shows that in fact it changed virtually nothing but names. More cogently, this decree did no more than formalize the manner of government that had existed since the army took over and ruled through the Supreme Military Council, very much a unitary body.

The Unification Decree was then used as the excuse for a series of most violent massacres of Easterners across the Northern Region. It started with a student demonstration at Kano. Within hours it had turned into a bloodbath. Again, although as advocates of unification the Yorubas of the Western Region had been almost the equals of the Ibos of the East, it was exclusively the Ibos and their fellow-Easterners that the Northern mobs sought out. Shortly after the start of the demonstration in Kano hundreds of armed thugs swept across the space between the city walls and the *Sabon Garis* where the Easterners lived, broke into the ghetto and started burning, raping, looting and killing as many men, women and children from the East as they could lay hands on.

Any idea of spontaneity was dispelled by the spread of the riots. In lorries and buses thoughtfully provided by unnamed donors, waves of former party thugs spread out through the North, to Zaria, Kaduna and elsewhere. By the time it was all over Nigeria was again on the verge of disintegration. Although no figures were ever published from either Federal or Northern Government sources, the Easterners later calculated they lost three thousand dead in those massacres.

It may well be that some thought they were just demonstrating their feelings -- which they had every right to do. But the butchery that went with it, the degree of the organization, and the ease with which it could be accomplished should have given warning of a deep underlying danger which constituted a dark portent for the future. Again the warning was overlooked.

Many Northerners were probably quite convinced after several months of quiet indoctrination that the Ibos really were trying to take over Nigeria, to colonize the backward North, and use their undoubted talents to run the country from end to end. Again the secessionist demand of the North became an open issue. Demonstrating civil servants in Kaduna carried banners proclaiming: 'Let there be secession.' In the same city Colonel Hassan called a meeting of all the Northern Emirs, and many arrived with clear mandates from their people at home asking for secession of the North. In Zaria the Emir was mobbed by crowds begging for secession.

After the meeting the Emirs sent Ironsi a secret memorandum telling him, in effect, to abrogate the Unification Decree or they would secede. General Ironsi replied by going to great lengths to explain that the decree involved no changes of boundary, and that indeed it hardly changed the *status quo* at all; he pointed out that it was a temporary measure to enable the army, accustomed to a unified command, to rule; and that there would be no permanent changes made without the promised referendum. The Emirs declared themselves satisfied.

In June Colonel Ojukwu, welcoming the Emir of Kano, his contemporary and friend, with whose aid he had been able to keep Kano without bloodshed in January, as the new Chancellor of the University of Nsukka, publicly called on his people to return to their homes and jobs in the North. Many of these Easterners had fled after the May massacres to seek safety in the East. Colonel Ojukwu asked them to believe that these killings had been 'part of the price we have had to pay' for the ideal of One Nigeria.

Throughout June the Ironsi Government groped for a remedy to the problem of the rising tension in Nigeria. To none did it occur, and least of all to Colonel Ojukwu, that the Northerners might be permitted to fulfil their age-old wish and set up their own state. Eventually General Ironsi left for a tour of the country to sound out local opinion, on the broadest possible basis, as to the future form of Nigeria that its people wished to see. He never returned to Lagos.

4. The Second Coup that Failed

SOME of those seeking to explain away the coup of the junior army officers of Northern origin on 29 July 1966, have suggested it was motivated by ideas of righteous revenge for the deaths in January of three senior army officers of Northern birth. Certainly, prior to the second coup there were growing cries in the North for the execution of the mutineers of January, not as retribution for the deaths of the politicians, whose passing remained largely unregretted, but for the shooting of Brigadier Maimalari and Colonels Pam and Largema.

This argument is not convincing. Apart from these three, two Yoruba colonels and two Ibo majors were also killed in January. It seems far more likely that the key to the motives of the officers who mutinied in July is to be found in the code-word that triggered the operation – ARABA. It is the Hausa word for 'Secession'; and although there was undoubtedly a strong element of revenge inside the movement and the subsequent activities of its perpetrators, their political aim was to fulfil the long-standing wish of the mass of the Northern people and quit Nigeria once and for all.

In this and in other points the two coups were utterly different. In the first coup there had been a fiery zeal to purge Nigeria of a host of undoubted ills; it was reformatory in motivation; bloodshed was minimal – four politicians and six officers. It was extrovert in nature and non-regional in orientation.

The July coup was wholly regional, introverted, revanchist and separatist in origins and unnecessarily bloody in execution.

A few years earlier it had been noted that although the great majority of the infantry were of Northern origin, and about eighty per cent of this majority were Tivs, almost seventy per cent of the commissioned ranks were from the East. This was no accident; but neither was it the design of the Easterners that this should be so, as has since been alleged. In its early days the Nigerian Army had emphasized the importance of education when granting commissions. As can be seen from the dispersion of primary schools (mentioned earlier) the North was chronically short of educated personnel.

In 1960, independence year, there had been only six commissioned officers from the North in the army. The new Defence Minister, Alhaji Ribadu, a Hausa, had decreed there should be fifty per cent Northerners in the commissioned ranks; but this could not be done overnight. By 1966 there were however far more junior officers of Northern origin in the army; and although the planning of the July coup was undoubtedly done by a small group of senior officers, the execution fell to these lieutenants.

Inside the army the dispersion of the officers reflected regional characteristics, again not deliberately, but on the basis of education and tendency. The great majority of the Northern officers were in infantry battalions, while the technical sections – stores, radio, engineering, maintenance, armoury, transport, medical, intelligence, training and ordnance – were the preserve of the Easterners. When the July coup came the mutineers had only to take possession of the various garrison armouries and to arm their men to have the rest of the army and therefore the country at their mercy. This in fact was what they did.

General Ironsi was dining on the evening of 28 July with Lieutenant-Colonel Fajuyi, Military Governor of the West, at the latter's residence in Ibadan. Ironsi had just completed his nation-wide tour. With them was Colonel Hilary Njoku, the Ibo commander of the Second Battalion based at Ikeja outside Lagos.

The coup started with a mutiny at Abeokuta Barracks in the Western Region where a Hausa captain led a group of troops into the officers' mess at 11 p.m. and shot three Eastern officers, a lieutenant-colonel, a major and a lieutenant. They then besieged the barracks, disarmed the Southern soldiers among the guard, seized the armoury and armed the Northerners. They also sounded the call to action, which brought the garrison from its sleep to line up on the parade ground. The Southern soldiers were singled out and locked up in the guardroom, while the Northerners made a house-to-house search for those not present. By day-break most of the Southern officers and senior N.C.O.s had been rounded up. They were led out of the guardroom at dawn and shot.

Meanwhile the mutineers had apparently telephoned the adjutants (both Northerners) of the Second Battalion at Ikeja and the Fourth Battalion at Ibadan to inform them of the news. But at 3.30 a.m. an Ibo captain among the prisoners at Abeokuta escaped: he too telephoned, but to Army Head-quarters in Lagos. He reported what he thought was a simple mutiny. At A.H.Q. the man in charge in the absence of Ironsi was his Chief of Staff, Lieutenant-Colonel Gowon.

It was he who now took charge. Whether he did so to better the direction of the coup and the massacres that it entailed, or whether he tried to prevent it, is still hotly debated. He claims he had nothing to do with the coup, but his subsequent be-haviour would appear to cast doubt on this and he may have been a not-too-hesitant accomplice during and after the fact.

The news also reached General Ironsi. The three officers con-ferred shortly after midnight and agreed that Njoku should return to Lagos in a civilian vehicle and in mufti to take over control and counter the 'mutiny'. He left in order to return to his chalet and change. Once outside he noticed troops dis-mounting from two parked Land Rovers. They gave him a burst from Sten guns, and he ran off, wounded in the thigh. Later, after treatment at Ibadan Hospital he wended his way back to the East disguised as a priest, while patrols scouted the West for him and roadblocks had orders to shoot on sight. It was the tenacity of the hunt for Eastern officers, and the duration of it long after Colonel Gowon had taken over supreme con-trol in the name of the mutineers, that cast doubts on both the political aspect of the coup and Gowon's innocence of events.

In fact the Southern troops in Ironsi's bodyguard had been disarmed before midnight by their Northern counterparts who had been stiffened by twenty-four extra Northern troops sent from the Fourth Battalion headquarters in Ibadan. This bat-talion, after the death of Colonel Largema in January, had been under the command of Colonel J. Akahan, a Tiv from the North. The newly-arrived party was commanded by Major Theophilus Danjuma, a Hausa, who is now Second-in-Command of the First Division of the Nigerian Army and Garrison Commander of Enugu.

Inside the house Ironsi and Fajuyi heard the shooting and sent down Ironsi's Air Force A.D.C., Lieutenant Nwankwo, to find out what was going on. (Ironsi's Army A.D.C., Lieutenant Bello, a Hausa, had quietly disappeared, although there is no evidence to connect him with the coup.) Downstairs Nwankwo was arrested and his hands tied. After waiting almost till dawn Colonel Fajuyi descended to find out what had happened to Nwankwo. He too was arrested. Finally at 9 a.m. Major Danjuma went upstairs to find General Ironsi, and arrested him. He too was brought downstairs.

Among those who know what happened after that, only Lieutenant Nwankwo has ever given testimony. From the Federal Government side a discreet veil is drawn over everything. What follows then is Nwankwo's evidence.

All three men were stripped and flogged with horsewhips. After being put into separate vans the convoy set off with Major Danjuma leading. At the Mokola road junction where the roads divide, one going to Oyo town and the other to Letmauk Barracks, garrison of the Fourth Battalion, the convoy split. Danjuma headed back to Letmauk after giving whispered orders to Lieutenant Walbe, the commander of General Ironsi's escort. The rest of the convoy proceeded. After ten miles the three detainees were ordered down and made to march along a narrow footpath in the bush. They were stopped, and were beaten and tortured again so badly that they could hardly walk. After being pushed on they came to a stream which in their weakened state they could not jump across. They were carried over the stream and a few yards down the path, where they were laid face down and given another beating. At this point Nwankwo had managed to untie the wire round his wrists, and made a dash for it. He got away. The other two men, nearly dead from their sufferings, were finished off with bursts of Sten gun. Later the police found the bodies and buried them in Ibadan cemetery, from where they were taken six months later and laid to rest in their respective home towns.

After dawn on 29 July the massacre of officers and men of

55

Eastern origin took place all over Nigeria with a speed, precision and uniformity of pattern that took away any subsequent excuse of spontaneity. At Letmauk Barracks, Ibadan, the commanding officer Colonel Akahan claimed at sunrise that he had known nothing of the midnight movements against General Ironsi. But it is unlikely that the troops, transport, arms and ammunition used for the siege of Government House were removed without the C.O.'s knowledge. At 10 a.m. Colonel Akahan called an officers' conference, from which he himself stayed away. When the officers were assembled the Easterners were taken away to the guardroom, then later to the tailor's workshop. At midnight that night thirty-six hand grenades were lobbed through the windows. The survivors inside were shot down. Eastern soldiers were then made to wash the blood away, before being taken out and shot. The Easterners in Ironsi's retinue were also finished off. On the afternoon of the 30th Colonel Akahan called together the Northern soldiers and congratulated them, saying at the same time that there would be no more killing 'since events had now balanced out'.

On the basis of this statement Eastern soldiers in hiding came out; but that night they too were hunted down and those caught were killed. The killing went on for several days, accompanied by the raping of the wives of Eastern men and the spreading of terror to the city of Ibadan itself. Colonel Akahan later became Gowon's Army Chief-of-Staff.

At Ikeja things went much the same. About breakfast time on the morning of the 29th Colonel Gowon arrived from Lagos fifteen miles away. From five in the morning onwards Northern troops of the garrison had been rounding up the Easterners, including scores of civilians, policemen and customs officials of Eastern origin working at the nearby airport. By midday of 29 July there were 200 held in the guardroom. In the evening Lieutenant Walbe arrived and reported to Colonel Gowon the capture and death of General Ironsi. The next day the civilians in the guardroom were released while the names of the soldiers were taken. From this list the execution squad called out the officers and men in order of seniority. Eight officers ranging from Major to Second Lieutenant and fifty-two other ranks from Warrant Officer downwards were killed. The killing was accompanied by the usual beatings, but after one Ibo corporal escaped (and lived to tell the tale), the rest were handcuffed and led away to the killing ground behind the guardroom. When weary, the Northern soldiers exchanged knives and carried on cutting throats. Before death many of the prisoners were whipped, made to lie in puddles of urine and excrement and consume the mixture. Captain P. C. Okoye was on the way to attend a course in the United States when he was caught at Ikeja Airport and brought to the barracks. Tied to an iron cross he was flogged almost to death, then thrown into a cell, still tied to the cross, where he died.*

All this happened less than 200 yards from the office where Colonel Gowon had set up his headquarters and from where he had been vested with the title of Supreme Commander of the Armed Forces. It was from this office that he told the world he was trying to hold the country together in a time of crisis.

Despite subsequent assurances that it was a quick and short-lived affair, there is eye-witness testimony that it went on sporadically for four weeks. On 22 August a young Northern officer brought from Benin prison the detainees who had been concerned in the January plot (ostensibly the reason for the July coup). The five of them were killed. The same day news came through that in the East Colonel Ojukwu had asked for the repatriation of all Eastern officers and men. Lieutenant Nuhu then gave orders that the remaining twenty-two Eastern prisoners, all N.C.O.s, be executed, which they were.

Long before that date Colonel Gowon had told the world that the killing had ceased and that 'conditions have returned to normal'.

Colonel Akahan and Major Danjuma were not the only ones to achieve promotion after acts which customarily lead to the gallows. At Makurdi in the heart of Tiv-land a detachment from the Fourth Battalion at Ibadan had arrived between 11 and 14 August. Fifteen soldiers of Eastern origin were arrested and detained. On the 16th the detachment commander Major Daramola told them they would be driven to Kaduna, then

---

* The evidence for the incidents at Ibadan and Ikeja barracks is in the Military Archives, National Defence H.Q., Umuahia, Biafra.

sent back to the East by air. The convoy set off along the road with Major Daramola bringing up the rear in a Mini-moke. After fifty miles the convoy stopped and reversed into the bush where a firing squad was waiting. One by one the men were called out for execution. Three escaped by darting out of the lorry and running off into the long grass, later to come home on foot and tell the tale. Lieutenant-Colonel Daramola today commands the Eighth Brigade of the Second Division, Nigerian Army, which garrisons the Enugu to Onitsha road from Abagana village to Udi.

Enough of the July massacres. They have been adequately detailed elsewhere. Suffice it to report that in all barracks and garrisons, in Lagos and throughout the Western and Northern Regions the pattern was the same. Northern soldiers took over the armouries and armed themselves; arrested and locked up their colleagues of Eastern origin; and subsequently led many of them out to execution. Some escaped and wended their way back to the East, to form the basis of the Biafran Army of a year later. Among the senior officers most of those in the infantry were killed; most of the survivors were in the technical cadres, which is why, of the present Biafran Army commanders who held the rank of Major or senior in the old Nigerian Army, the majority were in the technical rather than the combat units. By the time it was all over nearly 300 officers and men were dead or unaccounted for. As a coherent unit, as a truly Nigerian institution in which men of all tribes and nations, cultures and creeds, could live side by side and call each other comrade, the army was shattered beyond repair. And the army had been the last such institution. Despite what happened before and after, despite all the efforts (which might have succeeded) to hold Nigeria together in some form, if any moment can be identified as the moment when Nigerian unity died, it was when the General called Johnny Ironside crashed down in the dust outside Ibadan.

The aim of the coup was partly revenge on the Ibo for what had been an all-party coup in January, and partly the secession of the North. As soon as Lieutenant-Colonel Gowon set up base at Ikeja barracks a strange flag was seen flying from the main gate, and it remained there for eighteen days. It had lateral red, yellow, black, green and khaki stripes. It was the flag of the Republic of Northern Nigeria. For three days buses, lorries, cars, trains and planes were commandeered in Lagos and the Western Region to transport the enormous reflux of Northern families home.

The garrisons in Lagos, the West and the North were under the control of Northern-officered and -manned units. While the killing of the Eastern soldiers went on Lieutenant-Colonel Hassan Katsina, Military Governor of the North, rallied to the rebel cause, giving grounds for suspicion that if he had not been one of the instigators he had at least known roughly what was afoot. The West had no one to speak for it, Colonel Fajuyi being dead, and there was no one either to speak for Lagos.

In the Midwest, however, there had been no coup; but neither were there any soldiers stationed there. As usual it was too small to bother about. In the East there was a strong Governor, a loyal garrison, and no attempt at a coup. As a result the rule of the old régime continued unbroken in that Region.

When it became clear that the Northern officers intended to secede, a cold wind swept through several quarters, not least through the British High Commission. From the East Colonel Ojukwu saw the writing on the wall, and by telephone urged the Yoruba Brigadier Ogundipe, senior ranking officer in the army and *legally* the successor of General Ironsi, to take over and declare himself Supreme Commander. Ojukwu promised that if he did, he (Ojukwu) would recognize Ogundipe as such. The Yoruba did not rate his chances very highly, and after a crass radio speech of three minutes asking everyone to be calm, he disappeared to Dahomey and thence to London, where some months later he agreed to become the Nigerian High Commissioner. In the meanwhile frenzied efforts by the British High Commission and others had been going on to try to dissuade the North from seceding. But the Northern officers were not alone in their demand; separate independence, the message of the rioters' banners the previous May and of the Emirs' memoranda of June, was still the wish of the great majority of the North. There was only one way to keep them inside Nigeria; by putting into effect the old alternative, 'We rule the lot or we pull out'. According to later accounts from highly

59

placed civil servants then working in Lagos, the British High Commissioner Sir Francis Cumming-Bruce had a six-hour private session with Gowon on the morning of 1 August. Gowon then reported back to his fellow-Northerners. By the afternoon Colonel Ojukwu, telephoning from Enugu to ask Gowon what he intended to do, was told the group intended to stay in Lagos and take over the running of the country. When Ojukwu protested, Gowon replied: 'Well that's what my boys want and they're going to get it.' And stay they did. Gowon's first broadcast to the nation, already prepared and tape-recorded, had to be hastily but not very skilfully edited. What he said was:

I now come to the most difficult but most important part of this statement. I am doing it conscious of the great disappointment and heartbreak it will cause all true and sincere lovers of Nigeria and of Nigerian unity, both at home and abroad, especially our brothers in the Commonwealth. As a result of the recent events and of the previous similar ones, I have come to strongly believe that we cannot honestly and sincerely continue in this wise, as the basis for trust and confidence in our unitary system of Government has been unable to stand the test of time. I have already remarked on the issue in question. Suffice it to say that putting all considerations to the test, political, economic as well as social, the basis for unity is not there, or is so badly rocked, not only once but many times. I therefore feel that we should review the issue of our national standing and see if we can help stop the country from drifting away into utter destruction.*

The last sentence but one does not finish. After a phrase like 'so badly rocked, not only once but many times' one would expect the word 'that' followed by an announcement of the consequences of the rocking. Moreover, it is nonsensical to suggest that the peroration of stopping the country from drifting to destruction would be likely to cause disappointment and heartbreak to all true lovers of Nigeria. In fact before editing the speech *was* to have announced the North's secession.

Had it done so, there seems little doubt that the West, Midwest and East would soon have reached a suitable *modus vivendi,* and shortly afterwards North and South could have entered into a Confederacy of autonomous states or at the least

* Schwarz, op. cit., p. 211.

60

a Common Services Organization that would have put all the erstwhile economic benefits within the reach of all parties while avoiding the powder keg of the racial incompatibility of North and South.

By this time Gowon had either named himself or had been named Supreme Commander of the Armed Forces and Head of the National Military Government of Nigeria. In the East Colonel Ojukwu had no hesitation in refuting Gowon's right to either title. It is of vital importance in understanding why Biafra exists today to realize that after 1 August 1966, Nigeria did not have one legitimate government and one rebel régime, *but two separate de facto governments ruling different parts of the country*.

The July coup was radically different from the January coup in one other respect, as had become clear by 1 August. In the first coup the mutineers did not achieve power, but ended up in prison. In the second they took over the control at the Federal Government and in two Regions. The third Region recognized the new régime later. The fourth Region never did, nor was it obliged to in law.

That was why the coup failed. Its objects were to extract revenge (which it did) and then to secede (which it did not). Having opted to change the second objective into a take-over of all power, the coup leaders were then obliged to presume acquiescence by the two unaffected Regions. When they did not get it from the larger of these two, Nigeria was *effectively* divided into two parts.

But the British Commonwealth Office had got what it wanted, and recognition followed. In October, appealing to the Northerners to stop killing the Easterners in their midst, Gowon was able to use the argument that 'You all know that since the end of July God in His power has entrusted the responsibility of this great country of ours, Nigeria, into the hands of another Northerner. . . .'

THE QUESTION OF LEGITIMACY

One of the main bases of the Nigerian and British Government case against Biafra is that its Government is illegitimate while

61

that of Colonel Gowon remains the sole legitimate government inside the country. But legal experts exist, by no means all Biafrans, who maintain that in law both régimes have a case.

That of the present Nigerian Military Government is based on its effective control of the capital and three of the former Regions, a rule extending over seventy per cent of the population. The diplomatic world has an obsession with capitals, and control of the capital city counts for much. Had Lagos been in the Eastern Region and had Gowon taken over the three outlying Regions while Colonel Ojukwu kept the Eastern Region and the capital, possibly the diplomatic advantage would have swung the other way.

Colonel Ojukwu's claim that it is the Gowon Government rather than he that is in a state of rebellion and therefore illegitimate is based on the continuance of lawful authority in the Eastern Region after July 1966. Earlier General Ironsi had been appointed to his post as Supreme Commander and head of the Supreme Military Council by almost the entire existing Cabinet of Ministers. Had this cabinet sat after the death of Premier Balewa (at that time it was presumed he had only been kidnapped) under the chairmanship of an Ibo minister, it might have been later said that the appointment had been 'fixed'. But the chairmanship was taken by Alhaji Dipcharima, a Hausa, and senior ranking minister of the Northern People's Congress party.

Nor did General Ironsi bring undue pressure to bear on the politicians. He told them, quite realistically as it turned out, that he was unable to guarantee the loyalty of the army to the rule of law unless the army took over. With Nzeogwu marching south and many garrisons seething with unrest, this was no exaggeration. General Ironsi's appointment may therefore be judged to have been legitimate in law. It was he who appointed Colonel Ojukwu to govern the Eastern Region, which was a legitimate appointment.

For Colonel Ojukwu the only man who was entitled to the post of successor to General Ironsi was the next-ranking senior officer, Brigadier Ogundipe. If Ogundipe were not nominated, a plenary meeting of the Supreme Military Council would have had to name a successor. This did not happen. Colonel Gowon either named himself to the post, or he was named by the mutineers in the first three days after 29 July. Among these there was only one member of the Council, Colonel Hassan Usman Katsina, Governor of the North. Even the later meeting of the Council that confirmed Gowon in the post was not plenary, since it was held under conditions that made it impossible for Colonel Ojukwu to attend with more than a tiny chance of getting out alive.

Only in the East did government continue uninterrupted and undisturbed by the events of July 1966. The train of legitimate appointment remained unbroken. For the Biafrans their break from Nigeria in May 1967 was, in view of the treatment accorded to the Region and its citizens, legitimate in international law, and this claim is not without its international supporters.

5. Two Colonels

THE two men who now held effective power in the two so far unreconciled parts of Nigeria were utterly different. Lieutenant-Colonel Yakubu Gowon was thirty-two, the son of a Methodist minister and mission-trained evangelist from one of the smallest tribes in the North, the Sho Sho. He came from near the town of Bauchi. In early youth he too had had a mission-school training, and later went to a grammar school. At the age of nineteen he joined the army, and was lucky to be sent soon after for officer training first at Eaton Hall, then Sandhurst. He returned to Nigeria to take up the career of a normal infantry officer, and later attended more courses in England, notably at Hythe and Warminster. On his return again he became the first Nigerian Adjutant and later served like General Ironsi in the Nigerian contingent in the Congo. During the January coup he had been on yet another course in England, this time at the Joint Services Staff College.

In appearance too he was utterly different from his fellow officer across the Niger. He is small, dapper and handsome, always beautifully groomed and with a dazzling, boyish smile. But probably in nothing are the two leaders as different as in their characters. Those who knew Gowon well, and who served with him, have described him as a mild, meek man who would not hurt a fly – personally. But they also describe him as having a strong streak of vanity and a strain of spite behind the instant charm which has endeared him to so many foreigners since he came to power. In political terms the greatest reproach made by the Biafrans of moderate views is that he is weak and vacillating when confronted by the necessity to make firm decisions, a man easily swayed by stronger and more forceful spirits, cowed by a bullying, hectoring approach, and certainly no match for many of the army officers who led the July coup or the shrewd civil servants who saw in his régime a path to power within the country.

For the Biafrans Gowon has never been the real ruler of

Nigeria, but an internationally acceptable front-man, smooth with visiting correspondents and journalists, charming with diplomats, endearing on television.

Gowon's weakness of character became noticeable shortly after he took power. One of his first acts was to order a stop to the killing of Eastern officers and men of the Nigerian Army. However, as has been shown, the killing went on with little check until late in the month of August. Two years later he apparently had no more control over his armed forces. Time and again he swore to correspondents and diplomats that he had ordered his air force to stop bombing civilian centres in Biafra; but the rocketing, bombing and strafing of markets, churches and hospitals continued relentlessly.

Lieutenant-Colonel Chukwuemeka Odumegwu Ojukwu is an entirely different person. He was born thirty-five years ago at Zungeru, a small town in the Northern Region where his father was staying on a short visit. The father, Sir Louis Odumegwu Ojukwu, who died in September 1966 with a knighthood and several million pounds in the bank, started life as a small businessman from Nnewi in the Eastern Region. He built up a nationwide road haulage business, had the foresight to sell out for a high price when the railways were coming into their own, and put his assets into property and high finance. Everything Sir Louis touched turned to gold. He invested in building land in Lagos at a time when prices were low; by the time he died the tracts of marshy ground on Victoria Island, Lagos City, were being snapped up at fancy prices as Victoria Island was earmarked for the new diplomatic and residential suburb of the expanding capital.

The story of his second, but favourite son, can hardly be described as a rags-to-riches tale. The family dwelling where the young Emeka Ojukwu played before going to school was a luxurious mansion. Like most wealthy businessmen, Sir Louis kept open house and his mansion was a meeting place for all the moneyed elite of the prosperous colony. In 1940 the young Ojukwu entered the Catholic Mission Grammar School, but soon moved to King's College, the smart private academy modelled closely on the lines of one of Britain's public schools. Here he remained until he was thirteen, when his father sent him to Epsom College, set amid the rolling green hills of Surrey. He recalled later that his first impression of Britain was a sense of being completely lost 'amid this sea of white faces'. The isolation of a small African boy in such a totally strange environment caused the first moulding of the character that was to follow. Driven in on himself he developed a private philosophy of total self-reliance, an unyielding internal sufficiency that requires no external support from others. Despite frequent clashes with established authority in the form of his housemaster, he did reasonably well, played a good game of Rugby and set a new junior discus record which still holds.

He left at the age of eighteen and moved to Lincoln College, Oxford. It was here he had his first clash of will with his father, and won. Sir Louis was very much the Victorian father, a strong-willed head of the family who expected to have to brook little opposition to his wishes on the part of his offspring. In his second son he seemed to recognize something of himself, and he was probably right. Sir Louis wanted his son to study law, but after the statutory one year Emeka Ojukwu changed to Modern History which interested him much more. He still played Rugby, and almost got a Blue, and obtained a degree without excessive exertion. His three years at Oxford were the happiest of his life; he was coming up to twenty-one years of age, strong and good-looking, wealthy and carefree.

When he returned to Nigeria he was noticeable in Lagos, he remarks now, 'only for the impeccable cut of my English suits'. Then came the second clash with his father. The obvious thing would have been for Ojukwu to go into any one of the prosperous business concerns owned by his father, or one of his father's friends, where promotion would be automatic and work minimal. It says much for his independence that he sought a job where he could do something on his own without the too-influential pall of the Ojukwu name hanging over him. He opted for the civil service, and asked to be sent to the Northern Region, hoping thus to escape his name and paternity.

But the built-in regionalism of the civil service prevented it. The North was for the Northerners, and the young Ojukwu was sent instead to the East. Having his son enter the civil service in a humble grade was a blow to Sir Louis, but he put up with it. Going to the East was a blow to Ojukwu. He had hoped to escape his father's name, influence and prestige. Instead he found it everywhere. Sir Louis was the local boy who had made good, his name was magic, and the new Assistant Divisional Officer soon realized that whatever his performance his annual reports were bound to be glowing. No superior would dare send in a bad report on the son of Sir Louis. This was the last thing the young man wanted.

In an attempt to prove himself, he threw himself into the work with a vengeance, choosing to get out of town as much as possible and help in building roads, ditches, culverts among the peasantry. Ironically it was a vital apprenticeship for his present position, and one on which he draws constantly. In those two years the favoured young man from Lagos learned to know his own people, the Ibo, at the level of the common man, to understand their problems, hopes and fears. Most important of all he is tolerant of their weaknesses and makes allowances for their failings, something that is often beyond the understanding of his other Western-educated colleagues and fellow officers. It is this bond with the people, a deep and two-way communication, that today provides the basis of his leadership of the Biafran people, and which still baffles his foreign opponents who wish he had been the victim of a coup long ago. The people know his understanding of them and their customs, and reply with an abiding loyalty to him.

But after two years in the civil service, working among Ibos and non-Ibos in the East, he decided to leave and join the army. The reason is an ironic one for the man now accused by some of 'breaking up the Federation'. He was such a convinced Federalist that the narrow confines of regionalism that strait-jacketed the civil service got on his nerves. In the army he saw an institution where tribe, race and standing at birth counted for nothing. It was also a framework in which he could lose the cloying prestige of the Ojukwu name and earn his promotion on his own merits.

He was immediately sent for officer training at Eaton Hall, Chester, and emerged as a second lieutenant. (He is sometimes wrongly referred to as having been at Sandhurst.) After further courses at Hythe and Warminster, he returned home and got his first posting – to the Fifth Battalion based at Kano in Northern Nigeria. Two years later he was promoted Captain and sent to Army Headquarters at Ikeja Barracks, Lagos. This was in 1960, independence year.

For the wealthy bachelor officer of Nigeria's darling army, life was very pleasant. In 1961 he was sent to the West African Frontier Force training school at Teshie in nearby Ghana as a lecturer in tactics and military law. Top of the class in tactics was Lieutenant Murtela Mohammed.

Later that year Captain Ojukwu returned to the Fifth Battalion at Kano, but was soon promoted Major and sent to the First Brigade Headquarters at Kaduna. The same year he served at Luluabourg, Kasai Province, Congo, with the Third Brigade of the United Nations peace-keeping force during the Katangese secession. From here he was selected for further military training and in 1962 attended the Joint Services Staff College in England. In January 1963 he was made a Lieutenant-Colonel and as such became the first indigenous Quartermaster General of the Nigerian Army.

It was while in this position that he took the decision and gained the experience that was later to enable him to give the lie to British Government claims that arms shipments from London to Lagos were only a part of 'traditional supplies'. While in office he operated a policy of 'buy the best at the price from whatever the source'. Under this policy most of the old arms contracts with British firms were cancelled, and fresh ones placed with more price-competitive manufacturers in Holland, Belgium, Italy, West Germany and Israel. By the time the present war broke out the Nigerian Army remained dependent on Britain for the supply of ceremonial dress uniforms and armoured cars only.

A year later he went back to the Fifth Battalion, this time as Commanding Officer. It was while he was at Kano during 1965 that the young Major Nzeogwu at Kaduna was plotting the January 1966 coup. No one has ever bothered to suggest that Colonel Ojukwu was party to, or knew about this coup. The plotters left him strictly alone. For one thing he was regarded as too much an 'establishment' figure; more important, however, was that it was known that his legalistic turn of mind would make the idea of rebellion against legally constituted authority repugnant to him.

When the coup of January 1966 exploded he was one of the few who did not lose his head. Gathering the Provincial Administrator and the Emir of Kano together in conclave he urged them both to join with him in keeping Kano and its province free from disturbance and bloodshed. They were successful; there was no rioting in Kano. Within hours he was on the telephone to General Ironsi pledging his support and that of the Fifth to the loyal side.

A few days later, when Ironsi needed an Eastern Region officer to become Military Governor of the East, he called on Colonel Ojukwu to take the job.

At the age of thirty-three Colonel Ojukwu was appointed to govern his own people and the five million non-Ibo people of the Eastern Region. The carefree days were over. Those who knew him in the old days say that a considerable change came over him. With the responsibilities of government and later of popular leadership the lively young army officer subsided and gave way to a more sober figure. He still takes the post, rather than himself, extremely seriously. Ahead, although he did not know it at the time, lay the massacres of May 1966 of his own people, another *coup d'état,* more race slaughter, hatred, mistrust, broken pledges, the decision to follow the people's wishes and pull out of Nigeria, war, starvation, the calumny of half the world, and possibly death.

But after taking over in January 1966 it did not look like that. Like Colonels Fajuyi and Ejoor, Colonel Ojukwu lost little time in tackling the corruption and venality he found in public life in the East. As elsewhere in the South, but not in the North, some of the top politicians of the old régime were detained while the spring-cleaning went ahead.

Even the massacres of May in Northern Nigeria did little to dim his hopes for One Nigeria. After General Ironsi had had an assurance from the Sultan of Sokoto that there would be no more killing, Colonel Ojukwu took the opportunity of the visit of his friend the Emir of Kano to Nsukka to ask his people who had fled the North to go back to their jobs. Later he was to regret this stand, and the sense of remorse when many of those who took the advice died in later massacres still pains him today.

In two things Colonel Ojukwu is almost unique in the present situation. For one thing he was not compromised by participation in the corrupt rule of the politicians; the present politicians of Lagos are largely those who wheeled and dealed in the old political circus where self-enrichment out of public funds was the order of the day. Again, he was not involved in either of the military coups; most of the present military musclemen behind the politicians in Nigeria today are the same group who put through the bloody coup of July 1966.

Secondly, he was a wealthy man in his own right. After his father died in 1966 he inherited large properties in Lagos and elsewhere. But the inheritance was not all in property. The old financier had large sums deposited in Swiss banks, and before he died he gave his second son the details and access to them. Had Colonel Ojukwu played things the way the Lagos clique wanted, following the July coup, he could have kept all that and still held office. By doing what he did he lost everything in Lagos and his entire fortune in Nigeria. As regards the money overseas, he insisted when the crunch came that the last penny of it should be spent on Biafra before any of the old Eastern Regions funds abroad were touched. The total fortune has been estimated at £8,000,000.

6. The Autumn Atrocities

THE situation following the July coup was complex and deeply unhappy. As news of the killing of the Eastern Region soldiers in barracks all over Northern and Western Nigeria got back to the East, feeling ran high. Without their weapons, disguised in civilian clothes, walking by night and hiding by day, the first groups of officers and men who had escaped from the killings began to cross the Niger and tell the tale.

For Colonel Gowon the week was crucial. Several reasons have already been cited as the basis for his choice as leader of the plotters. That he was the next senior officer in line was obviously not true. His own explanation on the radio on 1 August that he had been named by a majority of the existing Supreme Military Council was also quickly discounted in the East. For one thing the Council did not make majority decisions, and for another thing it had not met. A third reason given for his selection, notably by expatriate writers at the time, was that he was 'the only man who could control the rebels'.

The new régime was faced with three urgent unsolved problems: the killing inside the army had to be stopped, a Supreme Commander acceptable to everyone had to be found, and the future basis of association of the four regions had to be sought.

Colonel Ojukwu, although not prepared to recognize the supremacy of Colonel Gowon, nevertheless realized that if anything of Nigeria was to be saved from the mess he would have to try to cooperate with the new régime. Towards this end he proposed by telephone from Enugu that there should be a meeting of representatives of the Military Governors to try to get agreement on at least a temporary association of the regional military power blocks that the coup had created.

The controlling force in the North, West and Lagos was now the Northern Army. The Easterners in 'the army' (i.e. the Federal Army) had been killed or chased out, most Mid-

71

westerners (and there were not many) had been of the Mid-western Ibo group and had thus been classed as Easterners, suffering the same fate, and the Westerners in the army were little more than a handful. Traditionally the Yorubas seldom presented themselves as candidates for the army.

The meeting of representatives was duly held on 9 August, and the vital agreement it reached, with the Northerners concurring, was that all troops should return to their regions of origin. Although often overlooked by later writers, this agreement might have saved Nigeria had it been carried through. The coup in the West had had the support only of the ex-politicians of the Akintola days, who were still heartily disliked by the majority of the population. The return of the Northern soldiers to the North would have enabled the Westerners to speak their mind, something quite impossible so long as there were garrisons of Northerners in every barracks and squads of them manning the roadblocks.

Chief Awolowo, freed from prison, still had enough popularity to speak for the West. But the pledge was never fulfilled by the new régime. The excuse given was that there were virtually no Yoruba troops to replace the Northerners. In fact security could have been assured by the police, for the Westerners had no cause to run amok. As it turned out the Northern soldiers stayed put; to the Westerners, as to the Easterners, seeming like an army of occupation, and often behaving like one.

In the East Colonel Ojukwu stuck to the letter of the agreement. The Northern-born component of the garrison at Enugu was repatriated to the North by rail, and in accordance with the terms of the 9 August concordat, they were allowed to take with them their arms and ammunition as a protection against being waylaid en route. These arms were then supposed to be sent back after the troops had got home. But once in Kaduna the troops from Enugu kept their weapons and no more was heard about them.

Elsewhere Eastern-born troops were clamouring to return home. Apart from the fugitives of 29 July and the succeeding days, there were other groups who were still intact. From the North some of them were sent home, but without arms or escort, and were forced to submit to repeated molesting on the way from the by now hostile populations through whom they passed. The tension grew.

By late in the month it became clear that there were still hundreds unaccounted for. That was when Colonel Ojukwu asked that the outstanding personnel be allowed to return home, and the twenty-two at Ikeja were executed in consequence.

These events were not without their effect in the East. After the May massacres in the North a Commission of Inquiry under the chairmanship of a British High Court judge had been instituted by General Ironsi. In doing this he was following the practice laid down by the British after the Jos riots of 1945 and the Kano killings of 1953. But before this Commission sat, he had asked his Chief of Staff to conduct a brief preliminary inquiry. Pressed several times before the Supreme Military Council to produce his findings, Colonel Gowon had procrastinated, claiming the report was not yet ready. In fact it never was ready, and after taking power he dismissed the Commission, which consequently never sat. As a result there was no apportionment of responsibility for the May killings, no prosecution in law of those responsible, and no compensation for the victims.

Thus a deep suspicion of Colonel Gowon grew in the East: it looked as if he had never intended the background to the May killings to come to light. This impression was heightened when he subsequently caused to be published a document that claimed the riots had been caused solely by the publication of the Unification Decree of 24 May. In fact this decree was the unanimous decision of the Supreme Military Council, which had as its members two Northerners, Colonel Hassan Katsina and Alhaji Kam Selem.

Far more important, and often overlooked, was a complete *volte-face* in Eastern thinking on the question of the future form of Nigeria. Previously the Easterners had been the foremost advocates of One Nigeria, had put more effort into the realization of this concept than any other ethnic group, and had constantly promoted its cause at the political level. But between 29 July and 12 September the East swung through 180

73

degrees. It was not, for them, a happy experience, but one which they felt was dictated by recent events. A plaintive paragraph in one of the official publications of the Eastern Region Government in the autumn explains the conclusion the Easterners had come to:

Recent events have shown even more clearly that the belief of the Easterners that only a strong central authority could keep the people of the country together was presumptuous, and perhaps an over-simplification of the situation. Now, the whole basis on which the Easterner's conception of one nation, one common citizenship and one destiny was built, appears never to have existed.*

It was not an agreeable confession to have to make, and the sense of disillusionment was profound, almost traumatic. Even today it is still reflected in the tone of those in Biafra who were at the centre of affairs at that time.

Meanwhile in each region discussions at every level were taking place to decide the posture each region would adopt at the forthcoming Ad Hoc Constitutional Review conference to be held in Lagos starting on 12 September. At this conference the East proposed a loose association of states with a wide degree of internal autonomy, not because that was the Eastern dream, but because it seemed to be the only format which took cognizance of the realities of the situation. Three months later Colonel Ojukwu expressed this view in two sentences: 'It is better that we move slightly apart and survive. It is much worse that we move close and perish in the collision.'†

The North also opted for a loose federation, but even looser than the East had proposed. The Northern proposal was so loose that it amounted to a Confederation of States; and to leave no doubt about their wishes, the Northern delegation appended a detailed memorandum about the East African Common Services Organization, which it suggested as a model. In their proposals the Northern delegation had this to say about Nigerian unity:

Recent events have shown that for Nigerian leaders to try and

* *The Problem of Nigerian Unity: The Case of Eastern Nigeria*, p. 28.
† Verbatim Report of Proceedings of Supreme Military Council, Aburi, Ghana, 4–5 January 1967, p. 45.

build a future for the country on rigid political ideology will be unrealistic and disastrous. We have pretended for too long that there are no differences between the peoples of this country. The hard fact which we must honestly accept as of paramount importance in the Nigerian experiment especially for the future is that we are different peoples brought together by recent accidents of history. To pretend otherwise would be folly.*

The similarity of conclusion in that passage and the one quoted earlier from the Eastern publication are obvious. For the first time ever it appeared that East and North were agreed on the self-evidence of their own incompatibility.

The North went even further, asking that in any new Nigerian Constitution a secession clause should be written, adding: 'Any member state of the Union should reserve the right to secede completely and unilaterally from the Union, and to make arrangements for cooperation with the other members of the Union in such a manner as they may severally or individually deem fit.'†

Unlike the Eastern attitude, the North's viewpoint was completely in accord with decades of tradition. That was when the second *volte-face* occurred. There seemed after a few days in Lagos to be a crisis inside the Northern delegation. Colonel Katsina arrived from Kaduna; the delegates hurriedly left for the North; the conference was adjourned. When the Northerners arrived back after consultations, they presented an entirely different set of proposals. This time they wanted a strong and effective central government, thus diminishing the autonomy of the Regions; they agreed to the creation of more states in Nigeria (the idea had always been abhorrent to them before); and they agreed to cut out any mention of secession.

There have been various explanations offered for this extraordinary break with all traditional Northern attitudes. One is that the Middle Belt elements, whose infantrymen composed

* Original memorandum submitted by the Northern Delegation to the Nigerian Ad Hoc Constitutional Conference which opened in Lagos on 12 September 1966. Quoted in full in *The North and Constitutional Developments in Nigeria*, p. 23.

† Ibid., p. 25.

the bulk of the army, made plain that they did not want a return to regional autonomy, since that would reimpose on them the hegemony of the Emirs which they found so irksome; and that they pressured both the North and the central government with their preponderance in the army, on which both sets of rulers now depended, to get their way. If this is true, then it brought a new force into Nigerian politics, the minority tribes, and caused what Mr Walter Schwarz refers to as 'the third coup'.

Another explanation is that it occurred to the Emirs, or was explained to them, that virtually autonomous regions would depend largely on their own revenue, and that the North would then be left to repay the massive loans owing for the Kainji Dam project and the Bornu Railway Extension, while the East would collar most of the oil revenue.

A third explanation is that once again the British diplomats got to work and used their undoubted influence in the North to urge that it was certainly not Whitehall's wish that Nigeria should become a Confederation of States.

Fourthly, it is possible that the Northern rulers realized that they could afford to let minority tribe figures take the front of the stage in a unified Nigeria, and could even afford the creation of new states, provided they remained the true power base in the background by making sure that the central government remained dependent of its power on the army, and the army remained the tool of the North. Some evidence to support this view came later when, after the North had ostensibly been divided into six states, Colonel Katsina was asked by a B.B.C. correspondent whether this change in any way affected the traditional power structure in the North. He replied, 'Not in the slightest'. When, half way through the present war, Gowon looked as if he might assert himself, Katsina moved a brigade of Hausas to the northern approaches of Lagos and calmly appointed himself Army Chief of Staff in succession to another northerner, Colonel Bissalla.

Whatever the reason for the change, it was so sudden and so out of character that it smacked of a 'deal' somewhere behind the scenes, and the satisfaction of Whitehall at the change was so evident in Lagos that one is at pains to believe the British

High Commission was content to remain an idle bystander throughout.

As it turned out the Constitutional Conference came to nought; for it was interrupted and stultified by another outbreak of killings of Easterners in the North, the worst ever, and of such an intensity that it destroyed once and for all any illusion that the hatred of the North towards the East could be dismissed as a passing phase in a new nation, and laid the grounds for the Eastern feeling that their only hope of ultimate survival as a people was to get out of Nigeria.

In later explanatory literature published by the Nigerian Military Government (not surprisingly Federal literature is strongly pro-Northern), several reasons are given for these massacres, and the size and character of them is strongly played down. An examination of these excuses reveals them to have been adduced or invented after the massacres, and a comparison of the pertinent dates and an examination of contemporary evidence from European eye-witnesses proves their falsehood. The main excuse was that there were killings of some Northerners in the East, and that this triggered the massacre of the Easterners in the North. In fact although there was some violence shown against Northerners living in the East, it was first manifested a full seven days after the killings of Easterners in the North.

As in May the massacres were plotted and organized by much the same elements that had been discredited in January; ex-politicians, civil servants, local government officials and party hacks and thugs. Again they were seen driving in hired buses from town to town in the North, exhorting the populace to violence and leading them in their attacks on the *Sabon Garis* where the Easterners lived. There was one significant difference; in the late summer the police and the army not only joined in but in many cases actively led the killing gangs, spearheading the looting of the victims' properties and the raping of their womenfolk.

These outbreaks started between 18 and 24 September, that is, within a few days of the opening of the Constitutional Conference in Lagos, in the Northern cities of Makurdi, Minna, Gboko, Gombe, Jos, Sokoto and Kaduna. The Fourth

Battalion at Kaduna left its barracks and went on the rampage with the civilians. Colonel Katsina issued a warning to the soldiers to desist, with not the slightest effect.

On 29 September 1966 Colonel Gowon made a radio broadcast apparently intended to bring the violence to an end. In it he said: 'It appears that it is going beyond reason, and is now at a point of recklessness and irresponsibility', giving the impression to his listeners that up to a certain point the killing of Easterners might be regarded as a reasonable practice. In any event his intervention was fruitless. Far from abating, the pogrom on that day exploded from a blaze into a holocaust.

Lest descriptions of what happened should be regarded by the reader as a figment of imagination, a theory that has subsequently come close to being postulated in some British and Nigerian Government circles, three European eye-witnesses had better tell the tale of what they saw.

The correspondent of *Time* magazine, 7 October:

The massacre began at the airport near the Fifth Battalion's home city of Kano. A Lagos-bound jet had just arrived from London, and as the Kano passengers were escorted into the customs shed a wild-eyed soldier stormed in, brandishing a rifle and demanding 'Ina Nyamiri' – the Hausa for 'Where are the damned Ibos?'. There were Ibos among the customs officers, and they dropped their chalk and fled, only to be shot down in the main terminal by other soldiers. Screaming the blood curses of a Moslem Holy War, the Hausa troops turned the airport into a shambles, bayonetting Ibo workers in the bar, gunning them down in the corridors, and hauling Ibo passengers off the plane to be lined up and shot.

From the airport the troops fanned out through downtown Kano, hunting down Ibos in bars, hotels, and on the streets. One contingent drove their Landrovers to the rail-road station where more than 100 Ibos were waiting for a train, and cut them down with automatic weapon fire.

The soldiers did not have to do all the killing. They were soon joined by thousands of Hausa civilians, who rampaged through the city armed with stones, cutlasses, matchets, and home-made weapons of metal and broken glass. Crying 'Heathen' and 'Allah' the mobs and troops invaded the Sabon Gari (strangers' quarter) ransacking, looting and burning Ibo homes and stores and murdering their owners.

All night long and into the morning the massacre went on. Then, tired but fulfilled, the Hausas drifted back to their homes and barracks to get some breakfast and sleep. Municipal garbage trucks were sent out to collect the dead and dump them into mass graves outside the city. The death toll will never be known, but it was at least a thousand.

Somehow several thousand Ibos survived the orgy, and all had the same thought: to get out of the North.

Mr Walter Partington of the *Daily Express*, London, 6 October:

But from what I have been told on my journey by chartered plane to towns to which the North civil airline would fly, and hitching a lift through this desolate land, the horror of the massacre at times seems to equal that of the Congo. I do not know if there are any Ibos left in the Northern Region ... for if they are not dead they must be hiding in the bush of this land which is as big as Britain and France.

I saw vultures and dogs tearing at Ibo corpses, and women and children wielding matchets and clubs and guns.

I talked in Kaduna with the Airline Charter Pilot who flew hundreds of Ibos to safety last week. He said, 'The death toll must be far in excess of 3,000'. . . . One young English woman said, 'The Hausas were carting wounded Ibos off to hospital to kill them there.'

I talked to three families who fled from the bush town of Nguru, 176 miles north of here [the dispatch was datelined Lagos]. They escaped in three Landrovers from the town where about fifty Ibos were murdered by mobs drunk on beer in some European shops. Another Englishman who fled the town told of two Catholic priests running for it, the mob after them. 'I don't know if they escaped; I didn't wait to see.' ... A lot of the massacred Ibos are buried in mass graves outside the Moslem walls.

In Jos charter pilots who have been airlifting Ibos to Eastern safety talked of at least 800 dead.

In Zaria, forty-five miles from Kaduna, I talked with a saffron-robed Hausa who told me: 'We killed about 250 here. Perhaps Allah willed it.'

One European saw a woman and her daughter slaughtered in his front garden after he had been forced to turn them away.

Mr Colin Legum of the *Observer*, London, 16 October 1966:

While the Hausas in each town and village in the North know

what happened in their own localities, only the Ibos know the whole terrible story from the 600,000 or so refugees who have fled to the safety of the Eastern Region – hacked, slashed, mangled, stripped naked and robbed of all their possessions; the orphans, the widows, the traumatized. A woman, mute and dazed, arrived back in her village after travelling for five days with only a bowl in her lap. She held her child's head, which was severed before her eyes.

Men, women and children arrived with arms and legs broken, hands hacked off, mouths split open. Pregnant women were cut open and the unborn children killed. The total casualties are unknown. The number of injured who have arrived in the East runs into thousands. After a fortnight the scene in the Eastern Region continues to be reminiscent of the ingathering of exiles into Israel after the end of the last war. The parallel is not fanciful.

To continue with descriptions of the type and scale of the atrocities perpetrated during those weeks of late summer 1966 would be to invite criticism that one was glorying in the bestiality of the affair. The eye-witness descriptions later put together from the victims' accounts run to several thousand pages, and in parts the nature of the atrocities perpetrated baffles human understanding. The same applies to the descriptions offered by the European doctors who were among those tending the wounded at Enugu airport and railway station as the refugees arrived back in the East.

But no less awe-inspiring has been the subsequent attempt by the Nigerian and British Governments to brush all this under the carpet, as if by lack of mention the memory of it would the more easily pass away. For the Nigerian Government the subject is taboo; in Whitehall circles it is the best conversation-stopper since Burgess and Maclean.

Many sophisticated newspaper correspondents also appear tacitly to have agreed not to mention the killings of 1966 in regard to the breakaway of Eastern Nigeria from the Federation, and to the present war. This is unrealistic. One can no more explain the present-day attitude of Biafrans to Nigerians without reference to these events than one can account for contemporary Jewish attitudes towards the Germans without reference to the Jews' experience in the Nazis' hands between 1933 and 1945.

7. Aburi – Nigeria's Last Chance

THERE is no doubt that the aim of the pogrom of 1966 was to drive the Easterners out of the North and perhaps even out of Nigeria. In both it was remarkably successful. In the wake of the killing the Easterners came home in droves, convinced once and for all that Nigeria neither could nor would offer them the simple guarantees of security of life and property that are habitually the inalienable rights of citizens in their own country.

They have since been accused of playing up the scope and effect of the massacres. Ironically no playing up was necessary. The facts spoke for themselves and were witnessed by too many independent minds to be discountable. Mr Schwarz, who can hardly be accused of sensationalism, refers to them as 'a pogrom of genocidal proportions'.

Nor were they directed solely against the Ibos. The word 'Ibo' is a single generic term in the North – actually the Hausa word is 'Nyamiri', which is derogatory as well as descriptive – for all Easterners regardless of racial group. Thus not only the Ibos suffered, though they were undoubtedly in the majority. Efiks, Ibibios, Ogojas and Ijaws were also singled out for butchery.

As they came home and told their tales, a wave of rage swept across the East, mingled also with despair and disillusion. There was hardly a village or town, family or compound in the Region that did not take into its fold one of the refugees and listen to what he had to say. Thousands of the refugees were maimed for life by what they had gone through either mentally or physically. Almost everyone was penniless, for the Easterner traditionally invests his money in his business or in property, and few could bring away more than a small suitcase when they fled.

Houses, businesses, prospective earnings and salaries, savings and furniture, cars and concessions – for many people the sum total of a lifetime of effort, all had to be left behind. Not only were the refugees refugees, they were without any

81

visible means of support when they arrived back in the East, for many of them a place they had never seen.

Naturally there was a reaction. While the killings were going on in the North there were sporadic retaliatory acts of violence against Northerners living in the East. Expatriates have told of Hausas being set on in Port Harcourt, Aba and Onitsha. But the same eye-witnesses stressed that these were occasional acts born of the fury of the moment. There were never more than a few thousand Northerners in the East, and Colonel Ojukwu's reaction to the news of violence against them was fast. As the toll mounted in the North and the news started to come through of just what was going on, it became clear that the future of Northerners in the East was problematic to put it mildly.

The Military Governor ordered that those that there were should be escorted northwards over the border, and should have police protection all the way. His ability to command his own people contrasted with the impotence of Gowon and Katsina. Though as human beings they may have hated their charges, the Eastern Region police did their duty. On only one occasion, when a train was stopped by rioters at Imo River Bridge, was violence done to a handful of Northerners while they were under police protection. The overwhelming majority left the East intact.

As regards the totals, very much a question in dispute ever since, Mr Legum hit the nail on the head when he observed that 'Only the Ibos know the whole terrible story'. Faced with the obvious disinclination of the Federal Government to conduct an inquiry, the East ordered its own. It was conducted by Mr Gabriel Onyiuke, the former Nigerian Attorney-General, who had also fled from Nigeria. It took a long time to complete. Many of the refugees had scattered throughout the Region and were difficult to reach. Others failed to respond to an appeal to come forward and testify. Moreover the influx continued for months as the aura of violence and fear spread from the North to the West and to Lagos.

Taking their cue from their counterparts in the North, Northern soldiers in the West also started marauding through the streets seeking Easterners to harass. They haunted the streets of Lagos at night picking up stray Easterners and taking them out on to the Agege Motor Road for execution. Some of the top men in Nigeria fled with a car full of belongings from their houses and flats in the capital in an effort to cross the Niger and reach safety.

By January the inquiry had established a figure of 10,000 dead in the North, but it was provisional, and had been reached by adding together the large units of those killed in the major cities. There had been hundreds of small settlements of Easterners out in the open country of the North, sometimes no more than ten or a dozen of them in a village otherwise inhabited solely by Hausas or Tivs. When evidence of what had happened to these small units had been collated, the total of dead, including those who died in the West and Lagos, topped 30,000. Added to that there were several thousand more maimed and mutilated, and others demented for life.

Even the Eastern population of the North exceeded known estimates. Altogether, when they were all back, the figure was put at 1,300,000, while those coming in from the other regions came to close to 500,000.

By necessity there was an element of estimation in the figures, for many people had given evidence that they had known of a family living at a certain place, but had heard nothing of them since. The cross-tabulation of evidence to pin down the fate of those who were known not to have returned would ideally have needed a computer.

A visitor to the East three months after such an enormous influx of refugees would have expected to find great camps of displaced persons living off charity; it would have been perfectly normal for appeals to have been made to the United Nations Refugee Fund to import aid and relief to prevent the refugees from dying of starvation. Ironically, if that had been the reaction of the East, their refugee problem might then have become a world conscience-issue, like the Gaza Strip, and the sympathy they might have received could have carried them through into separate independence with the blessing of the world. Alternatively, if they had opted to break with Nigeria there and then, they might have received instant support from a wide circle of sympathizers.

But the Eastern Nigerians were not the Arabs. They would tolerate no festering sore like the Gaza Strip on their land scape. The extended family system – the traditional structure under which everyone is obliged to take in any relative in distress, no matter how distant he may be – came into full play. Almost miraculously the refugees disappeared, finding shelter with long unseen grandparents, uncles, cousins, in-laws. In each case the breadwinner simply took on the added burden of more mouths to feed. This was the reason why, on the surface, the problem appeared to have been coped with so quickly.

But under the surface the problem was there, and it was enormous. The influx had caused an unemployment problem of hardly manageable proportions; health and social welfare services were unable to cope; medical services were overwhelmed with the casualties; educational services suddenly found several hundred thousand children of school age to teach. In most other countries in the world the central government would have felt itself obliged to launch a massive aid programme, either through an assisted rapid expansion of all services, or through wide-operating fiscal relief. Bearing in mind that the damage had been done by fellow-Nigerians pretty extensive compensation would also have been the order of the day. Being Nigeria under Colonel Gowon, nothing of the sort happened.

There was no expression of regret; there was no demand by the central government that the North voice an expression of regret or remorse; there was no compensation, no recompense, no offer to make good the damage in so far as it could be made good. So far as is known, not one soldier was ever given a day's 'confined to barracks' punishment, not one officer was court-martialled, not one policeman was ever retired, and not one civilian ever faced a court of law, although many had been identified.

The attitude of the Gowon Government in Lagos answered Easterners' questions about the impartiality of the centre with discouraging finality. The tension was by this time electric and the demand for a complete break with Nigeria, starting as a small murmur, grew to a hurricane.

Of the three original regions, the East was the last even to mention the word. The threat to secede had come from the North periodically for twenty years. In 1953 at the talks in London that gave rise to the 1954 Constitution, Chief Awolowo heading the Action Group had threatened the West would secede if Lagos was made Federal Territory rather than a part of the Western Region. He was only dissuaded from this course by a sharp warning from the Colonial Secretary Mr Oliver Lyttleton, later Lord Chandos.

But by now most Easterners were convinced that the old Nigeria in which they had participated was dead. That is to say, the spirit of it was dead. Only the format remained, and without the spirit, the format was an empty shell, and a badly shattered one at that.

By contrast Colonel Ojukwu thought there remained a chance that Nigeria could be saved. He fought the separatist demands with all his authority, even though aware that in the process he might lose his authority. He could go so far but no further. He was convinced that on the basis of reality alone the best that Nigeria could get for herself would be a structure where a temporary loosening of the existing regional ties would allow time to elapse for a cooling-off process, later to be followed by further discussions in a less feverish atmosphere.

But in Lagos Gowon was apparently being advised by a group of men who had not been to the East since the massacres in the North, and presumed that the aggrievement of the Easterners was a passing tantrum which could reasonably be discounted, or at least overcome if they later proved trouble-some. This ability to underestimate the degree of the damage that had been done, and the reaction in feeling it had caused east of the Niger, also seems to have infected the British High Commission, whose subsequent advice to Whitehall was to pooh-pooh the crisis as a temporary brush-fire.

One precaution Colonel Ojukwu did feel obliged to take nevertheless was to import some arms. The departure of the Enugu garrison with all its weaponry and the arrival back home of the Eastern troops without any had left the East defenceless. Moreover Colonel Ojukwu had come into posses-sion of a document from an Ibo diplomat in Rome showing that a Northern Army Major, Sule Apollo, was in Italy buying large quantities of arms.

In the meantime invitations had been issued to resume the constitutional talks. In view of the violence with which Northern troops were still threatening Easterners in the streets of Lagos, Ojukwu regarded these invitations as somewhat unrealistic unless adequate safeguards could be guaranteed. None was forthcoming, and as all the other three regions and the capital were under the heavy control of Northern troops, Ojukwu could not see how he could reasonably ask the Eastern delegates to risk their lives by returning. Gowon responded by dismissing the constitutional talks as being able to serve no further purpose, and announced that a committee would draft a new constitution based on a Nigeria composed of between eight and fourteen states.

Ojukwu was aghast, but knew his former colleague well enough to know that the weakling Supreme Commander had got into fresh hands and was being emboldened by a new group of advisers. Sure enough he had and was.

Before the autumn killings some of the top positions in the civil service in Lagos had been held by Easterners who had reached the top through their talents. The Permanent Secretary – that is, the top civil servant in a Ministry – is a powerful man even in a democratic society. He knows his Ministry and the business of that Ministry often better than the Minister. By advising the Minister one way or the other he can often influence policy or even create it indirectly. In a military government of young and not-too-bright soldiers, happy enough behind a gun but bewildered when the bullets have finally brought them to power and faced them with the complexities of government, the Permanent Secretary becomes even more influential. When the leader of the military clique in power turns out to be a man of straw, he (the civil servant) runs the show.

After the killings the Ibos and other Easterners had fled, leaving their posts vacant. There were not enough Northerners to fill them, and in any case a talented Northern civil servant is so valuable back home that he is likely to rate a better job in the Northern Region than he could get in Lagos. The Yoruba from the West tend to stick to their own Regional affairs. The men who had moved in when the Easterners left in the autumn and early winter of 1966 were mostly minority-tribe men. As has been explained earlier, they had their own reasons for not wishing to see a return to the powerful Regions of yesteryear. So long as Nigeria remained a multi-state complex with weak regions and a powerful centre, and so long as they ran the centre, the power was theirs for the first time in history. It was a chance not to be missed.

By the early winter of 1966 Colonel Gowon had taken on the aspect in Eastern eyes of a highly suspect individual who either could not or would not honour his agreements. This impression was later to be so heightened that today it forms one of the major obstacles to peace in Nigeria. The bases for this mistrust may be summarized as follows:

The unanimous agreement of the representatives of the Military Governors of 9 August had been for the repatriation of troops to their regions of origin, which had not been implemented; for the repatriation of the arms and ammunition they carried with them, which had not been implemented. Gowon had pledged that the killing of Eastern soldiers would stop, but it had not. He had promised that the inquiry into the May massacre set up by General Ironsi would 'certainly go on as scheduled'. It was never heard of again.

In early September a number of Northern troops from Ibadan, capital of the West, had raided Benin City in the Midwest and snatched from prison a number of officers in detention for their part in the January coup. The Northerners among the detainees were released in the North, while the Easterners were murdered. Gowon had promised immediately that those responsible would be punished, but this too went by the board.

Finally his dismissal of the Ad Hoc Constitutional Conference on 30 November on the grounds that the Eastern delegates had not attended it since the original adjournment on 3 October was seen in the East as dictatorial, since the reason for the non-attendance was the quite genuine fear of violence at the hands of Northern soldiers in Lagos. The bald announcement that a committee would draft a new constitution based on between ten and fourteen states was seen in the same light. In the same broadcast on 30 November Gowon felt bold enough for the first time to threaten to use force 'if circumstances compel'.

The weeks rolled by without any spontaneous offer from central government of aid to alleviate the social problems caused by the tide of refugees in the East, and by early December Colonel Ojukwu told a journalist: 'I cannot wait indefinitely for Lagos, so I have to make other arrangements'.*

There was increasing popular pressure that the Regional Military Governors should meet to sort the problems out, a view strongly shared by Colonel Ojukwu. But since there was nowhere within Nigeria he felt he could go in personal safety, it was agreed to hold the meeting at Aburi, Ghana, under the auspices of General Ankrah.

It was there in ex-President Nkrumah's luxurious country seat in the hills above Accra that the Supreme Military Council of Nigeria met on 4 and 5 January 1967. Present were: Lieutenant-Colonel Gowon, the four Regional Military Governors – Colonel Robert Adebayo (successor to the dead Colonel Fajuyi), and Lieutenant-Colonels Katsina, Ojukwu and Ejoor. Four others were also on the Council, representing the Navy, Lagos Territory, and two from the Federal Police; but the real talks hinged on the five colonels.

Intellectually Ojukwu towered above the rest, and they seemed to know it. To make sure there were no later misinterpretations as to what had been decided, a complete stenographic record and a tape recording was made of the entire discussion. Later when Gowon reneged on the agreements, Ojukwu released the entire text of the two-day discussions as a set of six gramophone records.

A study of these records leaves no doubt that only one man had a clear idea of the single way in which Nigeria could be preserved as a political entity, and that was the Military Governor of the East. Gowon's performance reveals that he wished the Federation to stay together, but beyond that had little or no ideas. The other three soon found themselves

* *West Africa*, 24 December 1966.

forced to agree with the compulsive logic of the Easterner's arguments.

On the question of the repatriation of troops Gowon, confronted with his failure to implement, lamely explained that he had only meant that Easterners should be repatriated to the East, and Northerners in the East should go back to the North. Although the Western Leaders of Thought Conference* had unanimously agreed with the East's firm stand on the repatriation from the West as well, Gowon said he had to keep Northerners there as there were no Yoruba troops. At this Adebayo protested.

But the main question was the form of Nigeria and of its army in the immediate future. Here Ojukwu argued that

As long as this situation exists, men from Eastern Nigeria would find it utterly impossible to stay in the same barracks, feed in the same mess, fight from the same trenches as men in the Army from Northern Nigeria. . . . For these basic reasons the separation of forces, the separation of population is, in all sincerity, in order to avoid further friction and further killing.

Katsina agreed, as did Adebayo and Ejoor.

On the question of Ojukwu's non-recognition of Gowon as Supreme Commander, the Eastern leader argued that as the fate of General Ironsi was not known, there was no one who could succeed him. But in his absence there were at least six officers senior to Gowon, and that the next senior should manage the affairs of the country. And thirdly the East had never been a party to the nomination of Gowon to the post. At this point Gowon revealed what had happened to General Ironsi, admitting that he had thought it 'expedient' not to announce it sooner, although he must have known the details since Lieutenant Walbe reported back on the evening of 29 July the previous year.

* The Leaders of Thought were first summoned under the Ironsi régime to advise each military Governor on local affairs and feeling. They comprised leading figures in the professions, business, commerce, administration and the chiefs and elders. But they were nominated by the Governors; hence Ojukwu preferred to listen to the popularly mandated members of the Consultative Assembly, which did not exist anywhere else.

The question was finally resolved by the decision to submit the army to the Supreme Military Council, which would have a chairman who would also be 'Commander-in-Chief of the Armed Forces and Head of the Federal Military Government'.

On the constitutional side the meeting agreed that the Ad Hoc Conference should resume its sitting as soon as practicable to begin from where they left off.

On the subject of the East's big headache, the refugees, the meeting agreed that Permanent Secretaries of Finance should meet within two weeks to submit their recommendations on how to help rehabilitation of the dispossessed go forward; that civil servants and Public Corporation staff (including daily paid employees) should receive full salary up to the end of the financial year, 31 March, unless they had been re-employed; and that Regional Police Commissioners should meet to discuss the problem of recovery of property left behind by the refugees. These were the decisions Ojukwu had to take home to the people, for they were vital elements in calming tempers down. For instance, there were 12,000 railway workers alone among the East's refugees.

The meeting also agreed that future meetings should be held in Nigeria at a *mutually* agreed place, and that government information media should be restrained from publishing inflammatory or embarrassing statements or documents.

With that the meeting broke up in goodwill and champagne toasts. Back in the East Ojukwu gave a press conference to reassure the Easterners (many of whom had been far more in favour of immediate secession than in parleying) that the Aburi meeting had been worthwhile; he told them that provided the arrangements made were implemented, much progress would have been made towards relieving tension and banishing fear in the country.

Aburi was Nigeria's last chance. It has been said since that there was something rather 'unfair' in Ojukwu being cleverer than the other four colonels, as though he had in some way taken unfair advantage. It was also put forward, notably by English writers, that Ojukwu failed to play the gentleman because he went to Aburi with a clear idea of the agreements he wanted, a cogent brief in his head, while the others went under the assumption the meeting was just a friendly get-together of brother officers.

It is somewhat disingenuous to claim that the other four colonels could not be expected to be aware the first meeting of the Supreme Military Council after the holocaust of the summer would be other than a fireside chat. It must have been perfectly clear to one and all that Aburi was a historical occasion. The other colonels could have gone prepared if they had wished, and Colonel Ojukwu firmly expected that they would be prepared. They had their civil servants and advisers too.

Within a few days of Gowon's return to Lagos the Aburi agreements began to die on the vine. The minority-tribe civil servants previously mentioned took one look at what had been agreed and realized that their witless chief had gone far further than they would have wished him to go. The drawing apart of army and populace for the cooling-down period gave the regions in their view far too much autonomy, thus weakening their own authority. The Permanent Secretaries set to work on Gowon to get him to back-track on the agreements.

In ten days the Federal Government had published a booklet called *Nigeria 1966* which gave the Federal, that is to say Northern, version of everything that had happened since the January coup. It is to this day a remarkable exercise in distortion. At the time it caused a furore in the East. When Colonel Ojukwu protested over the phone that it had been agreed not to publish any more official versions, Gowon told him after some flustering that there had been a leak. Later Ojukwu learned that far from being a leak, the booklet had appeared simultaneously in London, New York and several other capitals with all the usual publishers' ballyhoo, including cocktail parties at the High Commissions and Embassies. When he again remonstrated by phone, Gowon again flustered until he was cornered, then lost his temper and put the phone down. (These conversations have been tape-recorded at the Enugu end.) Colonel Ojukwu also put the phone down, but with an icy foreboding. For he knew that his own position inside the East would make it impossible for him to back down on Aburi.

On 26 January Gowon held a press conference in Lagos in which he purported to reveal the agreements of the Aburi meeting. The text of the press conference appears to be based not on the minutes and final agreement of Aburi, but on the criticisms of those documents by the Permanent Secretaries. Reading the two (press conference and Aburi minutes) side by side, one wonders whether Gowon was really present at Aburi.

First he disagreed with the submission of the army to the Supreme Military Council, objecting that it took the control of the army out of his hands and placed it in the corporate body of the Council. He went on to add that the Military Area Commands (covering the areas of the existing regions) would be under the Military Headquarters 'which will be directly under me as the Supreme Commander of the Armed Forces'.* Actually the conference at Aburi had agreed on no such thing as the phrase in quotes.

On displaced persons, he said that when the Finance Secretaries met 'the principle of revenue allocation should not be discussed', although revenue allocation notably in the form of some fiscal relief, was vital to enabling the East to cope with its 1,800,000 refugees.

On payment of salaries, he intoned, 'The decision to continue to pay salaries to the end of March does not take into consideration economic factors which are linked to it ... secondly it does not make sense to include daily paid workers among those whose salaries should continue to be paid. The decision should therefore be reconsidered.' For good measure he warned that Federal Corporations would find it 'very difficult' to continue to pay their displaced employees.

On the constitution he dropped another bombshell. The Permanent Secretaries had advised him 'to stick to their previous recommendations and advice, namely: that the Ad Hoc Constitutional Conference should stand adjourned indefinitely; and that the immediate political programme announced to the nation on 30 November (i.e. the project for a Nigeria of ten to fourteen states) by the Supreme Commander should be implemented, and the country must be so informed'.

By the time he had finished with the small print there appeared to be little of Aburi left. He may well have disagreed with what he had signed; there might well have been a good

* *Nigerian Crisis*, Vol. 6, pp. 11–15.

case for reconsidering Aburi; but the fact remains that he and his fellow colonels had all voluntarily signed the document, after two days of talks, without any coercion, and the unilateral rescinding of so many of the important paragraphs, particularly the ones most vitally sought after in the East, effectively dealt a blow to Nigeria from which it never recovered.

In Enugu Colonel Ojukwu metaphorically rubbed his eyes on reading the transcript of the press conference. It has been said by many writers then and since that 'Colonel Ojukwu did this . . .' or 'Colonel Ojukwu refused to do that . . .' but little attempt seems to have been made to understand the pressures he was under. As far back as the massacres of the previous autumn the cry to pull out of Nigeria had been growing louder and more clamorous. More and more sections of the population joined in. The refugee problem, smoothly forgotten or bypassed in Lagos, was still a festering reality. The question of payment of salaries, for thousands of Corporation employees and civil servants a question of whether their families ate or not, was still a burning topic. He had fought the separatist clamour as far and as hard as he could.

'On Aburi We Stand' became the slogan in the East. Colonel Ojukwu refused to attend further meetings of the Supreme Military Council until the Aburi agreements had been implemented, partly because the meeting scheduled was in a Benin City liberally sprinkled with Northern soldiers, partly because he knew he could go no further. In a broadcast at the end of February he said, 'If the Aburi agreements are not fully implemented by 31 March, I shall have no alternative but to feel free to take whatever measures may be necessary to give effect in this Region to those agreements.'

On that day the departure of Eastern Nigeria was fully expected. Journalists arriving in Enugu for a press conference already had their headline mapped out. Instead, still playing for the last chance of staying inside One Nigeria, Colonel Ojukwu told them that he was issuing a Revenue Edict appropriating all Federal Revenue collected in the East as a means of paying for the rehabilitation programme. The decree did not affect oil revenues, as these were collected in Lagos. The reporters were stunned; they had expected fire and brimstone and were being confronted with a fiscal programme. Mildly Ojukwu told them the East would only pull out of Nigeria if she were attacked or blockaded.

The Federal Government replied with Decree Eight, a document that appeared at first glance to implement the major points of the constitutional agreements of Aburi, if not the fiscal arrangements. Decree Eight, like Aburi, vested the legislative and executive powers in the Supreme Military Council, and decisions on vital matters could only be taken with the agreement of all the Military Governors. Within their own regions the Governors were to have virtual autonomy.

It looked good, and was hailed as such, although it went no further than what had been agreed at Aburi four months earlier. Except for the small print. This was so skilfully worded that it looked fairly harmless until read a second time, when it was seen that the extra provisions reduced the main paragraphs to nothing.

One of the extra clauses was to the effect that the Regional Governors could not exercise their powers 'so as to impede or prejudice the authority of the Federation, or endanger the continuance of Federal Government'. Although it looks harmless, it was presumably up to the Federal Government, i.e. Gowon, to decide precisely what would 'impede or prejudice the authority. . . .' Another section enabled the Federal Government to take over the authority of a regional government which was 'endangering the continuance of the Federal Government', and again the criterion was apparently left to Lagos.

Most menacing of all to Eastern eyes was a paragraph under which a state of emergency could be declared in any region with the agreement of only three Military Governors. As the declaration of a State of Emergency usually implies sending in troops, and as the other three Military Governors were either Northern or governed regions occupied by Northern troops, Colonel Ojukwu saw this as being specifically anti-Eastern. He rejected the decree.

The growing unpopularity of the Gowon régime now sprouted elsewhere in the South. In the West there had been growing resentment over the failure to repatriate the Northern troops, a measure that Aburi had re-stated. Chief Awolowo led the revolt. His following had traditionally been among the proletarian and radical elements in the West, and these were the people who resented most the occupation of the Northern soldiers. At a meeting of the Western Leaders of Thought in Ibadan in late April he resigned as the West's delegate to the supposedly soon-to-be-resumed Ad Hoc Conference, stating in his letter: 'It is my considered view that whilst some of the demands of the East are excessive, within the context of a Nigerian union most of such demands are not only well founded but are designed for smooth and healthy association among the various national units of Nigeria.'*

Chief Awolowo had just returned from a visit to Colonel Ojukwu in Enugu and he had been able to witness for himself (which others scrupulously refrained from doing) the depth of feeling in the East. According to Colonel Ojukwu, Awolowo had asked if the East would pull out, and the reply had been that it would not until and unless it was absolutely offered no other alternative.

After seeing the situation for himself, Awolowo sympathized with the sufferings of the Eastern people, and asked that if the East was going to pull out he be allowed twenty-four hours forewarning and he would do the same for the West. This he was promised. Later he got his forewarning, but by that time he had been swayed round by other attractions, and failed to fulfil his intent. From the point of view of the Yorubas it was a pity, for if Awolowo had stuck to his guns the Federal Government, unable to face two simultaneous disaffections, would have been forced to fulfil the Aburi agreements to the letter.

Had it done so, Nigeria would probably be at peace today, not as a unitary state of twelve provinces, but as a Confederation of quasi-autonomous states living in harmony. The civil servants at the centre might have lost much of their power, but a lot more people would have stayed alive; including many Yoruba, for today the West is as ever occupied by Northern troops while the hastily recruited Yoruba are used as cannon fodder against the Biafran machine-guns. Exactly what their casualties have been in this war the Biafrans do not know and

* Schwarz, op. cit., p. 227.

the Federal Army declines to say, but Biafran Military Intelligence is convinced that of all ethnic groups in the Federal Army the Yoruba have taken higher casualties than any other.

Thus at Ibadan in late April 1967 Awolowo added to his resignation that if the East pulled out, the West would feel free to follow suit. He was followed by Colonel Ejoor of the Midwest, a region with over a million Ibo normally resident in it. He wished to avoid being caught in any future clash and called for a demilitarized zone in his Region.

At this point yet another thunderbolt came from the North. The Northern Emirs, for decades virulent exponents of their own domination of Nigeria, suddenly issued a call to the effect that 'the North should be irrevocably committed to the creation of states – whether or not they are created elsewhere – as the basis of stability in the North and also in the entire Federation; and urges the Federal Government to take immediate steps to set in motion the machinery for the creation of these states'.*

Like the *volte-face* of the Ad Hoc Conference, the decision was so out of character that one is led to the conclusion either that the minority tribes in the infantry had again given voice, or that the Emirs had decided they could use the creation of new states to break up the growing solidarity of the South while themselves remaining united behind the façade and across the state boundaries.

The decision effectively underpinned the Gowon régime and broke up the solidarity of the three Southern Regions. Awolowo, a long-time advocate of the creation of more states as a means to *break up* the North, jumped at the chance. His change of heart coincided with being made Commissioner for Finance and Deputy Chairman of the Supreme Council in a new mixed government of soldiers and civilians. Chief Enahoro, a minority-tribe Midwesterner, and Joseph Tarka, champion of the Tivs, also got ministerial appointments. Ejoor subsided.

With his ranks once more closed Gowon felt strong enough to go for a showdown with the East. It appears by this time that he was being assured that if there was to be any fighting,

* *West Africa*, 13 May 1967.

it would be over very quickly, in his favour, and there is a strong possibility that if he had foreseen the long and horrible war that was to follow he might have stayed his hand. But there were voices in the background persuading that in the event of a military showdown a simple military solution could be imposed, and this may have appealed to his simple, military mind.

Early in May he imposed a partial blockade on the East – it extended to postal and postal order services, but also affected telephones, cables, telex machines and other forms of communication, all of which were routed through Lagos. The effect was to leave the East cut off from the outside, the more so as Nigeria Airways flights were also banned.

In Enugu Colonel Ojukwu confided to Reuters: 'I think we are now rolling downhill. It will take a great deal to halt the momentum. We are very close, very, very close.'

There was one last peace move. A group calling itself the National Conciliation Committee, headed by the new Federal Chief Justice Sir Adetokunboh Ademola, a Yoruba, and including Chief Awolowo, visited Colonel Ojukwu on 7 May. They listened to his views, accepted all his demands, and called on the Federal Government to implement them. These demands included little more than the implementation of the agreement of 9 August to post the troops back to their regions of origin, and to call off the economic sanctions.

On 20 May Gowon accepted all the recommendations. But it was another illusory hope. He announced that the ban on Nigeria Airways flights to the East was lifted, along with other sanctions. But the Director of the Airways privately admitted that he had had no order to resume flights. As for the troops, Colonel Katsina flew from Kaduna to Ibadan to inform the troops they were to be moved – but only to the town of Ilorin, about a stone's throw over the border between West and North, and lying on the main road to Lagos. To have brought them back would have been the work of a moment.

The clamour in the East to get out of Nigeria became too strong even for Colonel Ojukwu to bear. On 26 May the 335-member Consultative Assembly of Chiefs and Elders gave him a unanimous mandate at the end of a noisy session to pull the

East out of what was now regarded as the defunct Federation of Nigeria 'at an early practicable date' by declaring the Eastern Region 'a free, sovereign and independent state by the name and title of the Republic of Biafra'.

One of the cardinal errors of the Federal Government was to threaten to use force. The most charitable interpretation is that those in Lagos were blissfully unaware of the depth of feeling in the East. To the Easterners, knowing the Federal Army to be largely composed of those same Northerners who had massacred their fellows barely eight months previously, it looked like (and still does today) a threat to send the hated Northerners to finish off the job of extermination they had left half-done the previous year.

The mandate did not mean secession, but Gowon activated his plans the next day. He declared a state of emergency and simultaneously published a decree dividing Nigeria into twelve new states and abolishing the existing Regions. He could hardly have behaved more provocatively. For one thing there had been no consultation, which was in itself contrary to the Constitution. It went back on all the promises that each Region would have its full say in any future format of association. More important was the division of the East into three tiny states, each of them impotent, and the wrenching of Port Harcourt away from the Ibo State to become the capital of the Rivers State. It has been described as 'an open challenge to secede'. In the same broadcast Gowon announced the reimposition of the blockade, the abrogation of Decree Eight, and accorded himself full powers 'for the short period necessary to carry out the measures which are now urgently required'.

In the small hours of 30 May diplomats and journalists were called to State House, soon to be renamed Biafra Lodge, to hear Colonel Ojukwu read the Declaration of Independence. Here is the text:

Fellow countrymen and women, you, the people of Eastern Nigeria:

Conscious of the supreme authority of Almighty God over all Mankind; of your duty to yourselves and posterity;

Aware that you can no longer be protected in your lives and in your property by any government based outside Eastern Nigeria;

Believing that you are born free and have certain inalienable rights which can best be preserved by yourselves;

Unwilling to be unfree partners in any association of a political or economic nature;

Rejecting the authority of any person or persons other than the Military Government of Eastern Nigeria to make any imposition of whatever kind or nature upon you;

Determined to dissolve all political and other ties between you and the former Federal Republic of Nigeria;

Prepared to enter into such association, treaty or alliance with any sovereign state within the former Federal Republic of Nigeria and elsewhere on such terms and conditions as best to subserve your common good;

Affirming your trust and confidence in me;

Having mandated me to proclaim on your behalf and in your name, that Eastern Nigeria be a sovereign independent Republic,

NOW THEREFORE I, LIEUTENANT-COLONEL CHUKWUEMEKA ODUMEGWU OJUKWU, MILITARY GOVERNOR OF EASTERN NIGERIA, BY VIRTUE OF THE AUTHORITY, AND PURSUANT TO THE PRINCIPLES RECITED ABOVE, DO HEREBY SOLEMNLY PROCLAIM THAT THE TERRITORY AND REGION KNOWN AS AND CALLED EASTERN NIGERIA, TOGETHER WITH HER CONTINENTAL SHELF AND TERRITORIAL WATERS SHALL HENCEFORTH BE AN INDEPENDENT SOVEREIGN STATE OF THE NAME AND TITLE OF 'THE REPUBLIC OF BIAFRA'.

With these words the Eastern Region of Nigeria entered into a self-stated independence, and the word 'Biafra' entered the contemporary political vocabulary – in the view of most political observers at that time, only temporarily.

Three sentiments dominated the outlook of the people of Biafra. Firstly a deep sense not of rebellion, but of rejection, and this feeling lasts until today. For the Biafrans, they did not leave Nigeria but were chased out of it. They firmly believe that the impulse of separation came from the Nigerian side. For most of them it was the shattering of the illusions of their lifetime that after being the foremost of the 'One Nigeria' actors and thinkers, it was finally they who were not wanted. The subsequent attempt of Nigeria to hammer them back into the country has always appeared illogical – among other things. They are convinced that there is no place for them inside

Nigeria as equal citizens with the Nigerians; that the latter do not want them as people, but only their land for the oil it bears and the riches it can produce. They are convinced that it was the Nigerians, not they, who broke the bond that links the contractual society whereby the citizenry have a duty of loyalty to government, which government repays with a guarantee of the protection of life, liberty and property. They remain convinced the only role they could ever play in Nigeria henceforth would be that of victim in the first instance and work-slaves ever after; ironically, despite protestations to the contrary from General Gowon (he had in the meanwhile promoted himself to Major-General), the behaviour of the Nigerian Army, numerous statements from senior Lagos officials, and the propaganda from Kaduna, far from assuaging this fear, have completely confirmed it.

Secondly the Biafrans felt and still feel an utter mistrust for anything the Lagos Government may say or promise to do. Here again precedent gives succour to their belief, for General Gowon has repeatedly shown over the past eighteen months that he cannot impose his will on his army or air force commanders, nor they theirs on the troops in the line. Repeated pledges from Gowon that the soldiers would behave decently, that the air force would desist from bombing civilian centres, have turned out to be hot air. As a result all peace proposals based on a 'Hand over your guns and then we'll be nice to you' promise from the Federal side have met with complete disbelief. As for future constitutional guarantees of safety inside Nigeria, lately offered by Gowon and heavily backed by Britain, the Biafrans reply that they had these guarantees in the Constitution of Nigeria before, but they did not change anything during 1966. This mistrust makes any peace formula proposed by the *present* Nigerian régime highly unlikely to succeed.

Thirdly the Biafrans were possessed of a deeply held conviction that the advent of the Nigerian Army into their land would mean the execution of another pogrom of such massive proportions that it would constitute genocide, that in the planning of the Northern rulers (hence of the Lagos Government) the Biafrans were destined for extinction once and for all, and that the North, avid for the oil royalties of the coast, would continue Balewa's promised 'interrupted march to the sea' over their dead bodies. Outside, this fear was contemptuously put down to 'Ojukwu's propaganda', particularly in British Government circles. The subsequent months, far from robbing this fear of its base, confirmed it in the eyes of most Biafrans without a word being necessary from Colonel Ojukwu.

A number of explanations were immediately postulated to explain the breakaway of Biafra from Nigeria, and were subsequently presented to the world by Lagos, London and correspondents of what might be called the 'establishment press'. One was that Biafra was 'Ojukwu's revolt', the attempt by a single man, backed by a small clique of army officers and civil servants, to create a rebel state through motivations of ambition and personal greed. The facts soon invalidated this explanation, though it is still clung to in a few corners. For one thing the Biafran leadership, in contrast to the people, understood the magnitude of the task that had been undertaken, the risks involved, and most of them had given up positions of power to return home and live in more straitened circumstances in the service of Biafra. It was clear to all of them that the road to ease and luxury, power and prestige, lay in cooperation with the powers-that-be, that is, Lagos. Colonel Ojukwu, if he had chosen to cooperate with Gowon against the wishes of the Eastern people, could have kept his fortune, enjoyed a high position in Nigeria and probably still kept his Governorship of the East, not as a popular leader but as a hated quisling surrounded by Federal Army soldiers. Alternatively, if power had been his motivation, he could have bided his time, intrigued with other Southern leaders among whom he had considerable standing, nursed into being a new Southern Army, and led his own coup at a later date. With his acumen he would probably have been more successful as a coup leader than those who led the previous two insurrections.

For another thing, the unanimity among notable men of Eastern origin in supporting the Biafran cause indicated fairly soon that they believed in the justice of the cause. Hundreds of Easterners who had made the top in their various professions, at home and abroad, offered their services, which they would not have done to an ambitious colonel willing to risk the ruin of his people for his own advancement. Later, when Gowon sought Governors for the three states he had created in the former Eastern Region, he was unable to find a single man of note to take the jobs. For the Ibo East Central State he had to pick an obscure lecturer in social studies from Ibadan University, Mr Ukpabi Asika, who was disowned by his entire family (the ultimate shame in Africa). For the Rivers State Gowon had to boost a twenty-five-year-old junior naval officer, Alfred Spiff, to the rank of Lieutenant Commander. He too was disowned by the Spiffs of Port Harcourt. For the Southeastern State Gowon chose a Mr Essuene, a totally unknown junior officer from Lagos who had not seen his home region in years.

And lastly, the performance of the Biafran people in defending their own land, which even their worst enemies have been forced to admit has been remarkable, indicated that they believed in what they were doing. A single officer or group of officers, bullying a lukewarm, half-hearted, reluctant folk into rebellion would never have been able to keep control as the sufferings of the people passed all known levels in Africa. Such a potentate would long ago have seen his kingdom overrun by the Federal Army as the reluctant defenders threw down their weapons and ran. More likely, such a man would long since have fallen to a coup based on popular resentment of the pass into which he had led the people. This has not happened; the Biafrans have fought tooth and claw for every inch of their country while on the home front there has not been a single anti-Government riot, something it would have been impossible to prevent had the people been disgruntled; for as the British found out in the late twenties, when Biafrans are discontented they permit their feelings to be known.

Another excuse sought to explain the Biafran obduracy was that it was due to 'Ojukwu's propaganda'. This is still being bandied about in some places. While it might have been possible by shrewd manipulation of the public relations media to sway the broad mass of the populace (for a while) it is difficult to imagine the host of top-grade brains who have offered to serve Biafra in far less important capacities than they previously enjoyed being deceived by smooth propaganda.

Such men include former President Dr Nnamdi Azikiwe, former Premier Dr Michael Okpara, former civilian Governor of the East Dr Francis Ibiam, former Judge of the World Court Sir Louis Mbanefo, former vice-Chancellor of Ibadan University Professor Kenneth Dike, and men like Professor Eni Njoku, probably one of the finest academic minds ever to come from Africa. Added to these must be a host of academics, lawyers, teachers, doctors, surgeons, administrators, businessmen, engineers and civil servants. General Gowon would have loved to have been able to show the world one defector among the men listed above.

Within a few months of the declaration of independence, a remarkable array of forces had ranged themselves to crush the new country. General Gowon launched the Federal Army behind the slogan 'To Keep Nigeria One – Is a Job That Must be Done'. Phrases like 'One Nigeria', 'to preserve the territorial integrity of Nigeria' and 'crush the revolt' were soon bandied about, though little constructive thought appears to have been done by anyone to consider a lasting solution beyond the slogans. Dark hints of the immediate balkanization of Africa were mentioned, seemingly without reference to the breakaway from Britain of the Republic of Ireland which miraculously failed to bring about the balkanization of Europe. 'Secession' was roundly condemned, though no one bothered to mention that partition had for years been an accepted political formula where two distinct populations had proved to be incompatible.

Nigeria received immediate backing from a number of countries, notably 'Socialist' Britain, Fascist Spain and Communist Russia. These three countries still provide the military wherewithal for the execution of the biggest bloodbath in Africa's history.

But on 30 May 1967 all this was a part of the unrevealed future. Seeing that war was imminent, both sides went forward with feverish preparations, the Biafrans to defend themselves, the Nigerians to bring about a quick finish to what they regarded as a childishly easy task. The first shells were fired over Biafra's northern border at dawn on 6 July.

Part Two: The Fight To Survive

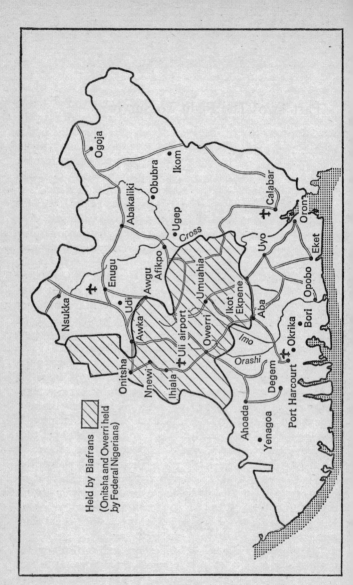

Held by Biafrans

(Onitsha and Owerri held
by Federal Nigerians)

Biafra

8. The Character of Biafra

IN area Biafra is not large, about 29,000 square miles. Yet in most other statistics it comes in the top three in Africa. The population is the most dense in Africa, over 440 to the square mile. In every sense it is the most developed country in the continent, with more industry, the highest per capita income, the highest purchasing power, the greatest density of roads, schools, hospitals, business houses and factories in Africa.

In potential it has been variously described as the Japan, the Israel, the Manchester, and the Kuwait of this continent. Each appellation refers to one of the many facets that cause surprise to the visitor who thought all Africa was uniformly backward. Years of under-exploitation, as factories, investment and public services were sited elsewhere in Nigeria, though often staffed by Easterners, left the Eastern Region a long way short of its full development potential. Even in the south the major petroleum companies failed to boost oil production to its potential, preferring to keep the oil fields there ticking over as a useful reserve while Arabian fields were sucked dry.

The use of the comparison with Japan refers to the population. Rarely among Africans, they have the gift of unceasing hard work. In the factories the workers turn in more man-hours per year than elsewhere, and in the farms the peasants produce more yield per acre than in any other country. It may be that nature's necessity has bred these traits; but they are also backed by the ancient traditions of the people. In Biafra personal success has always been regarded as meritorious; a successful man is admired and respected. There is no hereditary office or title. When a man dies his success in life, his honours, his prestige and his authority are buried with him. His sons must fend for themselves on the basis of equal competition with the other young men of the society.

The Biafrans are avid for education and particularly for qualification in one of the technical professions. It is not unusual to find a situation like this: a village carpenter has five sons. The father works from dawn till dusk; the mother has a stall in the market; the four junior sons sell matches, newspapers, red peppers, all so that the senior son can go through college. When he is qualified he is duty-bound to pay the way through college of the second brother; after which the pair will pay for the education of the third, fourth and fifth. The carpenter may die a carpenter, but may leave five qualified sons. For most Biafrans no sacrifice is too much for education.

Communes of village farmers will club together to build a structure in their village – not a recreation centre, swimming pool or stadium, but a school. A village that has a school has prestige.

Because they are convinced that 'no condition is permanent in this world' (an Ibo motto) they are adaptable to a degree and prepared to learn new ways. Where others, notably the Muslim communities of Africa, are content to accept their poverty or backwardness as the will of Allah, the Biafran sees both as a challenge to his God-given talents. The difference in attitude is cardinal, for it spells the difference between a society where Western influence will never truly take root, and where investment capital will seldom bear fruit, and a society destined to succeed.

Ironically it is their hard work and their success that have contributed to make the Biafrans so unpopular in Nigeria, and notably in the North. Other characteristics are adduced to explain the antipathy they manage to generate; they are pushful, uppity and aggressive say the detractors; ambitious and energetic say the defenders. They are money-loving and mercenary says one school; canny and thrifty says the other. Clannish and unscrupulous in grabbing advantages, say some; united and quick to realize the advantages of education, say others.

The reference to Manchester refers to their flair for trade. Rather than work for a boss on a salaried wage scale the Biafran would prefer to save for years, then buy his own lock-up shop. This he will keep open all hours of the day and night so long as there is a chance of a customer. Having profited, he will plough the money back into the enterprise, buy a brick-built shop, then a store, then a chain of shops. With several thousands in the bank, he can be found going about on a bicycle. Throughout Africa one will find Arab traders (Lebanese or Syrian), or Indians. These peoples have wandered across the world with their talent for trade, under-cutting local traders and driving them to the wall. But they will never be found where the Biafrans operate.

The reference to Israel refers obviously to the persecutions that have touched them sooner or later wherever they have set up shop. Mr Legum's reference to the gathering in of the exiles into Israel after the last war was perhaps closer than he realized at the time; having got their backs to the wall the Biafrans have now got nowhere else to go. That is why they prefer to die in their homeland than give in and live (the survivors among them) like the Wandering Jew. Colonel Ojukwu once told correspondents: 'What you see here is the end of a long road; a road that started in the far North and has led finally here into the Ibo heart-land. It is the road to the slaughterhouse.'*

'Kuwait' refers to the oil beneath Biafra. It has been postulated that if the Biafrans had had as their homeland a region of semi-desert and scrub they would have been allowed to depart from Nigeria with cries of 'Good riddance' in their ears. One foreign businessman remarked succinctly during a discussion about this war 'It's an oil war', and felt obliged to say no more. Beneath Biafra lies an ocean of oil, the purest in the world. You can run Biafran crude straight into a diesel lorry and it will work. Approximately one tenth of this field lies in neighbouring Cameroon, about three tenths in Nigeria. The remaining six tenths lies under Biafra.

The government of Biafra is a disappointment to those who come seeking a totalitarian military dictatorship. Colonel Ojukwu rules with a surprisingly light hand, but this is incumbent on any man who rules the Biafrans. They do not take kindly to government without consultation. Soon after taking power as Military Governor in January 1966 Ojukwu realized he had to have a closer line to the broad masses of the people, partly because of their characteristics and partly through his own predilections.

* Colonel Ojukwu to James Wilde and the author, Umuahia, 17 August 1968.

He could not reconstitute the discredited Assembly of the old politicians, and General Ironsi was against (for the moment) other forms of assembly, preferring to let the Military Régime find its feet first. So Ojukwu quietly began drawing up plans for a return to civilian rule, or at least a joint consultative body through which the people could let their wishes be known to the Military Governor and in which he could seek the wishes of the people.

After the coup of July he got his chance, and the plans went ahead. From each of the twenty-nine Divisions of the Region he asked for four nominated representatives and six popular delegates. The nominated posts, although named by his Office, were *ex officio* nominations, such as the Divisional Administrator, the Divisional Secretary, etc. The six popular delegates were chosen by the people through village and clan chiefs, and the 'Leaders of Thought' conferences. This gave him 290 persons. To these he asked for another forty-five representatives of the professions to be added. Delegates were chosen and sent from the Trade Unions, the Teachers' Conference, the Bar Association, the Farmers' Union, several other sections of the community, and, most important, the Market Traders' Association – imposing and outspoken Market Mammies who had kept the British in order in 1929, when they led the Aba riots.

This group formed the Consultative Assembly, and was soon regarded, with the Advisory Council of Chiefs and Elders, as the parliament of Biafra. Colonel Ojukwu has since taken no major decision without consulting them, and has inevitably followed their wishes on national policy. For immediate administration he has the Executive Council which meets every week and of which only one member other than Colonel Ojukwu is in the Armed Forces.

From its first meeting on 31 August 1966, thirty-three days after the Gowon coup, the Assembly was consulted at every stage of the road to partition. In view of subsequent claims that the Ibos dragged the non-Ibo minorities unwillingly into their act of separation, it is significant that of the 335 members of the Assembly 165 are non-Ibo minority group men as against 169 Ibo-speaking members. This gives the

110

minorities a higher proportional representation in the Assembly than their respective populations inside the country.

The decision to mandate Colonel Ojukwu to pull out of Nigeria nine months after the first meeting was unanimous. Far from being unwilling victims of Ibo domination and from being coerced into partition against their will, the tribal representatives of the minorities had their full say, and were active participants in the policy to pull out. Without doubt there were those among all groups who did not agree with the decisions, and a number of these have since been used by the Nigerians as spokesmen to claim a great degree of oppression inflicted by the Ibos against the minorities. But those who travelled or lived among the minority groups at the time noticed not only that the opposition appeared to be comparatively small, but that the same spirit of effervescence that marked partition in Ibo-land was also to be observed in the minority areas.

The minority regions fell first to the advancing Federal Army, being the peripheral areas of Biafra, and quite a lot of changing of sides took place. This is habitual when lands are conquered by armies at war. For most people, seeing the Biafran Army pull out and the Nigerian Army march in, to lift the right hand and cry 'One Nigeria' was more a gesture of self-preservation than of political conviction.

Nor were collaborators hard to find. By and large the leaders among the minority groups, having given their allegiance to Biafra, were forced to flee to escape persecution when the Federals came in. This left vacant good jobs, houses, offices, cars, privileges. It was not difficult for the Nigerians to find other local people to fill these vacancies on the condition of full collaboration with the occupying forces. But an examination of the men who now fill the posts allocated to local people under the Nigerian rule will normally reveal that they were very small fry when their more talented kinsmen ran the province for Biafra.

Immediately after conquest many local people stayed behind in the minority areas, converted by previous Federal publicity to the view that Biafra had been a mistake and that cooperation with the Nigerian Army would be better. Some of these local dignitaries sincerely believed in their conversion; others saw self-advancement or self-enrichment from the property of the dead or fled leaders of yesterday. But since the midsummer of 1968 more and more reports have come into Biafra of a growing dissatisfaction with life under the conquerors.

Very often the biggest wave of refugees into unoccupied Biafra came not with the fall of a province, but a few weeks later when the Nigerian Army's methods had been tasted. Later still more alienation of the local leaders took place, as the Federal soldiers killed goats, chickens, cattle and pigs for their own kitchens; harvested unripe yam and cassava crops for their own diets; took local girls and used them as they wished; stopped protests at this behaviour by punitive raids against the protesters; forced villagers to watch public executions of honoured village chiefs and local elders; closed down schools and turned them into barracks for the army; enriched themselves in black market deals in relief food supposed to be destined for the needy; looted desirable property and sent it back home; and generally let it be known that they were there to stay and intended to live off the land, and live well.

Before the summer an increasing number of chiefs were sending emissaries through the lines to Ojukwu, convinced by now, if not before, that his rule was infinitely preferable to that of the Nigerians. One of the reasons why Colonel Ojukwu's rule was appreciated – there had certainly been grievances under the former rule of the politicians – was the change in status of the minorities. When the politicians were in power the Ibo-speaking groups dominated the Assembly and some minority areas felt neglected in the apportionment of funds, facilities and investment. Colonel Ojukwu stopped that.

One of the first proposals of the Consultative Assembly was for the abolition of the British-drawn twenty-nine Divisions and their replacement by twenty provinces, the boundaries to be drawn along tribal and linguistic lines. The Proposal came from Mr Okoi Arikpo, one of the members for Ugep, a minority area inhabited by one of the smallest groups, the Ekoi. If there had been such a thing as 'Ibo domination' so widely referred to in Nigerian propaganda since the war

112

started, this idea would have cut it to the bone, since the plan also called for a wide degree of autonomy within each province, and eight of the twenty provinces had non-Ibo majorities inside them. Yet the plan was hailed by the Assembly (with its Ibo majority), welcomed by Colonel Ojukwu and it soon became law.

On the basis of this Mr Arikpo told Ojukwu that he deserved a ministerial post, but the latter thought otherwise. Arikpo then disappeared to Lagos where he is now Commissioner for Foreign Affairs.

Not that Ojukwu has anything against minority men in top posts; on the contrary, minority spokesmen have a greater say in government than ever in the previous history of the Eastern Region. The Chief of General Staff and acting Head of State in the absence of Colonel Ojukwu, Major-General Philip Effiong, is an Efik. The Chief Secretary and Head of the Civil Service, Mr N. U. Akpan, is an Ibibio. The Commissioner for Special Duties, one of Colonel Ojukwu's closest confidants, Dr S. J. Cookey, is a Rivers man, as is Mr Ignatius Kogbara, Biafran representative in London. The Executive Council, the foreign missions, the ministerial posts, the civil service, the peace negotiating teams, have all been heavily staffed with minority men.

Ironically the massacres of 1966 and the similarly brutal treatment accorded during the present war by the Nigerian Army to Ibo and non-Ibo populations has done more to weld Biafra into a single nation than any other factor. The displacement of millions of refugees, the intermingling, the common suffering, the collective impoverishment, have together done what other African leaders have been trying to do for years; they have created a nation out of a collection of peoples.

9. Thirty Months of Fighting

NEVER in modern history has a war been fought between armies of such disparity in strength and firepower as the Nigeria—Biafra conflict. On the one hand has been the Nigerian Army, a monstrous agglomeration of over 85,000 men armed to the teeth with modern weapons, whose government has had uninhibited access to the armouries of at least two major Powers and several smaller ones, which has been endowed with limitless supplies of bullets, mortars, machine-guns, rifles, grenades, bazookas, guns, shells and armoured cars. This has been supported by numerous foreign personnel of technical experience who have concerned themselves with the efficiency of radio communications, transport, vehicle maintenance, support weapons, training programmes, military intelligence, combat techniques and services. To these have been added several scores of professional mercenaries, Soviet non-commissioned officers for operation of the support weapons, and ample replenishments of lorries, trucks, jeeps, low-loaders, fuel, transport planes and ships, engineering and bridge-building equipment, generators and river-boats. The war effort of this machine has been backed by a merciless air force of jet fighters and bombers armed with cannon, rockets and bombs, and a navy equipped with frigates, gun-boats, escorts, landing craft, barges, ferries and tugs. The personnel have been lavishly supplied with boots, belts, uniforms, helmets, shovels, pouches, food, beer and cigarettes.

Facing it has been the Biafran Army, a volunteer force representing less than one in ten of those who have presented themselves at the recruiting booths for service. Manpower has never been the problem. It has been that of arming those prepared to fight. Totally blockaded for over eighteen months, the Biafran Army has managed to keep going on an average, at least for the first sixteen months, on two or sometimes one ten-ton plane-load of arms and ammunition per week. The standard infantry weapon has been the reconditioned Mauser bolt-action rifle, supported by small quantities of machine-pistols, sub-machine guns, light and heavy machine guns, and pistols. Mortar barrels and bombs, artillery pieces and shells, have been minimal, bazookas almost non-existent.

Forty per cent of the Biafran fighting manpower is equipped with captured Nigerian equipment, including an assortment of highly-prized armoured cars taken when their crews were caught unawares and ran away. Also contributing to the fire-power have been home-made rockets, land-mines, anti-per-sonnel mines, stand-cannon, booby-traps, and Molotov cock-tails, and to the defence have been added devices such as tank-pits, tree-trunks, and pointed stakes.

Without a new vehicle for a year and a half, the Biafrans have kept going on repaired, patched and cannibalized trans-port and latterly home-refined petrol. Spare parts have been either taken from wrecked vehicles or machine-tooled.

As regards foreign assistance, despite all that has been said of hundreds of mercenaries, the score over the first eighteen months has been: forty Frenchmen in November 1967 who left in a hurry after six weeks, when they decided it was too hot for them; another group of sixteen in September 1968 who stayed four weeks before coming to the same conclusion. Those who have actually fought with the Biafran forces have been a small handful comprising a German, Scot, South African, Italian, Englishman, Rhodesian, American (one each), two Flemings and two Frenchmen. Another half-dozen indivi-dual soldiers of fortune have drifted in for varying periods of one day to three weeks. With rare exceptions the difficulty of the combat conditions, the enormous odds against, and a rooted conviction that there must be easier ways of earning a living have kept most visits down to short duration. The only two men who ever completed their six-month contracts were the German, Rolf Steiner, who suffered a nervous breakdown in his tenth month and had to be repatriated, and the South African, Taffy Williams, who completed two contracts and went on leave in the first few days of 1969.

Ironically the Biafran war story, far from consolidating the position of the mercenary in Africa has completely exploded the myth of the Congo's 'White Giants'. In the final analysis the contribution of the white man to the war on the Biafran side must be reckoned as well under one per cent.

Most have been revealed as little more than thugs in uniform, and the riff-raff of the Congo did not even bother to volunteer to come out to Biafra at all. Those who did fight at all, fought with slightly greater technical know-how but no more courage or ferocity than the Biafran officers. The lack of contrast between the two is underlined by Major Williams, the one man who stuck by the Biafrans for twelve months of combat, and the only one who emerges as a figure really worth employing. 'I've seen a lot of Africans at war,' he said once.* 'But there's nobody to touch these people. Give me 10,000 Biafrans for six months, and we'll build an army that would be invincible on this continent. I've seen men die in this war who would have won the Victoria Cross in another context. My God, some of them were good scrappers.' His assessment of most of the mercenaries, and notably the French, is unprintable.

The war began in a spirit of confidence on both sides. General Gowon told his people and the world he had undertaken 'a short, surgical police action'.† Victory was forecast in days rather than weeks. In the North Colonel Katsina sneered at the Biafran 'army of pen-pushers' and forecast a swift victory as the largely Northern Nigerian Federal infantry marched in. The Biafrans, confident of their greater speed, ingenuity and resourcefulness, felt if they could resist for a few months the Nigerians would realize the folly of the war and go home, or negotiate. Neither proved to be correct.

Fighting started on 6 July 1967, with an artillery barrage against Ogoja, a town near the border with the Northern Region in the northeast corner of Biafra. Here two Federal battalions faced the Biafrans in what Colonel Ojukwu realized was a diversionary attack. The real attack came further west opposite Nsukka, the prosperous market town recently endowed with the handsome University of Nsukka, renamed University of Biafra.

* To the author, 25 August 1968.
† Quoted in *Time* magazine, 1 September 1967.

Here the remaining six battalions of the Nigerians were massed on the main axis, and they marched in on 8 July. They advanced four miles and then stuck. The Biafrans, with about 3,000 men in arms in that sector against the Nigerians' 6,000, fought back tenaciously with Eastern Nigeria Police 303 rifles, an assortment of Italian, Czech and German machine-pistols, and a fair sprinkling of shotguns, which in close bush country are not as harmless as they sound. The Nigerians captured the town of Nsukka which they then destroyed, university and all, but could advance no further. In Ogoja province they took Nyonya and Gakem, brought Ogoja into range of their artillery and forced the Biafrans to cede the township and draw up a line of defence along a river south of the town. Here too the fighting bogged down, and the situation looked, and might have remained, stationary.

After two weeks, discomfited by this immobility of their redoubtable infantry, Lagos began to broadcast the fall of numerous Biafran towns to the Federal forces. To those living in Enugu, which included the whole population, expatriates included, it appeared someone in Lagos was sticking pins at random in a map. At the Hotel Presidential it was tea on the terrace as usual, water-polo with the British Council staff, and jackets for dinner.

After three weeks the Nigerians got into trouble when two of their battalions, cut off from the rest, were surrounded and broken up to the east of Nsukka between the main road and the railway line. Two more scratch battalions composed of training staff and trainees were hastily armed and thrown into the Nsukka sector from the Nigerian side.

In the air, activity was confined to the exploits of a lone Biafran B-26 American-built Second World War bomber piloted by a taciturn Pole who rejoiced in the name of Kamikaze Brown, and to six French-built Alouette helicopters piloted by Biafrans from which they rained hand-grenades and home-made bombs on the Nigerians.

On 25 July the Nigerians staged an unexpected sea-borne attack on the island of Bonny, the last piece of land before the open sea far to the south of Port Harcourt. In prestige terms it was a spectacular coup in an increasingly newsless war, due to the fact that Bonny was the oil-loading terminal for the Shell-BP pipeline from Port Harcourt.

But militarily it was unexploitable, for once warned the Biafrans relentlessly patrolled the waters north of Bonny and subsequent Nigerian attempts to launch further water-borne attacks northwards on to the mainland round Port Harcourt were beaten back.

On 9 August the Biafrans struck in earnest with a coup that shook observers both in Biafra and Lagos. Starting at dawn, a mobile brigade of 3,000 men they had carefully prepared in secret, swept across the Onitsha Bridge into the Midwest. In ten hours of daylight the Region fell, and the towns of Warri, Sapele, the oil centre at Ughelli, Agbor, Uromi, Ubiaja, and Benin City were occupied. Of the small army of the Midwest nothing was heard; nine out of eleven senior officers of that army were Ica-Ibos, first cousins to the Ibos of Biafra, and rather than fight they welcomed the Biafran forces.

The capture of the Midwest changed the balance of the war, putting the whole of Nigeria's oil resources under Biafran control. Although she had lost about 500 square miles of her own territory in three small sectors at the perimeter, she had captured 20,000 square miles of Nigeria. More important, the whole of the Nigerian infantry was miles away opposite Nsukka, with the broad Niger separating them from the road back to the capital and helpless to intervene. For the Biafrans the road to Lagos was open and undefended.

Colonel Ojukwu was at pains to placate the non-Ibo majority of the Midwest and to assure them that he bore them no harm. For a week delegations of tribal chiefs, bankers, traders, Chamber of Commerce stalwarts, army officers and church dignitaries filed into Enugu on invitation to see the Biafran leader and be reassured. Colonel Ojukwu hoped that an alliance of two of the three Southern regions would swing the West into agreement and force the Federal Government to negotiate.

After a week it appeared this was not going to happen, and Colonel Ojukwu gave the order for a further advance westwards. On 16 August the Biafrans reached the Ofusu River bridge which marks the border with the Western region.

Here there was a brief scrap with Nigerian troops, who then withdrew. Inspecting the Nigerian dead, the Biafrans were elated; the Nigerian soldiers were from the Federal Guard, Gowon's own bodyguard of 500 Tivs, normally garrisoned in Lagos. If he had had recourse to using these, it was reckoned, there must be nothing else available.

On 20 August the Biafrans stormed into Ore, a town on a crossroads thirty-five miles into the West, 130 miles from Lagos and 230 miles from Enugu. This time the Tivs facing them took a worse beating, and disconsolately pulled back in disorder. To observers at the time it appeared that barely ten weeks after the Arab-Israeli war another military phenomenon was to be witnessed, with tiny Biafra toppling the government of the enormous Nigeria. A sudden motorized push at that time along any one of three major roads available would have put Biafran forces deep into the Yoruba heartland and at the gates of Lagos. Such was the order Colonel Ojukwu gave.

It was later learned from sources inside the American Embassy that on 20 August the Westerners were teetering on the verge of going over to a policy of appeasing the Biafrans to save their skins; that Gowon had ordered his private plane to be made ready, the engines warmed and a flight plan prepared for Zaria in the North; and that the British High Commissioner Sir David Hunt and the American Ambassador Mr James Matthews had had a long and serious talk with Gowon in Dodan Barracks, as a result of which the nervous Nigerian Supreme Commander agreed to carry on.

News of this intervention, if intervention it was (and it was reliably reported as such), reached Colonel Ojukwu within a week and caused anger among British and American citizens in Biafra, who felt their ambassadors were playing fast and loose with their safety, for if the news had got out to the Biafran public their reaction could have been violent.

The decision of Gowon to stay on saved his government from collapse and ensured the continuation of the war. Had he fled, there seems little doubt the West would have swung over, and Nigeria would have developed into a confederation of three states. Biafran suspicions since that day have been that the carrot that tempted Gowon and his fellow minority men to stay in power was the pledge of British and American aid. Certainly the aid followed hard and fast from that date.

The taking of the Midwest had one other by-product. It opened Nigeria's eyes to the fact that they were fighting a war. From the first they had underestimated Biafra and the latter, in taking advantage of this once-for-all opportunity, had got the war in her grasp. It was allowed to slip. In fact Ore was as far as the Biafran forces got, for in the meantime another remarkable about-turn had taken place. Unknown to all, the commander of the Biafran forces in the Midwest had turned traitor.

Victor Banjo was a Yoruba and had been a Major in the Nigerian Army, imprisoned by General Ironsi for allegedly plotting against him. His prison had been in the East, and it was from here, released by Colonel Ojukwu at the outbreak of war and offered a commission in the Biafran Army, that he came to join Biafra rather than go home to the West and face the possible danger of revenge from the Northerners ruling there. Why Colonel Ojukwu chose the one senior Yoruba in the Biafran Army to command the forces destined to march into Western Nigeria, he has never revealed, but the two men were known to have been close friends, and Colonel Ojukwu had implicit trust in him. With the rank of Brigadier, Banjo commanded 'S' Brigade when it moved into the Midwest.

According to his own confession when he was later unmasked, he decided soon after 9 August he wished to enter into talks with the leaders in the West, notably Chief Awolowo. He discovered the hideaway in Benin City of the Midwest Governor Colonel Ejoor, though he did not report this to Ojukwu, who wished to talk to Ejoor. Instead he asked Ejoor to act as intermediary between himself and Awolowo, but Ejoor declined to take the risk.

Banjo said later he relayed messages using the sideband radio of the British Deputy High Commission in Benin. A British official communicated the messages in German to another official in the High Commission in Lagos. The message was passed on to Chief Awolowo. The plot Banjo later revealed was typically Yoruba in its complexity. In conjunction with two other senior Biafran officers with political ambitions he was to cause the ruin of Biafra by withdrawing the troops from the Midwest on a variety of pretexts, arrest and assassinate Ojukwu, and proclaim the 'revolt' at an end. As a Nigerian hero he would then re-enter his home Western Region with all his past forgiven and forgotten.

He added that the second part of the plot, which was to come later, was that he and Awolowo were to rally the newly-recruited Yoruba Army to his standard, and depose Gowon, leaving the Presidency of Nigeria for himself, and permitting Awolowo his long-desired premiership. It seems unlikely that the Gowon government was informed of this postscript.

Banjo managed to recruit into his scheme Colonel Ifeajuana, also released from prison, a Moscow-trained Communist officer called Major Philip Alale, a Biafran Foreign Service official called Sam Agbam, who did some of the negotiating between the two sides while out of Biafra, and several other junior officers and functionaries.

By mid-September he was ready to move. In Enugu Colonel Ojukwu, although frustrated by the lack of action in the west, continued to trust Banjo and to accept his assurances of administrative difficulties, man-power shortage, lack of enough guns and ammunition, and so forth. It was true the Nigerians had grown stronger in the intervening three weeks. With a crash recruiting programme putting into uniform after a brisk one-week training course such diverse elements as college students and prison inmates, the Nigerians had formed first one fresh brigade and then another. These forces, named the Second Division and commanded by Colonel Murtela Mohammed, had been fighting back from the Western Region. The use of fast, motorized columns could still have put the Biafrans in a dominating position in the West as late as the first week in September, but on 12 September Banjo gave orders without authority to evacuate Benin City without firing a shot. Mohammed did not enter Benin until 21 September.

Banjo followed up with orders to withdraw from Warri, Sapele, Auchi, Igueben and other important positions without fighting. Baffled and bewildered Biafran junior officers did as they were told. Simultaneously the Biafran defences south of Nsukka collapsed and the Federal forces pushed several

121

miles down the road to Enugu, lying forty-five miles from Nsukka.

At this point Banjo decided to strike directly at Colonel Ojukwu. He conferred in the Midwest with Ifeajuana and Alale, and they worked out the final arrangements for the assassination, which was to take place coincidentally with Banjo's presence in Enugu on 19 September, where he had been summoned to explain what he was doing in the Midwest.

None of the three seemed to realize time had run out for them. Amazingly they had broached their plan to a number of other officers and civilians, without any attempt to check first to see if those people would not remain loyal to Ojukwu. In fact most did, and several had already been to see him with details of the plot.

He took a lot of convincing, but the facts were beginning to speak for themselves. Ifeajuana and Alale were summoned separately to State House where Ojukwu coldly confronted them, then ordered their arrest. Banjo was also summoned, but arrived with a strong escort of men loyal to himself, whom he wished to bring into the grounds. He was persuaded they could stay at the gate well within call, while he went in alone but armed. He agreed. While he was waiting in the ante-room Colonel Ojukwu's police A.D.C., a shrewd young Inspector, went out to the guard posse with a bottle of gin. After passing it round, he invited them to come to his house nearby and sample some more. They agreed and trooped off.

Inside State House watchers observed their departure, then swung their automatics onto Banjo. He was disarmed, then ushered in to see the Head of State. It was six hours to the time Colonel Ojukwu should have died, being close to midnight on 18 September.

It was impossible to keep the scandal quiet as the main culprits freely confessed their parts and the smaller fry were arrested. The effect on the army was traumatic, and swift demoralization set in. The entire officer corps was discredited in the eyes of the soldiery, themselves fiercely loyal to Colonel Ojukwu. Although torn by his one-time friendship with Banjo, and a relation by marriage to Alale, Colonel Ojukwu was heavily pressured by his army colleagues to the view that

122

examples had to be made to stop the rot. He gave his assent.

The four ringleaders were tried by special tribunal, sentenced to death for high treason, and shot at dawn. The date was 22 September.

The exact degree of complicity or awareness of some British officials in Nigeria remains a matter of speculation in Biafra. Banjo, in his confession (backed by a file of documentary evidence taken from Banjo which Ojukwu showed the author), heavily implicated the British Deputy High Commission in Benin and the High Commission in Lagos as having been his liaison men with Awolowo and Gowon. Correspondents in Lagos later remarked they had noticed a sudden buoyancy among British officials in the middle of September, confident assurances that 'it'll all be over in a few days'. This was in stark contrast to the near panic of 20 August, and a prophecy hardly merited by the military situation.

But after the attempted coup things did change. The damage in Biafra was enormous. By 25 September the Biafrans had withdrawn from Agbor in the Midwest, half way between the Niger River and Benin City, and by the 30th were back in a small defended perimeter around Asaba with their backs to the river. North of Enugu the demoralized infantry retreated disconsolately before the Nigerians coming south from Nsukka, and Enugu came within shelling range by the end of the month. On 6 October the Biafrans at Asaba crossed the Niger to Onitsha and blew up the newly completed £6,000,000 bridge behind them to prevent Mohammed crossing. They were highly disillusioned. Two days previously, on 4 October, the Nigerians had entered Enugu.

Abroad it was generally presumed that Biafra must collapse. Two things saved the country from disintegration; one was the personality of Colonel Ojukwu, who took a grip on the army and gave officers and men a talking to; the other was the people of the country who made it clear they did not intend to give up. As the soldiery was, and always has been, the people in uniform, the army soon got the message.

Colonel Ojukwu felt obliged to offer his resignation, which the Consultative Assembly unanimously refused. That marked the end of the Banjo episode; Biafra buckled down to getting

123

on with the job of fighting. The long, hard slog had begun.

By this time the enormous weight of firepower imported by Nigeria, notably from Britain, Belgium, Holland, Italy and Spain, was becoming overpowering. A further recruiting drive had enabled them to boost the Federal Army to over 40,000 men. The troops in the northern part of Biafra now formed the First Division, those across the Niger under Mohammed the Second. The First was commanded from Makurdi, miles away in the Northern Region, by Colonel Mohammed Shuwa. With Colonel Ekpo the Chief of Staff Armed Forces, and Colonel Bissalla Chief of Staff Army, four Hausas controlled the Nigerian Army. Bissalla's predecessor, the Tiv Colonel Akahan, had been killed in a helicopter in such odd circumstances that it was suspected a bomb had been planted.

The late autumn and winter was not a happy time for Biafra. In the north Enugu fell, while further east in the Ogoja sector the Nigerian troops had pushed down from Ogoja to Ikom, astride the main road to the neighbouring Cameroons. Then on 18 October the newly formed Third Federal Marine Commando Division under the command of Colonel Benjamin Adekunle, made a sea-borne landing at Calabar in the southeast. With Bonny still festering and the menace of Mohammed trying to cross the Niger, that made five fronts on which the Biafrans had to fight.

Despite fierce counter-attacks the Nigerians could not be dislodged from Calabar, and with massive backing their beach-head grew steadily stronger until Adekunle burst out and forged northwards up the eastern bank of the Cross River in an attempt to link up with the First Division at Ikom. In closing the second road (out of Calabar) to the Cameroons, the Nigerians cut Biafra off from road contact with the outside world.

The single air link that now remained had been transferred to Port Harcourt and the lone B-26 at Enugu, having been riddled with bullets on the ground, had been replaced by an equally lone B-25 flown by a former Luftwaffe pilot known as Fred Herz.

Throughout the autumn foreign correspondents glibly forecast that Biafra was finished. It was a cry that had been heard several times before and has been heard many times since. The Biafrans did not worry much about it.

During October and November, 1967, Colonel Mohammed tried three times to cross the Niger by boat from Asaba and capture Onitsha.

On the first occasion, on 12 October, he got across with two battalions. One of the operational commanders at Onitsha was Colonel Joe Achuzie, a tough and ruthless Midwesterner who had spent the Second World War with the British Army and had fought in Korea. He had been working as an engineer in Port Harcourt when the war started and had enlisted in the Militia. From there he transferred to the Biafran Army. Seeing Mohammed on his way across, he decided to ambush him.

The boats landed and the men disembarked with their armoured cars. Achuzie watched them from the timber yard of the Ministry of Works as the Hausa soldiers set fire to the Onitsha Market, the largest in West Africa and with a stock once valued at £3,000,000. After this senseless piece of destruction they got into line and marched off through the abandoned town. They went about a mile when the Biafrans counter-attacked. Losing both their armoured vehicles, the Nigerians were pushed back towards the river, and were finally destroyed near the landing stage.

Subsequently two more attempts were made to cross the Niger by boat, but on each occasion the craft were machine-gunned and sunk, causing heavy losses, mostly by drowning. The bulk of the losses were taken by the Yoruba soldiers in the Second Division, until their commander objected to further crossings. Leaving the Yoruba to keep watch at Asaba, Mohammed took his Hausas northwards, crossed into the Northern Region, and entered Biafra from that side, intending to take Onitsha from the landward approach.

From Lagos General Gowon had predicted a finish to the war by the end of the year, but when this became impossible he made another prediction for the crushing of Biafra by 31 March 1968. By the year's end the situation south and east of Enugu was stable, with Nigerian forces east of the town at a distance of about twenty miles, while to the south the Biafrans faced the Nigerians in the extreme outskirts of the town.

In the northeast the Federal forces possessed the whole of Ogoja Province, and were facing the Biafrans across the Anyim River, a tributary of the Cross. Further south, Adekunle's forces were half way from Calabar to Ikom, while in the deep south the Bonny sector was much as it had been five months before, several attempts at a water-borne push northwards having ended in disaster.

But with Nigeria receiving an ever-increasing supply of arms, while Biafra's supplies remained roughly static at two planes a week, fighting became increasingly hard. The Nigerian firepower, particularly in artillery and mortars, was getting steadily more murderous, while they had also got fresh supplies of armoured cars from Britain, not only to make up losses but to expand their armoured contingents considerably. It was habitually these armoured cars that made progress, for the Biafrans had nothing that could touch them.

In late December Colonel Mohammed, with his Division now swollen to 14,000 men, set off for the 68-mile march down the main road to Onitsha. He took with him enormous supplies. A document found in the pocket of a dead major of this division later revealed that the major's battalion alone had a reserve of 20,000 105-mm artillery shells. Just outside Enugu, close to the town of Udi, the Second Division met the Biafrans and one of the biggest running battles of the war was on.

True to Hausa tradition Mohammed massed his troops in solid phalanxes and thus they moved down the road. By mid-February he had reached Awka, still thirty miles from Onitsha. His losses had been enormous, since his path was known and the Federal soldiers did not like to move far from the main road. Throughout the war they have been highly wary of going off into the bush where their heavy equipment cannot follow them, and in massed formation they made easy targets for the Biafrans.

When he had been teaching tactics at Teshie in Ghana, Colonel Ojukwu had had in his class the young Lieutenant Murtela Mohammed. Sitting in his office in Umuahia Ojukwu now plotted and schemed to outwit his greatly superior adversary. He had to; the Biafrans, lightly armed but highly mobile, could not take Mohammed from the front. They concentrated on attacking his flanks and rear, causing high casualties. But with scant regard for loss of life among his men, Mohammed pressed doggedly on. At Awka he missed his big chance. The Biafran forces were terribly thin in front of Mohammed, but strong at rear and sides. If he had pushed hard forwards at Awka he could have got straight to Onitsha. Colonel Ojukwu realized the danger and switched extra forces to the main axis. He needed forty-eight hours; Mohammed gave it to him. The Northerners spent three days totally destroying Awka township.

By the time they had finished the Biafrans had regrouped. Further north Achuzie with his crack 29th Battalion had been off on his own, marching 92 miles and taking from the rear the town of Adoru in the Northern Region. From there he recaptured Nsukka also from the rear, having first vetted the defences from inside. Posing as an elderly farmer anxious to cooperate with the Nigerians, he entered the town alone and was even greeted in passing by the Nigerian commander of Nsukka. Ten hours later, back in uniform, Achuzie and the 29th swept in on the undefended side.

From Nsukka he marched south towards Enugu and linked up at Ukehe, a midway-point town between Nsukka and Enugu, with Colonel Mike Ivenso who had cut across country. The episode greatly heartened Biafrans and upset the Nigerians at Enugu, for that road was their main supply route. But the demands of stopping Mohammed were too pressing. Reluctantly Ojukwu called both colonels south to help the fight going on between Awka and Abagana. Mohammed made it to Abagana, sixteen miles to Onitsha, in the first week of March.

The fighting got tougher with the arrival of the two extra battalions of Achuzie and Ivenso. Mohammed desperately called for more men, and got another 6,000 from Enugu, stripping the town bare of its garrison. Had Ojukwu had a spare battalion he could have retaken Enugu for the asking. But Mohammed pressed on to Ogidi, eight miles from Onitsha, leaving his main force at Abagana.

The spearhead of two crack Hausa battalions, the 102nd

and the 105th, with Mohammed leading them, burst through to Onitsha on 25 March. Achuzie realized they could not be stopped, but decided to swing in behind them and follow into Onitsha so closely that the Nigerians would have no time to dig in. He hoped to rush them straight into the River Niger. It might have worked, for the two Federal battalions were exhausted. But on the road another Biafran battalion mistook Achuzie's men for the Nigerians. When that had been sorted out Achuzie pressed on. At the Apostolic Church he and his men came across the 300 corpses of the congregation, who had stayed behind to pray while others fled, and who had been dragged out and executed by the Hausas. The Biafran soldiers were so stunned they refused to move on. It was their officers who had the unpleasant task of moving the bodies out of the way.

When the road was again clear Achuzie moved on, but with an eighteen-hour delay. He found the Nigerians well dug-in already. He had two choices, to try to force the Nigerians out of their positions, or to turn back towards Abagana. The first would have exhausted his own men and their ammunition supplies, leaving them unable to cope with the larger force he was sure was following down the road. An argument developed between Achuzie and the other Biafran commanders, who maintained there was no larger force. Achuzie got his way and set up an enormous ambush outside Abagana. Into it the next morning rolled the main force, a 102-lorry convoy with 6,000 men on board and 350 tons of equipment.

The Abagana ambush was the biggest ever. A chance mortar bomb hit the 8,000-gallon petrol tanker and the vehicle exploded backwards, shooting a tongue of blazing fuel 400 yards down the road and covering 60 vehicles behind, which were soon burnt out. The surviving soldiers panicked, jumped down and ran. The waiting Biafran infantry got them. Very few got out alive.

Mohammed had made Onitsha, but out of 20,000 men he had brought 2,000 into Onitsha and lost most of the rest on the way. Lagos was not pleased when Mohammed crossed the Niger in a small boat, motored to Lagos and reported. He has not commanded a Division since. The 102nd and 105th in

Onitsha were relieved, and fresh troops sent across the river from Asaba. Soon there were 5,000 more Nigerians in Onitsha and despite repeated efforts to retake the city, they remained in control of it, boosting the garrison by November 1968 to 8,000 men.

April 1968 was a disastrous month for Biafra. The previous February a large number of technical assistants, believed by the Biafrans with some corroborating evidence from sources in London to be British N.C.O.s 'on attachment for training purposes', had arrived in Nigeria, and the effect was felt in April. Nigerian radio communications became infinitely better, and the Biafran monitors heard clipped English voices issuing instructions across the ether. Complex coordinated manoeuvres previously beyond the scope of the Nigerians became the order of the day. Vehicle maintenance on the Nigerian side increased at the same time and their shortage of transport of a few weeks previously was solved. More important, by April they were constructing Bailey bridges to cross rivers which had previously baffled them for months. The Engineering Corps of the Nigerian Army had previously been almost entirely composed of Easterners, and the Biafrans were aware that building Bailey bridges at that speed was beyond the capabilities of the Nigerians alone.

East of Enugu the Nigerians crossed a steep and narrow gorge at Ezulu and their armoured cars raced the last twelve miles to capture Abakaliki. This cut off the Biafrans east of Abakaliki facing the Nigerians across the Anyim, and they withdrew to a new line south of Abakaliki. Within days the Nigerians in Ogoja province had crossed the Antim on another Bailey bridge and linked up with Abakaliki. For the first time the two wings of the First Nigerian Division had made contact and possessed an east-west strip running along the north of Biafra.

Adekunle's Third Division, using two battalions of black mercenaries from Chad, called Gwodo-Gwodo, had pushed up the valley of the Cross River on the eastern bank to Obubra, the last major town in Ekoi country. They had been held along the river line for twelve weeks by the redoubtable presence on the far bank of Major Williams, a hundred of his personally trained Commandos, and seven thousand franc-tireur volunteers of the Ibo clan with whose chief Williams had established a personal friendship. These bush warriors of the Cross River, fiercely pro-Biafran, armed with blunderbusses and machetes, held seventy miles of river bank under constant surveillance.

But Williams' withdrawal in early April for training purposes gave the Chads across the water the chance they needed. In late April they crossed at two places and captured Afikpo, the main town in that area on the western side.

It was further south that Adekunle got his big break. In the last days of March, with the assistance of a handful of British amphibious experts he staged two landings across the Cross river at its broadest point, almost a mile of water. Capturing Oron and Itu within a few days, his fast-moving mercenary-led columns swept through the land of the Ibibios within a week taking Uyo, Ikot Ekpene, Abak, Eket and Opobo in quick succession. Their task was made easier by the provision of guides who knew the bush tracks, the hardness of the ground after the winter sun, and a certain degree of collaboration on the part of some of the local chiefs. Later, after several weeks and finally months of occupation by Adekunle's men these chiefs were to send pathetic appeals to Colonel Ojukwu. Eventually no people in Biafra suffered greater brutalization under Nigerian occupation than the Ibibios and Annangs.

At the northern fringe of Ibibio territory, where Ibo-land begins, about thirty miles from Umuahia, the Nigerians were halted. In any case Adekunle's main target was not northwards but west – the glittering prize of Port Harcourt.

From April onwards the First and Second Divisions quietened down, and attention switched increasingly to Adekunle in the south. The Second Division made repeated attempts to link up from Onitsha to Abagana, while the First Division fortified the series of towns along the main Enugu-Onitsha road. They could motor as far as Abagana but could not make the link-up to Onitsha. This failure inhibited any more major moves south, though the First Division attacked southwards in June and took Awgu, to the south of this main road, on 15 June.

But Adekunle throughout the summer of 1968 became the most important of the Nigerian commanders and was favoured with the majority of the arms and ammunition from Lagos. While the strength of the First Division remained stable at about 15,000 men and that of the Second Division at about 13,000, Adekunle's Third Division, responsible for the whole of the south, grew to over 25,000 by the end of 1968.

Relying again largely on foreign amphibious experts for his water-borne operations, Adekunle's advance units crossed the Imo River, the last barrier to Port Harcourt, in the second fortnight of April. He had forty miles to go to the biggest city in Biafra.

At the point of Adekunle's twin crossings the Imo flows south from Umu Abayi to its estuary at Opobo. Upstream of Umu Abayi the river flows in a west-to-east direction forty miles from Awaza. This oblong of land, forty miles long and thirty miles from north to south, is completed in the west by the Bonny River on which Port Harcourt stands and in the south by the creeks, a myriad of swamp and tangled mangrove which in turn gives way to the open sea. Inside this block of land, apart from Port Harcourt, lie the natural-gas-driven generating station at Afam, lighting the whole of the south of Biafra, the petroleum town of Bori, the £10,000,000 Shell-BP refinery at Okrika, and numerous oil wells. Although Port Harcourt itself was largely an Ibo city, the surrounding land is that of the Ogonis, Ikwerres and Okrikans, with the Rivers folk living down in the creeks and along to the west on the other side of the Bonny River.

At this time Biafra was already sheltering some four million refugees from other occupied areas, about one and a half million Ibos and two and a half million minorities. Port Harcourt and its food-rich surrounding countryside was a favourite shelter, and the pre-war population of half a million had swollen to close to a million.

After a swift build-up on the western bank of the Imo, beating off counter-attacks aimed at dislodging the beach-heads, the Third Division launched itself at Port Harcourt in the last days of April. The Biafran forces took the onslaught of the usual spearhead of armoured cars, a drenching in shells and mortars, and then the Nigerian infantry. In a lone last stand with an empty magazine, the Italian fighting for the Biafrans,

131

Major Georgio Norbiatto, was lost, missing presumed killed.

By the middle of May Afam, Bori and Okrika had fallen. The Biafran defence was hindered by thousands of refugees, while the Nigerian advance was assisted by small groups of local levies, volunteers and guides. Some of these had been imported from Lagos, including the former insurgent student, Isaac Boro, who appeared this time as a Major in the Federal Army. He was killed outside Bori.

With a fast right hook the Nigerians cut the road northward out of Port Harcourt towards Aba, and on 18 May advance units occupied the eastern outskirts of the city. A fierce shelling bombardment had been going on for days, and the road northwestwards from the town towards Owerri was choked with nearly a million refugees pouring out for safety. This human tide immobilized Colonel Achuzie, the newly appointed commander to the sector, and by the time it was cleared the Nigerians had ensconced themselves in the town and occupied one side of the airport, with the Biafrans at the other. Here both sides paused for a month to take breath.

Early in April Major Steiner, the German ex-Foreign Legion sergeant, who ranked senior among the four mercenaries (the fourth was an Englishman who like Williams had operated along the Cross River, but had left) was ordered by Colonel Ojukwu to train and bring into being a brigade of shock troops along the lines of the small, tough bands the four Europeans had been separately leading up to that time. Steiner, who had had his own band of guerrillas operating around Enugu airport to the great discomfiture of the Nigerians, set up camp and ordered Williams to join him. The two began to put together the Biafran Fourth Commando Brigade, a controversial unit which was nevertheless to play a widely publicized part in Biafran operations against the Federal Army.

Williams wanted to remain on the Cross River, but was overruled. A fortnight after he left the Gwodo-Gwodo crossed over, which Williams thought they could not have done if he had stayed. With his contract expiring, and desolated by the overrunning of his beloved Ibos, Williams returned to London in early May, but a week later he was asking to

132

come back. He returned for his second contract on 7 July. By this time Steiner had trained up 3,000 men divided into six small battalions or strike-forces, and was ready for action. When offered a sector he chose the Enugu to Onitsha road, and went back to the North, where Williams joined him on his return.

Throughout July the Commandos raided the positions of the Second Division along that road with some success. Later, when asked why he had not joined with the First and Third Divisions in the 'final assault on Iboland', Colonel Haruna, commanding the Second, admitted that all his preparations had been stultified by these Commando raids which forced him to keep switching large units from place to place wherever the raiders struck. The activities of the Commandos at Amansee, Uku, and Amieni proved the validity of Steiner's nonconformist theories of small fast-moving bands of men being more effective in African terrain than solid phalanxes of infantry, but although Colonel Ojukwu agreed with the principle, circumstances later forced him to bring the Commandos back to an infantry role.

During June Adekunle in the south launched out of Port Harcourt with orders to capture the remains of Gowon's Rivers State lying west of the Bonny. At this point Colonel Ojukwu asked the tribal chiefs of the two southern Provinces, Yenagoa and Degema, to come and see him. He told them the nature of the terrain they lived in was so unsuitable for defence that he could not offer great hopes of the Biafran Army being able to prevent the Nigerians from overrunning them. Therefore he offered the chiefs the chance that if they wished to opt for Nigeria and save themselves from eventual reprisals, he would draw up his defensive line north of the two provinces and cede the remainder of the Rivers area to Nigeria.

The chiefs wished to reply at once, but Ojukwu told them to go back home and talk it over in council. The next day a messenger arrived with the Rivers people's answer. They wanted to stay with Biafra; they hoped for every defence possible, and would help all they could; they realized this would bring reprisals, and were ready for them.

Adekunle later made the Rivers pay a stiff price for their

loyalty to Biafra. As Ojukwu had predicted, the territory was impossible to defend against a force equipped with scores of boats and ships. Defending units had to be split into penny-packets to watch every spit of land and island. The Nigerians could pick their spot and move in off the sea. By the middle of July landings had been made at Degema, Yenagoa, Brass and a score of other places. On the mainland Nigerian infantry forces moved through Igritta, Elele and Ahoada, to capture the rest of the 'Rivers State'.

So far Colonel Adekunle had never operated outside the minorities areas. He had never set foot in Ibo-land, while the other two Nigerian Divisions had never operated outside Ibo-land except for the First Division's campaign to capture Ogoja Province. In some ways therefore, despite his enormous weapons advantage, Adekunle had had it easy.

This is not to say that fighting was any less severe in the minorities areas than in Ibo-land, nor that most of the chiefs of the minority groups did not remain loyal to Biafra. But in the minorities areas it was easier to find dissidents prepared to collaborate either through genuine conviction or desire for advantage, and these Nigerian agents had done enormous work guiding the Nigerian forces and revealing to them hidden byways which only the local people could know.

It had also been easier to introduce into the minorities areas some weeks before an attack scores of agents imported from the Eastern minority communities in Lagos. Some of these agents nevertheless defected once they got among their own people again, and told of large sums of money being seeded around the minority areas to buy over the local chiefs, of *agents provocateurs* preaching hatred of the Ibos, and of threats of violent reprisal in the event of the local people re-maining loyal to Biafra when the forthcoming attack took place.

The techniques were not unsuccessful in some parts, though few of the original promises made were ever fulfilled and the behaviour of the Nigerian soldiery usually brought swift dis-illusionment. Violence habitually came in two waves. The Federal combat troops moved through first, shooting every-thing on sight regardless of tribe, destroying and looting property regardless of ownership. The violence of the soldiery was usually in proportion to the casualties they had had to take in order to capture a position. Thus where a town fell easily without a shot being fired, and the population swung rapidly into a pro-Nigerian attitude commensurate with the brisk change in the power balance, there sometimes occurred periods of amity between the infantry and the local population. This never happened in Ibo-land, but no one in Ibo-land had very many doubts that their fate was in any case sealed.

After the infantry moved on, the second-rate garrison troops moved in. Within weeks the local indigenes had learned that 'One Nigeria' was a fine slogan but an unattractive reality when it involved a seemingly limitless occupation by soldiers who had not been discouraged from thinking anything in occupied Biafra was theirs for the taking. That was why by the end of 1968 some of the most fertile breeding grounds in the whole country for the budding Biafran guerrilla movement were those minority areas that had been longest under Nigerian occupation.

In July Adekunle prepared to make his first move into Ibo-land and began to push towards Owerri. He had developed his 'O.A.U. plan', the capture of Owerri, Aba and Umuahia in quick succession. Somewhat intoxicated by the sense of his own importance and under serious illusions about his competence, Adekunle had vaunted his intentions for a quick kill of the remainder of Biafra far and wide. His increasingly erratic behaviour caused a tide of complaints and General Gowon was repeatedly forced to apologize on his behalf. But he could obviously twist Gowon round his finger when he wanted anything, and he remained at the head of the Third Division to build up his one-man kingdom.

Towards the end of July his forces had pushed up the Port Harcourt to Owerri road as far as Umuakpu, twenty-three miles south of Owerri. Colonel Ojukwu, wishing to go to Addis Ababa but not liking to see Owerri fall while he was away, ordered Steiner and his Commandos to leave Awka and come down to Owerri.

By this time it had become clear that Steiner was content to command the Brigade and do the operational planning, at which he was good, while leaving the actual combat to Williams. This lean Welsh-born South African, cheerfully admitting he was half mad, had a habit of proving he was bullet-proof by standing amid a hail of fire while men were shot down around him, waving a walking stick and shouting obscenities at the Nigerian machine gunners, which drove them frantic with rage. But the Biafran Commandos responded to this bravado by imitation, and 'Taffy's boys' got a reputation as hard fighters. At any rate Nigerian prisoners admitted their infantry did not like to find itself up against the Commandos, which pleased Steiner and Williams enormously. By this time they had been joined by three newcomers, a burly Scot, a lean, soft-spoken but highly dangerous Corsican, and a handsome young Rhodesian called Johnny Erasmus, no intellectual but a wizard with explosives.

South of Owerri, in the face of Umuakpu, Steiner put Erasmus to work to build a ring of obstacles in the path of the Nigerians. After three days, and having felled two hundred trees, dug pits, planted mines, linked booby traps, arranged arcs of fire, dug bunkers and wedged everything wedgeable with grenades with the pins taken out, Erasmus announced that the Nigerians could either stay at Umuakpu or use paratroopers. In fact they never did breach those obstacles; they were eventually outflanked and dismantled from the rear.

Leaving the Biafran infantry ensconced behind this Maginot Line, Steiner sent Williams and five hundred Commandos round the side. They struck on 4 August not at Umuakpu, but at Nigerian battalion H.Q. at the next village down the road, Amu Nelu. Within an hour Williams had destroyed the H.Q., recuperated a large quantity of equipment, arms and ammunition, left over 100 Nigerian dead on the road, and departed in time for breakfast. The effect of Amu Nelu was not long in coming. The Nigerians sent an emissary through the lines to the Biafran infantry asking for a local truce.

Within a week the Commandos had to be transferred again, this time to Okpuala, half way along the road from Owerri to Aba. The Nigerians were moving from the south against this road junction as well, and the Scot and the Corsican were detailed to stop the advance. A series of fierce battles ensued during which both were wounded. But a mixed force of Commandos and infantry held the Nigerians short of Okpuala until after Aba had fallen.

Aba, shielded from the south and west by the curve of the Imo River, was presumed to be safe from attack. It was the biggest city left, now overflowing not only with its original refugees but many of those from Port Harcourt. It was also the administrative centre of Biafra. Across the Imo there had been two bridges, one at Imo River Town on the main road from Aba to Port Harcourt, the other at Awaza further west. The first bridge had been blown up, the second was intact but mined. It was the Awaza bridge the Nigerians chose. When they appeared on the far bank, the Biafrans blew the charges, but they had been badly placed. It was one of the most serious errors of the war. The bridge went down, but a gas pipeline a few yards to one side escaped the blast. Along the top of this pipe ran a catwalk, and the Biafrans, out of ammunition, watched helplessly as the Nigerians started to cross on foot in single file. This was on 17 August. Williams was sent for with 700 men, but he could not get there until the morning of the 19th. By this time the Nigerians had put across three battalions.

The Commandos fought for two days to try to get the bridge-head back, but while two Federal battalions held them a mile from the water, the third marched south and captured the northern bank of the other, bigger bridge. Seeing that it was useless, Williams pulled back to the main Aba–Port Harcourt road. For six days the Biafran Twelfth Division assisted by Williams' men, now made up to 1,000, fought back as a tide of Nigerians crossed the Imo on foot. Feverish work was in progress, reportedly with Russian engineers, to re-build the Imo River Bridge to bring over the heavy equipment.

Williams, holding the main axis, did not rate the Nigerians very dangerous so long as they lacked their armour and artillery, although they still outnumbered the Biafrans many times in guns, bullets and mortars. On 24 August the bridge was completed and the attack column rolled across. The ensuing battle was the bloodiest of the war. Williams threw in his 1,000 Commandos in attack rather than wait in defence. The impertinence caught the Nigerians off guard. They had a reported three brigades in the main column up the main road, and the intention was to march easily to Aba, brush aside the resistance, and move on to Umuahia.

For three days Williams and Erasmus led less than 1,000 young Biafrans clutching bolt-action rifles against the pride of the Nigerian Army. They had no bazookas, no artillery, precious few mortars. The Nigerians threw in a rain of shells and mortars, five armoured cars and a monsoon of bazooka rockets. Their machine-guns and repeater rifles did not stop for seventy-two hours. The backbone of the defence was the 'ogbunigwe', a weird mine invented by the Biafrans. It looked like a square cone with dynamite packed into the narrow end and the rest stuffed with ball bearings, nails, stones, scrap iron and metal chips. The base is placed against a tree to absorb the shock, the trumpet-shaped opening, covered over with plywood, faces down the road towards the oncoming forces. It is detonated by a wire, and experts advise the firer to stand well back. On exploding, the ogbunigwe sweeps clear a ninety-degree arc in front of it, with a maximum killing range of over 200 yards. Such a device let off at short range will normally destroy a company and stop an attack in its tracks.

The Nigerians came up the road standing upright with no attempt at taking cover, chanting their war cry, 'Oshe-bey'. They were swaying oddly from side to side. Williams, who had done time in the Congo, took one look and said, 'They're doped to the eyeballs'.

Erasmus started to let go the ogbunigwes at point-blank range. The Nigerians were cut down like corn. The survivors swayed, moved on. On the first day Erasmus triggered over forty ogbunigwes. One of the Saladin armoured cars had its tyres shredded and withdrew. Biafran ammunition ran out, but the leading Nigerian Brigade had been ruined. Impeded by anti-tank ditches, they had filled them in with shovels, one relay team taking over from the previous one as the teams were cut down. Faced with fallen trees weighing many tons, they lifted them bodily out of the way, the team doing the work being blown to fragments as the mine beneath the tree went off automatically.

As the leading Nigerian brigade was changed, Williams urged his exhausted men to take advantage of the disorder in front of them and charge. They won back the three miles they had lost during the day and returned to their original positions. Waiting for the next day the troops slept while Erasmus started preparing more booby traps and Williams returned to Aba for ammunition. But the ammunition planes were not arriving. Steiner, promoted Lieutenant-Colonel, who had moved his headquarters to Aba, appealed to the Army Commander, then to Colonel Ojukwu. There was no ammunition. Williams returned to the front. For Sunday 25 August his men had two bullets each.

That Sunday was a repeat performance of Saturday, and Monday followed suit. Then for six days there was calm. Later it was reported that Adekunle had filled the hospitals of Calabar, Port Harcourt, Benin and even Lagos with his wounded from the Aba column. How many dead never got off that road was not counted, but Williams put the number at close to 2,500.

After licking its wounds the Third Division launched another attack on Aba, but not up the main road. They took the Commandos' right flank and the flank crumbled as the armoured cars rushed through. Aba fell on 4 September, not from the front but from the side. Steiner fought his way out with a handful of cooks armed with machine pistols. Colonel Achuzie nearly had a head-on collision with a Nigerian Saladin as he swept round a corner. Williams was still six miles south of the town holding the axis when Aba fell behind him. He came out with his men across country.

Colonel Ojukwu ordered the Commandos to return to base camp, recruit fresh men, re-form and re-fit. From both axes, Aba and Okpuala, 1,000 returned of the 3,000 who had moved to Awka nine weeks previously. In mid-September Steiner went on leave for a fortnight and Williams took over acting command.

The assault on Aba of 24 August had been the signal for the all-round 'final assault on Ibo-land' which the British Parliament had been told would never happen. Every sector burst into flame, in the south from Ikot Ekpene which had already changed hands six times, to Owerri; in the north Haruna made one spirited attempt to burst out of Onitsha and link up with his men at Abagana, while the First Division threw all its force against the demilitarized Red Cross airstrip at Obilagu. This fell on 23 September.

On 11 September the Nigerians launched a fast attack by boat up the river Orashi towards Oguta, a lakeside town not far from Uli Airport. Unspotted, the boats crossed the lake and the men disembarked. Oguta was still full of people and there was a lot of killing. After the flight of the townspeople Oguta was systematically looted, and more Nigerians came across the River Niger from the Midwest. An angry Colonel Ojukwu called his commanders and told them to get Oguta back in forty-eight hours. Ojukwu himself directed the operation, with Achuzie as operational commander. The Biafrans swept back into the town and the Nigerians fled for the river, leaving several hundred dead behind them, including their commander.

But Oguta had a by-product. Some of the Biafran troops used there had been taken from the right flank at Umuakpu, and on 13 September a Nigerian patrol probing the flanks discovered the weak spot. An attack was launched which outflanked the defences and brought the Nigerians to Obinze, ten miles south of Owerri. From there, on 18 September, they ran on into the town, led by armoured cars.

In the north the First Division moved on from Obilagu and captured Okigwi town, also undefended as it had been the Red Cross distributing centre for the relief food arriving at nearby Obilagu. Here they distinguished themselves by shooting down a couple of elderly English missionaries, Mr and Mrs Savory, and two Swedish Red Cross workers. This was on 1 October.

From that date the situation began to change. The arms shipper who had let the Biafrans down over Aba and Owerri had been dismissed and a new air bridge set up from Libreville, Gabon. Pilots of British, South African, Rhodesian and French nationality ran it. Acquiring more funds, Colonel Ojukwu gained access to a wider European arms market and greater quantities began to flow in. The Biafrans went on to the counter-attack.

Steiner returned from leave, but he was still a tired man. Made commander of the newly formed Commando Division, he was clearly not up to the task. Suffering from nervous exhaustion, the mental illness of which he had a history began to reassert itself, giving him delusions of grandeur combined with a persecution mania. His behaviour became increasingly undisciplined, until he gave his men orders to hijack three Red Cross jeeps for his own use.

Summoned to explain, he chose to remonstrate with Colonel Ojukwu, and the Biafran Head of State had no choice but to order him to leave. Six others of the officers he had brought back from leave with him went also. Williams took over again as Acting Commander, later to hand over command to a Biafran Brigadier. But while he was in charge two more battles were fought under his direction. Between 10 and 12 November one of the Division's three brigades launched a series of attacks on Onitsha which, though they did not capture the town, cut the Nigerian perimeter down to a half its size and relieved the danger of a break-out.

The attacks might have gone on, had the Nigerians at Awka not launched an attack southwards to capture the villages of Agolo and Adazi, which threatened the Biafran heartland. The Commandos in the area fought back, assisted by two battalions of the Biafran infantry. The Nigerians took another beating and retired back to Awka.

Elsewhere it was the same story through November and December. The Biafrans counter-attacked in most sectors, notably at Aba and Owerri. At Aba Colonel Timothy Onuatuegwu pushed the Federal forces back to the outskirts of the town, then swung his men down the right and left flanks. At Owerri Colonel John Kalu retook 150 square miles of ground around the town and laid siege.

This bare recital of events over eighteen months may seem to give the impression that the Nigerian advances into Biafra were a smooth and steady progression. This was not the case. Apart from the occasional instance where Nigerian forces had an easy run, they fought for every foot of the way. Often objectives were not taken until the third or fourth attempt. Sometimes they were blocked for months. Their expenditure in ammunition is conservatively estimated at several hundreds of millions of rounds, their losses several tens of thousands of men.

Nor did they achieve an ability to control and administer what they had captured. Sticking closely to the main roads and the towns, avoiding the bush which covers over ninety per cent of the country, the Nigerians were able to draw lines on maps which bore little relation to the realities of the situation. Their own appointed administrators sitting in the towns vie for authority with the Biafran administrator sitting out in the bush in the overrun areas, and often the Biafran appointee's fiat covers the majority of the land and the bulk of the largely rural population.

The secret of Biafra's survival lies partly in the leadership of Colonel Ojukwu, but far more in the people of Biafra. Neither the leader nor the army could have fought without the total backing of the people. The support from behind has to be there before an army can do more than put up a token resistance. The people contributed everything they had got; poor villages took collections, rich men emptied their foreign accounts to donate dollars and pounds. Tailors made uniforms out of curtain material, cobblers turned out army boots from canvas strips. Farmers donated yams, cassava, rice, goats, chickens and eggs. Bushmen came forward with axes and blunderbusses. Taxi drivers and Mammy-wagon owners drove troop convoys, priests and schoolteachers handed over their bicycles.

There were some traitors, and cheats, defectors, profiteers and racketeers; they come to the surface in every war. But from the people there was not a riot, nor a demonstration, nor a mutiny. As they watched their land devastated and their kinsfolk killed two things were born among the debris; a sense of nationhood and a hatred of the Nigerians. What had started as a belief was transmuted to total conviction; that they could never again live with Nigerians. From this stems the primordial political reality of the present situation. Biafra cannot be killed by anything short of the total eradication of the people who make her. For even under total occupation Biafra would sooner or later, with or without Colonel Ojukwu, rise up again.

Throughout the year 1969 there occurred remarkably few large territorial changes and by the end of that year the shooting war had degenerated into stalemate. The year started with the transfer on 3 January by Colonel Ojukwu of two brigades of the 'S' Division from the Aba front under the command of Colonel Onuatuegwu to the Owerri front to help Colonel Kalu and the Fourteenth Division in the siege of Owerri.

For the rest of that month, their forward units being inside the northern outskirts of the town, both commanders attacked the Federal garrison head on. They suffered casualties without gaining very much, since as usual the Nigerians were well dug in and excellently supplied with all the arms and ammunition they needed, which came up the main road from Port Harcourt to the south. At the end of January, in a conference with Colonel Ojukwu and Colonel Kalu, Onuatuegwu proposed that these head-on tactics should be abandoned, and what fire-power the Biafrans had should be used to try to clear the flanks of Owerri and close the Nigerian supply line – a tactic he had been using against Aba when he was transferred.

The plan was agreed to, and throughout the month of February both commanders cleared the Nigerian-occupied villages to the east and west of Owerri, finally penetrating in force round to the south of the town. The completion of the encirclement and the final cutting of the last Nigerian supply road to the south came on 28 February. Throughout the month of March, despite repeated attempts from the Federal forces to break through the cordon and relieve the brigade surrounded in Owerri, the encirclement held, and the Nigerian Air Force had to resort to supplying the imprisoned garrison with air drops of ammunition. As they were unskilled in this kind of operation, about seventy per cent of the supplies thus dropped fell outside the perimeter and into the hands of the Biafrans. These supplies included large quantities of brand-new Russian Kalashnikov AK-47 light assault guns, with ammunition to match.

Early in April even these supplies were stopped, and the Biafrans, realizing that no more manna from heaven was likely to fall, resumed their attacks on the increasingly demoralized Federal garrison, often using the Nigerian supplies that had unwittingly been dropped to them.

During March a particularly strong relieving force had been sent up the road from Port Harcourt to re-open the way to Owerri, but had been sidetracked to the west of the main tarred road and had come to rest at Ohuba, some nine miles south of Owerri. Here it remained until the end of 1969.

After twenty days of unremitting attack from the Biafrans during April, running short of food and ammunition, the Nigerian commander inside Owerri, Colonel Utuk, held a meeting with his battalion commanders on the evening of 22 April. It was decided that despite orders from Colonel Adekunle in Port Harcourt to stay put, they would instead pull out. During that night the entire garrison, including wounded who were loaded onto lorries, lined up in a column inside the town facing south. Previous patrols probing the southern outskirts of the town had revealed a rather weak Biafran battalion guarding a road heading south. This was not the main tarred road, but another earth road slightly to the east. On the morning of 23 April, spearheaded by their two Saladin armoured cars, the column hit this Biafran battalion and broke through. From then on the column headed out of town and back towards the main body of the Nigerian Third Division, whose advance units were at Umuakpu and Amu Nelu, where Taffy Williams had halted them ten months earlier.

Hearing that the Federal garrison had slipped out of the net, Colonel Onuatuegwu hastily dispatched two battalions to chase them. These two caught the tail of the Federal column five miles south of Owerri, and from then on the latter fought a bitter rearguard action as it retreated southwards. Assailed from rear and sides, ambushed constantly, the column was cut to pieces and it was finally no more than scores of groups of stragglers who arrived in safety at the Nigerian positions around Umu Nelu, twenty-three miles south of Owerri. They had lost most of their equipment and almost half their men.

The Biafrans reoccupied Owerri the same day, 23 April, and started to put the shattered and spoliated town back together again. A fortnight after the loss of this town, which hurt Nigerian morale badly, Colonel Adekunle was relieved of his command and returned to a training assignment in Lagos. Until the end of November 1969, despite repeated attempts to advance, the Federal forces were still respectively at Chuba and Umuakpu, and Owerri had become the new capital of the Biafran Government.

The Biafrans' joy at recapturing this important and strategic town was marred by the recent loss of their previous capital, Umuahia. While the reoccupation of Owerri had been long and laborious, the Federal capture of Umuahia represented the culmination of another short all-out attack supported by an enormous quantity of hardware. During the three spring months, as the rainy season approached, the Federal Government's concern had been to build up not the prestigious Third Division in the south, but the less renowned First Division in the north. Throughout the last three months of 1968 and the first three of 1969 large quantities of the newly arriving Russian arms were being fed to the First Division, and on 26 March, to coincide with the arrival in Nigeria of Mr Harold Wilson, the First Division launched itself out of Okigwi and Afikpo simultaneously.

Both spearheads were tipped with half a dozen armoured cars, and supported by large amounts of artillery and mortar fire. By 1 April the towns of Bende and Uzoakoli had been reached and fierce fighting was taking place in both areas. Uzoakoli was a particularly heavy loss for the Biafrans, because it was the site of the oil refinery they had built after losing Port Harcourt the previous May. This refinery was turning out about 30,000 gallons of refined petrol a day at full production and was on its way to coping with the fuel shortage that had bedevilled the Biafrans since stocks had been expended the previous November.

For a few days it seemed as if the Federal forces might be held at these two towns. Holding Bende was also important because this town dominates a ridge of hills from which the path to Umuahia is a downhill run. But on 7 April a Nigerian column cutting across country took the town of Ovim, lying on the railway line leading straight to Umuahia. By 10 April

Federal shells started to fall on the outskirts of Umuahia and the town was evacuated by its population.

Umuahia fell on 15 April, although sporadic firing went on for a few days after that. The last man out of the town was Colonel Ojukwu, who had directed much of the fighting personally from his house at the end of Okpara Road.

Despite the capture, the Nigerian hold on the town remained tenuous. As usual in such cases, the Biafrans, having been disorganized as the town fell, regrouped and counter-attacked a week later. The Federal supply lines to Umuahia, running through miles of hilly country north and north-east of the town, were highly vulnerable, and several times during the early summer the garrison had to ask for air drops to keep going. By the end of the year Umuahia, like Aba, was still surrounded on three sides, an outpost at the end of a long and very vulnerable corridor of hostile territory.

Apart from these two major campaigns, all the fronts remained stable. In early March the Federal Second Division, based on Onitsha, attacked simultaneously out of Onitsha towards Awka and from Awka towards Onitsha in an effort to close the six miles of road held by the Biafrans that still separated the two halves of the Division. They succeeded in closing this gap and establishing road contact, and held it for about a fortnight. The counter-attacking Biafrans regained that portion of the road, and eventually in June re-entered the eastern outskirts of Onitsha itself.

Apart from this nothing happened in the north throughout 1969. In the south it was the Biafrans who, for the first time, were on the attack in almost all sectors. Learning their lesson from the new tactics used at Owerri, nowhere did they launch massive frontal attacks, but concentrated on clearing one by one the Nigerian occupancy of small villages. Thus by the end of the year it was possible to drive the whole length of the Owerri to Aba road, which had previously been in Federal hands, up to a point five miles short of Aba. The Federal garrisons had been swept out of Okpuala, and Father Kevin Doheny had been able to reopen his seminary there. Owerrinta had also been cleared and the leading Federal forces were back in Amala, five miles south of this road where the Scottish and

Corsican mercenaries, leading a detachment of the Commandos, had fought them back in August 1968. In all about 1,000 square miles of territory in the southern sector had been quietly recaptured by the Biafrans during 1969.

The reasons for these successes, although limited, were five-fold. Firstly, they were due to the change in tactics, the abandonment of head-on clashes with a better-armed enemy and the greater reliance on attacks from the sides, on ambushes and on commando tactics; in short, on the tactics for which Williams, who had left in February without his contract being renewed for a third term, had unavailingly pleaded. Secondly, they were due to a steadily decreasing morale among the Federal infantry; throughout the year, as the summer rains poured down and the appalling Nigerian Army logistics caused the front-line men to go short of food and ammunition, captured prisoners complained that the men on the Federal side were fed up, wanted to go home, and did not wish to risk dying in yet another suicidal attack ordered by senior officers who kept themselves well to the rear. A general war-weariness set in on both sides, but the Biafran soldiers were at least on their home territory, supported by the peasantry behind them, and considerably better armed than they had ever been.

The last three reasons for the changed situation concern weapons. In the first place, the main Federal advantage in all its attacks up to the late spring of 1969 had lain in its armoured cars, with which the Biafrans had been quite unable to cope. During 1969 they acquired a substantial number of good-quality bazookas, and rockets to go with them. Some were of the Soviet type, an extremely light and efficient bazooka, accurate up to 300 yards and easy to maintain. Others were the more complex French LRAC bazookas made in the Western world. Whereas in 1968 training for use in these weapons had been rudimentary in the extreme, during 1969 two European officers trained the Biafran bazooka crews to use their weapons properly, with the effect that the Biafran infantry soon lost their fear of Saladins and Ferrets; it became rare for these vehicles to show their noses too prominently as their life expectancy became shorter and shorter.

Secondly, the general level of Biafran weapons and firepower went steadily up during 1969. Speaking at a press conference on 4 November in Owerri, General Ojukwu (he had accepted promotion to the rank of General from the Consultative Assembly in March 1969) said: 'We are infinitely better off in firepower than at any time since the war began.' He added that the main increase had been in support weapons, that is, bazookas, artillery, mortars and heavy machine guns. Again, training in the use of these weapons was more general in 1969 than in 1968. The effect of these two changes in the Biafran situation was almost to nullify the advantages the Federal Army had possessed so long that they had almost come to be regarded as built-in.

Lastly, the difference was made by the new Biafran Air Force, which made its first raid on 22 May and grew steadily stronger for the rest of the year. The story of the Biafran Air Force cannot yet be properly told since so much of it is still unknown, but most of its activities and its successes lie in the personality of a remarkable Swedish veteran pilot, Count Carl Gustav von Rosen.

This aviator (see Chapter 11, p. 211) was the man who, while flying as senior pilot for the Nord Church Aid relief scheme, brought in the first daylight hedgehopping aircraft from São Tomé on 10 August 1968 to show that Wharton's monopoly of the relief route could be broken. By the end of September, after several differences of view with his direct employers, Transair, and his more recent masters in Nord Church Aid, he resigned from his post at São Tomé and returned to Sweden.

He next appeared in Umuahia, Biafra, at Christmas 1968 having brought a letter from the Emperor Haile Selassie, a personal friend, to Colonel Ojukwu. On Christmas Day he came to the author's caravan in Umuahia almost in tears, having witnessed the scene of devastation and carnage that had been left behind after one of the three separate bombing raids carried out by the Nigerian Air Force on Umuahia that day. Some of the bombs had hit a house full of children, and the spectacle had badly upset the Count, just as it had already upset various journalists who had previously seen similar sights.

In subsequent conversation over coffee, the elderly Swedish

pilot, within one year of a pensionable retirement from Trans-air, spoke of his determination to return to Biafra and smash the Egyptian-piloted Federal Air Force. As the hours dragged by he elaborated step by step, visualizing and solving the problems as he went along, a plan to buy light aircraft of an extremely manoeuvrable type, fit them with rockets or bombs, and use them at tree-top level to destroy the MiGs and Ilyushins on the ground. Escape, he maintained, would be afforded by the element of surprise and the low altitude of the planes. Painted green on top, blue underneath, flying scarcely above the tops of the palm trees, they would be undetectable until they struck, and impossible to follow afterwards.

At the time it seemed like such general talk as pilots often indulge in. But he did exactly what he said he was going to do. On 22 May Count von Rosen led his first strike against Port Harcourt airport, destroying with rockets fired from Swedish-made MFI Minicon light monoplanes one Ilyushin and two MiGs parked on the tarmac. There were five Minicons in that raid, three flown by Swedes and two by Biafrans whom von Rosen had trained in Gabon.

In succeeding months the Minicons pounded away at the Federal airfields, destroying by the end of the year some thirty war and transport planes, including three of the bombers that almost nightly harassed Uli airstrip as the relief aircraft came in. After hitting the airports, the Minicons, by now flown by Biafrans alone, started in mid June on the oil installations that provided Nigeria with most of its foreign currency and credit with which to buy war weapons.

By the end of the year this tiny force of hedgehoppers had done enough damage to have persuaded Shell–BP temporarily to suspend its operations from mainland Nigeria. As other companies followed suit after watching their installations rocketed, oil flow out of Nigeria slowed to a trickle and caused the first serious rethink in British commercial circles since the war started.

By mid summer Count von Rosen had handed over the flying role to enthusiastic young Biafrans, trained by his two Swedish associate pilots in Gabon, and had taken on a more organiza-tional role. This bore fruit on 2 November 1969, when two

Harvards flew into Uli airport to join the Minicons in the bush fighter strip where they were based. There were by now fifteen Minicons. The two-seater Harvards, single-engined low-wing monoplanes, were originally built as advanced trainers for the Canadian Air Force, but later proved sufficiently powerful and adaptable to be flown against the Simbas in the Congo crisis with great effect. Equipped with bombs, rocket or machine guns, they form an ideal platform for air-to-ground operations in the African type of war, better than jet fighters.

The pilots were both Germans, one of them being Fred Herz, previously the pilot of the old B-25 back in January 1968. On 10 November the two Harvards, accompanied by three Minicons to take care of the anti-aircraft fire, made their first attack on Port Harcourt, destroying three of the new MiGs, three freighter aircraft including the latest of the Uli-bombers, the main hangar, fuel dump and control tower. By the end of the year two British Meteor jet fighter-bombers were expected to join what General Ojukwu referred to as Biafra's mini-Air-Force.

The raids against the oil installations, representing throughout 1969 Ojukwu's top Nigerian and British Government policy to exert pressure for a ceasefire, were conducted only partly by the Minicons. These were backed up with commando-style attacks on lonely installations in the bush.

Partly with this in mind, in March 1969 General Ojukwu gave Colonel Joe Achuzie the task of going back into his home region, the Midwest, with a force of commandos to raise an insurrectional movement among the Ica-Ibos, who since the Biafrans had left the Midwest in October 1967 had led a precarious existence, mainly hiding out in the dense bush on the western bank of the Niger. Little was heard of Achuzie apart from rumours in Lagos of mounting guerrilla activity in the Ibo-speaking parts of the Midwest, until 9 May.

On that day, in the half-light before dawn, a unit of Achuzie's troops stormed into an oil settlement at Kwale and captured it. The Nigerian Army company that was supposed to guard the place ran away, leaving to their fate the twenty-nine whites employed there. Of these, eleven, ten Italians and a Jordanian, were killed in the mêlée. Eighteen others, fourteen

Italians, three Germans and a Lebanese, were taken prisoner and sent back across the Niger.

Some of the prisoners, having allegedly been found in possession of weapons, were tried as mercenaries, found guilty and sentenced to be executed. When the story broke, the European Press nearly went into hysterics. It remains extremely doubtful whether General Ojukwu ever intended anything to happen to these men; the evidence is that he did not. The sentencing, however, caused a furore, shook the oil chiefs to the extremities of their patent leather pumps and caused the heads of the Italian Agip petroleum combine, which employed the men, to enter into dialogue with Ojukwu. It also collected for Biafra some of the worst publicity imaginable.

Despite this, Ojukwu was on balance content with the outcome. He had got what he wanted, which was some direct reaction from the oil chiefs. He had impressed on them all that the Nigerian Army, despite his promises, could not protect their staff, and it was no accident that subsequently all the oil companies made substantial withdrawals of staff from oil installations in Nigerian-occupied Biafra. The remaining question was what to do with the eighteen sentenced oilmen.

In the outcome, Ojukwu yielded to a plea for clemency from the Pope and on 6 June at a ceremony outside Owerri jail, where the men had been held, they were handed over to a delegation of Caritas, the World Council of Churches, and representatives from Gabon and the Ivory Coast. The same night they were flown out to Gabon, and thence home to their families.

The only other person to fall into Biafran hands in unusual circumstances was a British nurse, Miss Sally Goatcher, who was working for the Save the Children Fund on the Nigerian side of the firing line, and who accidentally motored through the lines south of Uli on 29 May and was captured. She was kept until 16 June, when she was also released and flown out via Libreville, Gabon. Once out, neither she nor the oilmen manifested any grudge against the Biafrans, and all agreed they had been well treated during their captivity.

During the autumn, reports continued to come from Nigeria that the Federal Army was slowly cranking itself up for yet another 'final assault'. Despite the gullibility of some reporters who were content to tell their readers that the six-month inactivity of the Nigerian Army from April until October was due to the kindliness of General Gowon in refusing to give the order to advance and crush the remainder of Biafra, those willing or capable of looking beneath the surface of propaganda descried two reasons for the lull in the fighting. One was the rainy season: after two light rainy seasons in 1967 and 1968, the season of April until October 1969 was exceptionally heavy. Not only were bush paths and tracks reduced to a sticky quagmire in which nothing on wheels could safely move, but even large parts of the tarred roads were washed away. The other reason was that the Federal Army's logistics and supply situation, not very efficient at the best of times, deteriorated during the summer to a state as bad as it had ever been. This again was due partly to the rains making convoys difficult to move long distances, partly to the state of maintenance of the trucks which, after two years almost without maintenance, spent much of their time immobile, and partly to the effect of the increasing guerrilla ambushes, which required the Federal forces to guard their supply convoys with substantial escort parties.

Nevertheless, by mid October they were at last ready, and the attack was launched. It failed more miserably than any of its predecessors.

It had always been usual before any 'final assault' for broadcasts of exhortation to the troops to be beamed from Lagos, backed up by further pep talks from divisional and brigade commanders. On this occasion, using the forces' network, General Gowon repeatedly urged his troops into one last, final onslaught. He was at pains to repeat several times that this would have to be the last assault, that for the troops it was now or never. This he had not done before.

That the attack failed was due in part to the lack of enthusiasm of the men in the front lines, partly to the superior Biafran weaponry, and partly to sheer mismanagement. It started with the First Division in the North, now newly under the command of Colonel Bissalla, launching its two finest brigades out of Okigwi on 22 October. This battle raged with great ferocity for ten days. At one juncture the Nigerian forces seemed to have broken through the defensive line, and to have opened the road towards Orlu and the all-important Uli airport. The deciding factor, ironically, was the Nigerian Air Force.

According to European eye-witness reports, the East German pilots, now flying the MiGs with great accuracy, mistook the advancing Federal forces for the Biafrans, and twice within three days pulverized them so badly that their morale was broken and they pulled back to their own original lines. The other two fresh factors, apart from the higher level of Biafran firepower, included a new mine designed and built by the Biafrans. It was called the 'flying ogbunigwe' and took the form of a thirteen-inch rocket some seven feet long, tipped with a massive landmine of the type described earlier. This contraption was thrown by rocket fuel some six hundred yards, to explode in the air fifty feet above the oncoming troops while pointing downwards. It spread death and destruction over a large area, and as usual the First Division, being mostly Hausas and other Northerners, were advancing in solid phalanxes of packed soldiery. An American who examined the scene afterwards estimated that out of 6,000 men who took part in the attack, nearly 4,000 failed to return.

The other contributory factor in the defeat was the new Biafran Air Force, whose Minicons found the lorries bearing the Nigerians' supplies neatly lined up in columns along the roads behind the front. These were rocketed and strafed, and in the case of the lorries not destroyed, the drivers fled into the bush and left their vehicles immobile. After ten days of charging repeatedly into heavy machine-gun fire which they did not expect to meet, being subjected to the flying ogbunigwes and finally the attentions of their own air force, the two battered brigades withdrew on 2 November to their former positions.

Had the several attacks from the Nigerian side been launched simultaneously they might have had some effect. But as usual the divisional commanders declined to co-operate with each other. Hardly had the First Division attack failed than the Third Division in the south, now under the command of Colonel

Obassi (Adekunle having been relieved of command following the loss of Owerri) went on the warpath. At Ohuba, to the west of the main Owerri–Port Harcourt road, fierce fighting took place in the first week of November. Here the Biafrans not only held the attack, but by the time it had petered out in mid November they had pushed the Federal forces back out of most of the complex of villages called Ohuba.

Further east along the main tarred road there was more fighting and the Federal forces advanced four miles from Umuakpu village up towards Owerri. However, at the end of these four miles they were still sixteen miles south of the town on this axis.

In mid November another major push was launched towards Okpuala, and here there was a greater degree of success for the Third Division. They made nine miles, coming to rest at Amala village, some five miles south of the main Aba–Owerri road. Again, the advance cost them dear in men and materials. Simultaneously with the Okpuala axis attack, the Second Division at Onitsha made its single bid. This was the only time the attacks in various sectors were coordinated. From Onitsha eastwards the Second Division again managed to close the gap and link up with Ogidi village. At this point the Biafran divisional commander, Brigadier Amadi, was wounded in the stomach by a grenade splinter. The removal of their commander seemed to rally the Biafran Eleventh Division, for in the last week of November they fought back and regained not only the six-mile stretch of tarmac between the eastern outskirts of Onitsha and Ogidi, but some more as well.

The only crisis point came in the last of the Federal series of assaults. This was at Ikot Ekpene, in Ibibio country far down in the southeast. Ikot Ekpene had been quiet for over a year, but in the last week of November the Federal forces in that sector threw everything they had into a dive northwards to try to link with Umuahia and cut off the Biafran enclave containing the towns of Ohafia and Arochukwu, and their hold on the banks of the Cross River at Ikot Okpora.

Caught on the hop, General Ojukwu's forces were driven back six miles up the Umuahia road to Ito-Ndan, the point from which they had started their counter-attacks towards Ikot

Ekpene in May 1968. Missionaries working on relief programmes among the starving Ibibios were forced to evacuate Urho-Akpan, northeast of Ikot Ekpene, and the battle was still raging at the end of November. On 29 November General Ojukwu told the author that with a fresh consignment of arms imported the previous evening he expected to be able to hold the attack in this sector by the end of the first week in December. And so it proved.

By mid December the Nigerian fifth final assault on the inner perimeter of Biafra had failed to overcome the resistance, and Biafran imports of arms, far from seeming to shrink, gave every indication of continuing at a high level.

By the end of 1969 it had become clear to correspondents working on both sides of the firing line that a decisive outcome in military terms was highly unlikely. Neither side appeared to have the wherewithal to make substantial advances against the other, which threw the whole question of a peace settlement back into the diplomatic sphere. This was where it should have been since the first schism between Lagos and Enugu in 1967. Unfortunately in the intervening thirty months one and a half million people had died.

10. The Role of the Wilson Government

As has been observed, Britain's traditional interest in Nigeria had nothing to do with the good of the people of that country, and in that respect nothing has changed. The interest that did exist was borne by a small caucus of British politicians, civil servants and businessmen, and it was purely imperialistic. The policy was aimed at the maintenance of law and order, the raising of taxes to pay for the administration of the colony, the stimulation of the production of raw materials for British industry and the establishment of a consumer market to purchase manufactured goods from British industry. With independence the first two functions were handed over to selected and suitably friendly indigenes, while the latter two remained as before in the hands of the British. For those inside Britain who concerned themselves in any way with Nigeria, that country represented, like the others, not a land with a population of real people, but a market. Any tendencies inside Nigeria that might be viewed as harmful to the market were to be discouraged, and Biafra's desire for partition from the rest of the country fell squarely into that category.

When evaluating British Government policy towards the whole question of the Nigeria–Biafra war, two schools of thought emerge: one claims that the policy was in fact the absence of a policy, the hopeless outcome of a mish-mash of stupidity, apathy, indifference, callousness and ignorance in high places; the other maintains there was a policy from the start, that it was one of total support not for the Nigerian people but for the régime presently in power in Lagos, that it was carefully masked from public view for as long as possible, and that the stupidity of the politicians and the ignorance and apathy of the general public and the men controlling the mass-communication media were used either in the furtherance or the dissimulation of that policy. As an increasing amount of research into the growing pile of documentation available takes place, it is becoming plainer that the evidence supports the latter view.

That British leadership should privately wish to see a single and unified Nigeria so long as this was practically feasible is not blameworthy; but what happened was that in its total determination to see a single economic unit no matter what the cost in suffering to the people of the country, through the grossest interference in the internal politics of that country the British Government chose to ally itself not with the people or their aspirations, but with a small clique of army mutineers. The fact that this clique has shown itself throughout to be largely unrepresentative of Nigerian grass-roots opinion, far from changing the 'support' policy has merely hardened it until a point where British Government policy is so inextricably entwined with the survival of the present Nigerian régime as to be publicly committed to total complicity in anything that régime may do.

On the morning after Gowon's coup of 29 July 1966 it was clear that the British Government's advisers considered that Gowon's legitimacy was sufficiently doubtful to require a top-level decision whether or not to recognize his régime at all. This was quite different from the first coup in January 1966, which failed but which led to General Ironsi being asked by the rump of the Cabinet to take over control. On 25 January the British Commonwealth Secretary Mr Arthur Bottomley told the Commons that the British Government did not consider a formal recognition of General Ironsi even to be necessary.*

But in July when no semblance of legality attached to Gowon's government, when the partially successful mutineers only controlled the capital and two out of four regions, the position was quite different. Just when and by what reasoning it was decided to recognize Gowon has not yet been revealed. But it was not until November 1966 that Gowon's nominee as Nigerian High Commissioner in London, the fast-moving Brigadier Ogundipe, presented his credentials to the Court of St James. And, oddly, it was not until 20 December that the House of Commons was informed that Britain had

* *Hansard*, 25 January 1966, col. 21.

decided to give full recognition to Gowon's régime.* In February 1967, Sir David Hunt took over in Lagos as Britain's new High Comissioner to Nigeria. Gradually, he escalated a previously decided policy of unalloyed support for Gowon.

There seems little doubt that the motivating force behind the formulation of British policy in Nigeria since July 1966 has come not from the politicians but from the senior civil servants in the High Commission in Lagos and the Commonwealth Office in London who advise them. The then Commonwealth Secretary, Mr Bottomley, although acknowledged by those who knew him to be an agreeable soul, apparently knew little about the situation; his successor Mr Herbert Bowden was unable to make himself remarkable for his grip of the facts of the issue, and his successor, Mr George Thomson, showed publicly and privately that his greatest interest lay in efforts to solve the vastly more publicized Rhodesia issue. None of these three were at any time supported either in the Commons or the Lords by a Junior Minister of notable calibre, and those aware of what went on behind the scenes in Whitehall were not surprised to find that the formulation of policy on Nigeria, the writing of Ministers' answers to questions in the House, and the very important briefing of the accredited press correspondents, fell entirely to the civil servants. This did not displease the civil servants, many of whom are known to hold that the complexities of any situation more involved than catching a bus are above the intellectual level of professional politicians. Unfortunately the civil servants showed in the course of time that they too could only bring to bear on the issue a mixture of ignorance, misinformation, prejudice, cynicism and on occasion the traditional British upper-class contempt for all Africans and assertive ones in particular. It was out of this potpourri of crassness, which later became tinged with hints of viciousness, that Britain's support for an African military junta and for the latter's war policy, and for Britain's complicity in the bloodiest episode in Commonwealth history, was born.

Britain was set on the road to supporting Gowon by her then High Commissioner in Lagos, Sir Francis Cumming-

* *Hansard*, 20 December 1966, col. 263.

Bruce. He later told Professor Eni Njoku, the Chancellor of the University of Nsukka and leader of the Eastern Delegation to the Ad Hoc Constitutional Conference, that when it became obvious to him that Gowon intended to announce in his broadcast of 1 August 1966 the dissolution of the Nigerian Federation, he managed to persuade Gowon to strike out the words and substitute other ones. He had thus, he told the Professor, saved the unity of Nigeria. A month later he was gone. However, it seems likely his act set Britain on a course from which it became increasingly difficult to deviate, even though no real effort was made to do so.

In the ensuing months there appeared two occasions at least in which the British High Commissioner, had he been prepared once again to use the undoubted influence vested in his office, could have helped to avert disaster. The first was after the sitting of the Constitutional Conference when it became clear that the majority of Nigerians, from grass-roots level upwards, favoured a loose confederation with a weak central government. The second occasion was when the Regional Military Governors meeting at Aburi had jointly come to the same conclusion and had appended their signatures to the resolution.

There is no evidence at all to indicate that on either of these occasions the British Government's representative on the spot suggested that this course should be followed. On the contrary, there are indications that the British on each occasion instead of advising Gowon to go along with Nigerian popular wishes encouraged him to threaten the use of force if he could not get agreement to the course of action that he and his own senior civil servants wished to see. Ironically, the loose confederation in Nigeria would have offered Britain all the advantages of the single market which she favoured from her own point of view, since the four Regional Marketing Boards already in existence were so autonomous as to constitute a kind of confederation in the economic field even at that time. In the event what has happened is that Britain's annual turnover of £170 million worth of trade has been irreparably eroded and may yet be lost almost completely.

The most charitable interpretation that can be put on the High Commission's decision to back Gowon against all comers including his own people, and to persuade Whitehall to do the same, is that the British representatives out there shared Gowon's own view that the Nigerian Army could deal swiftly with any dissidence and that therefore opposition to the Gowon régime need not be taken seriously. At best this optimism was uninformed, at worst cynical.

The job of any ambassador is largely threefold: to maintain the most friendly relations possible between the country he represents and the country to which he is accredited, both on the official and at the popular level; to watch over the lives, safety, property and interests of his own fellow-nationals in the country to which he is accredited; to provide continuous reliable information to his own government on the state of affairs in all aspects within the country where he is stationed. No accepted order of priority of these three tasks ever seems to have been drawn up, but both the first two are likely to be profoundly affected by the policy adopted by the ambassador's own government towards the country in which he is stationed; and that policy is likely to be influenced by the information the diplomat provides. For although a diplomat may not formulate policy, it is unusual for his advice not to weigh heavily in the formulation of policy in his own country.

In the event of a policy review, the ambassador is habitually called home for consultations, and his account of the situation, political, economic and social, that prevails in the country to which he is accredited, is usually listened to with great and sometimes decisive interest. Consequently the 'information' aspect of an ambassador's job may be regarded as paramount among his functions. Thoroughly bad information not only is the hallmark of a poor diplomat, but may well influence his own country's policy into the path of disaster.

In the case of a British High Commissioner in Nigeria, drawing up factual accounts of what is going on should not be difficult. Nigeria abounds in British businessmen, civil servants, traders, journalists, travellers, missionaries, doctors, teachers, professors and engineers who collectively have centuries of experience and deep understanding. There is also a Deputy High Commissioner in each of the four regions.

To judge from Gowon's remarks before the war about a 'short, surgical police action' he genuinely seems to have thought the Nigerian Army could settle the Eastern Region's disaffection within a matter of days. That he should be uninformed is not surprising. All potentates in Africa are surrounded by sycophants, flatterers and opportunists who find it in their interest to tell the man of power what they know he would like to hear. Yet it appears that the British High Commission shared this euphoria; private conversations with journalists in Lagos at the time make clear the British officials were quite convinced that fighting when it broke out would be brief and almost bloodless, that Colonel Ojukwu would be brought down, and that the East would be reincorporated into Nigeria within a few weeks at most.

Officials, journalists, and socialites, refurbishing each other's illusions in the circular social sodomy of the diplomatic cocktail party round, had managed to convince themselves of this without any reference to what was actually going on in the Eastern Region.

That Gowon and his advisers should have been misled was understandable; that the British High Commissioner should have been wrong was not. For Sir David Hunt was fortunate in that he was served in the Eastern Region by a shrewd and well-informed Deputy High Commissioner called Mr James Parker. Mr Parker had widespread contacts with people of all nationalities and in all walks of life spread right across the Eastern Region. His American opposite number, Consul Robert Barnard, said of him, 'Jim's got his finger right on the pulse of this place.'* Mr Parker knew the terrain well enough, and the people involved, to realize that the sense of aggrievement and the people's ability and determination to defend themselves if they had to, made the situation far more dangerous than those in Lagos seemed prepared to accept.

Other sources in the British Deputy High Commission in Enugu made plain that Mr Parker had put his information and his warnings at the disposal of the High Commissioner in

* To the author, Enugu, July 1967.

161

Lagos over and over again. Pressmen in Lagos said later not only were these warnings from the East either cut out of the High Commission's reports before being forwarded to London, or forwarded with derisive addenda, but that Sir David was observed on the social circuit publicly disparaging his subordinate in Enugu as a 'white Ibo'.

(This vilification of anyone, even uninvolved reporters, who pointed out the misconceptions of the official assessment later became a pillar of High Commission and Commonwealth Office tactics in keeping attention off the Nigeria–Biafra issue.)

By the time the war started, as has now become clear in retrospect, the British civil servants at least had decided that the policy should be one of unalloyed support for Gowon's régime. That such support was not of a conspicuously practical nature in the early weeks of the war is due only to the presumption that Nigeria needed no help to crush Biafra. When it became clear that such help would be needed, there was a brief period of wavering as the politicians, though not particularly interested in an obscure African 'bush' war, asked their advisers 'Are you sure?'

The civil servants smoothly won the day, and from then on the aid for Gowon arrived in increasingly large quantities and in an ever wider variety of forms. It is a reflection on the attitude of the British people towards 'their' Commonwealth, reflected in their Press and their Members of Parliament, that the policy remained largely unquestioned for almost a year, that is, until the effect of the policy had enabled the Gowon Government to bring about the deaths of close to 200,000 Commonwealth citizens. It was only when the policy was firmly questioned that the official mask slipped for a moment and what was being done in the name of the British people was fleetingly discerned. The public then reacted violently, but too late. Government policy had by then so fossilized that even though the bases on which it had originally been formed, and the succeeding justifications, had all fallen into utter disrepute, the reputations of politicians and notably of the Prime Minister had all become hooked on a policy of crushing Biafra no matter what the cost might be.

That the British Government should decide to support the

Gowon régime was not in itself what disgusted the Biafrans. It was the hypocritical way in which it was done. For twelve months every possible effort was made to mask the facts of what was going on from the British Parliament, Press and people. In Parliamentary answer after answer the questioners and the House were misled, deceived, rebuffed and frustrated. Government spokesmen deliberately told the House that the British Government was neutral, only later to admit they were not and never had been. Poker-faced denials were given that the arms shipments to Nigeria had exceeded pre-war levels on occasions when those levels had already escalated many times. Ministers contradicted themselves, changed ground, vacillated and hedged, and for ten months a gullible House nodded and was satisfied.

While this was going on the arms shipments continued. The secrecy in which they were shrouded indicates something of the lack of confidence the perpetrators of the policy could expect from the British people if the facts ever got out.

Lorryloads of shells and bullets sped through the night in covered trucks to Gatwick Airport, where they were given permission to ride round the taxi-track (almost unprecedented at an international airport) in order to load up at a secret bay on the far side of the field. The story was eventually 'blown' by a reporter in Malta where one of the planes stopped to re-fuel. Much of the purchasing on behalf of the Nigerian Government was undertaken by the Crown Agents in Millbank, London, and not all arms orders fulfilled by this traditional purchasing agency for Commonwealth countries came from the British Isles.

In buying arms the important document is the export licence, usually only given after production of the 'end-user certificate' which states the ultimate destination of the cargo and avoids the possibility of the consignment falling into other hands. Thus a certificate signed in one country may well be valid for a purchase made elsewhere even though the ship carrying the arms does not stop over in a port of the country that signed the licence. Provided the seller is shown the licence and the end-user certificate, and provided his government has no objection, the deal may go through. Thus arms went to

Nigeria out of the British Rhine Army stocks at Antwerp, Belgium: notably mortars, artillery shells and armoured cars.

It is not the purpose of this chapter to list every one of the *known* arms shipments to Nigeria from Britain or through British offices.* The known shipments are a matter of record and available to study, mostly in newspaper files. Firm reports of a continuing and clandestine supply of arms by the British Government to the Nigerian régime usually in darkness and under a 'top security' classification appeared first on 9 August 1967, within thirty-three days of the start of the war, and have continued ever since, until they became so open that they ceased to be news. But the British Government's explanation of them is interesting.

For the first six months the Government had a fairly easy time; few questions were put and even fewer of their questioners were fully briefed on the subject. But on 29 January 1968 Lord Brockway put a question in the Lords to the Minister of State for the Commonwealth, Lord Shepherd. After the habitual answer that it was not Government policy to reveal arms shipments going to foreign governments, Lord Brockway reminded Shepherd that the Government had earlier claimed that 'only previous contracts and spares' would be supplied to Nigeria. Shepherd replied that he knew nothing of this but went on: 'While we deplore the tragic and sad civil war in Nigeria we have been supplying Nigeria with pretty well all its military equipment . . .'†

This was 100 days after the Nigerian commander at Asaba had used his share of 'pretty well all its military equipment' to order the execution of every Ibo male over the age of ten years.

The mask in London had slipped badly through Shepherd's unprepared answer and from then on the Government concentrated more on justifying the arms shipments to Lagos than denying them. But remarkable deceptions as regards to quantity still continued. Parliament was repeatedly told that

* References to these occur in the *Financial Times*, 9 August 1967; *Birmingham Post*, 15 August 1967; *The Times*, 3 January 1968; *Hansard*, 22 July 1968, col. 68.

† *Hansard*, 29 January 1968, cols. 599 and 600.

only 'traditional' supplies of arms, both in type *and quantity*, were being sent, yet on 16 May 1968 Mr Harold Wilson told the Commons:

'We have continued the supply – not the Government; I mean that we have allowed the continuance of supply of arms by private manufacturers in this country exactly on the basis that it has been in the past, but there has been no special provision for the needs of the war.'*

This was a remarkable statement, as Nigeria was proudly announcing that it had been able to increase the size of its army from 8,000 men at the start of the war to around 80,000 men. Apart from the weapons involved, the usage of ammunition by the Nigerians was so prodigal that correspondents from Vietnam were bemused by the way they threw their bullets around, needing constant re-supply with bullets at levels far beyond what pre-war supplies from Britain could have coped with. And thirdly, as regards the question of 'private manufacturers' mentioned by Mr Wilson, this author had during the entire spring of 1968 examined hundreds of Nigerian shell cases clearly marked 'U.K. Government explosives – War Department/Army' which also had their date of manufacture clearly stencilled on the sides – November 1967.

Finally it was admitted that Britain's supply of weapons to Nigeria had escalated 'because the war has escalated'. But even while politicians, when pressed hard enough into a corner, little by little permitted the Parliament, Press and public to realize that the arms shipments were very substantial, the façade was still kept up that they were justified for various reasons. It may be as well to examine these given reasons and seek to bring them into some form of perspective.

The main reason given was that Britain had been the traditional supplier of arms to Nigeria and that to have ceased supplies would have been a non-neutral act in favour of Biafra. This was not true. Colonel Ojukwu as Nigeria's first indigenous Quartermaster-General knew exactly what orders he had placed with Britain during his tenure of office, and which he had cancelled. He knew up to the date of Biafra's independence fairly accurately what purchases were being made or

* *Hansard,* 16 May 1968, cols. 1397 and 1398.

were pending. At a press conference on 28 April 1968 he stated the position. Significantly this was never denied by Lagos, nor has any subsequent Quartermaster-General of the Nigerian Army ever stated otherwise. What he said was that between 1964 and 1966 'the only supply of military equipment that came to the then Nigeria (from Britain) were twelve Ferret cars and two Saladins, with a further order of four pending delivery right up to 1966'.

He said he knew 'that Nigeria stopped the purchase of rifles and machine guns from Britain when Nigeria signed a contract with the German firm of Fritz Werner in 1964 for the construction of a munitions factory in Kaduna'. (Werner closed down at the start of the war rather than produce bullets for a civil war.) He stated that Nigeria bought recoilless rifles from America, sub-machine guns and rifles from Italy, light machine guns from Germany, 105-mm Howitzers from Italy, 81-mm mortars from Israel and boots and other equipment from Germany.

By July 1966, when General Ironsi was murdered, Britain had been so replaced as the traditional supplier of arms to Nigeria, that that country was dependent on Britain only for the supply of ceremonial dress uniforms and armoured cars.

A firm figure is available for the total cost of military aid from Britain to Nigeria during the course of the financial year 1965–6. It was stated by Mr Arthur Bottomley to the Commons on 2 March 1966 to be £68,000.* Yet on 12 June 1968 the Foreign Secretary Mr Michael Stewart told the House: 'It would at any rate have been wrong at the outset of the secession for us to have cut off supplies completely from the Federal Government. . . . At that time supplies from this country accounted for seventy-five per cent of Nigeria's supplies of arms from all sources.'† Earlier in the same debate Stewart had said that right up to the accession of power of General Gowon in Lagos, Nigeria 'was heavily dependent on us . . . in all her defence arrangements'.‡

Actually Nigeria's main defence purchase in 1966 was a frigate from Holland, and her embryo air force was being

* *Hansard*, 2 March 1966, col. 316.   † ibid., 12 June 1968, col. 290.
‡ ibid., 12 June 1968, cols. 289–90.

trained by West Germans on Dorniers. Mr Stewart's percentage becomes even more weird when it is recalled that Nigeria took delivery in May 1967 of a reported fifty French Panhard armoured cars. If the purchases of the frigate, the aeroplanes and the fifty Panhards are to be counted as part of the twenty-five per cent bought from sources other than Britain, then Britain's seventy-five per cent must have been a massive quantity of weaponry; yet Gowon's complete conviction that he could finish Biafra in a few days must make it extremely unlikely that he had placed such enormous orders. Of course, these alleged figures refer to the state of affairs pre-war.

On 22 July 1968 Mr George Thomson told the House that Britain's percentage of Nigerian weapons purchases by that time, after twelve months of war, represented only fifteen per cent of the total.* This figure is misleading. It refers to value only; by that time Nigeria had got very expensive jet fighters and bombers from Soviet Russia, along with Soviet technicians to maintain them and Egyptian pilots to fly them, later replaced by East Germans. Nor does the figure indicate whether it refers to weapons that came from the British Isles, or whether the arms from the Rhine Army stocks at Antwerp were included. Nor does it indicate whether the money referred to was the face value of the weapons or the downpayment made.

Even if what Mr Thomson said was true, he was contradicted by his own colleagues. Lord Shepherd had said six months earlier that Britain was supplying Nigeria with 'pretty well all its military equipment', while the indefatigable High Commissioner Sir David Hunt told an audience in Kaduna on 22 January 1968 that 'the bulk of the weapons in the hands of the Federal forces have come from Britain'.†

And so it went on and on. The 'traditional supplier' argument was quoted over and over again, although it had long been shown quite clearly that Britain was not the traditional supplier, and that the quantities involved would have been expended within a few hours if they had been at pre-war levels.

* *Hansard*, 22 July 1968, col. 106.
† B.B.C. Summary of World Broadcasts, Part 4B, Non-Arab Africa, ME/2677/B/2.

The 'maintenance of existing supplies' both of type *and quantity* was an untruth.

That was the first excuse. The second was that Britain was obliged to support the government of a friendly country. This was another misrepresentation. There was no moral or legal obligation to supply weapons to anyone in time of war, and there never is. It is habitual for any country, when deciding whether to sell weapons of war to a country at war, to decide two things first; is it in full agreement with the policies of the asking country which led that country into the position where it required weapons of war; secondly, is it completely satisfied as to the uses to which these weapons, if supplied, can reasonably be expected to be put?

On both counts the question of supplying Nigeria with arms to prosecute a war against the Biafrans must give anyone cause for misgivings. The background to the Nigeria–Biafra war has been described in previous chapters. Within a few weeks of the outbreak of that war the behaviour of the Nigerian infantry in the Midwest, amply witnessed, had indicated that any weapons supplied were likely to be used unhesitatingly on civilians.

Moreover, it is not unusual for the more scrupulous countries to refuse to sell weapons of war, even those necessary for defence purposes in time of peace, to a country of whose internal policies the supplier disapproves. Thus when Britain under a Conservative Government was on the point of selling warships to Spain, Mr Harold Wilson leapt to his feet with the cry 'No frigates for Fascists', and as his election was in the offing the Spaniards cancelled the deal.

Later, the Labour Government placed an embargo on the sale of arms to South Africa. While few like apartheid, not even the Labour Party stalwarts suggested that warships and Buccaneer bombers could be used against rioting Africans. The argument was, and it was sincerely felt, that by supplying arms to a country one sustains and strengthens that country's régime in power, even in time of peace; and that if one dislikes that régime, and the things it does on the domestic front, one should not strengthen it. The only logical conclusions from the continuing sale by the Wilson Government of arms to

Nigeria is that this Government does approve of the things the Gowon régime practises. These are described from eye-witness reports in a later chapter.

The third excuse was that if Britain had not sold the arms to Nigeria, then someone else would have done so. On the practical plane this is not probable. One by one the cash-and-carry suppliers of arms to Nigeria opted out as they and their peoples came to understand the use to which the arms were being put. One by one Czechoslovakia, Holland, Italy and Belgium decided not to supply any more. Belgium rushed through a special law banning even the fulfilment of tail-end orders. The idea that the Russians would automatically supply all that Britain failed to supply could have been knocked to pieces by any expert on weaponry. The Soviets use different weapon calibres on all types of arms from those used by Britain and NATO. Usually the Soviet calibres are one milli-metre bigger than NATO sizes, so that their forces can use Western captured ammunition, while NATO forces cannot use Warsaw Pact ammunition. For this reason Soviet ammunition could not have been supplied to Nigeria for use in NATO weaponry. A change of ammunition would have meant an entire switchover of all weaponry for an army of 80,000 men, a prohibitively expensive task. In fact, faced with the prospect of being reduced like the Biafrans to dealing on the black market for arms, there is a probability that Nigeria, in the event of a British withdrawal, would have been obliged to go to the peace table with meaningful proposals. By the time Britain and Russia had become the two sole suppliers a chance had been established that an agreement between the pair of them could have been the basis for the all-round arms ban to which Colonel Ojukwu had agreed in advance. But it was not even tried, perhaps because it was never intended to be an argu-ment, but simply an excuse for the gullible.

As regards the moral implications of the excuse, the Earl of Cork and Orrery, speaking in the Lords on 27 August 1968, said:

It is the same as saying that if somebody is going to supply the arms in any case, why not we? But unless you are going to insist that the purpose for which they are going to be used contains no evil –

and I do not see how you can say that – then this is an argument that no honourable Government can use, for it is the classic self-justification of the black marketeer, the looter, the drug pedlar . . . a burst of 9-mm bullets in an African stomach is an evil thing any way you reckon it, and if we send those bullets from England knowing that they may be so used, then that particular share in the general evil is ours, and that share is neither diminished nor magnified by a hair's breadth by the likelihood that if we did not send those bullets they would be sent by somebody else.*

The fourth and last excuse given for the supplies was that not to supply arms would destroy Britain's influence with Lagos. This excuse was not brought into play until the debate in the Commons on 12 June 1968, but was used increasingly thereafter. It was as threadbare as its three predecessors. During that debate Mr Stewart assured the House that if any final assault on the Ibo heartland were launched by the Nigerian Army, or if there were any 'unnecessary deaths', then in either case Britain would be forced to 'more than reconsider her policy'.

The pledges were meaningless. The influence Britain was supposed to have achieved through supplying arms was either never used or, more probably, never existed. In any event the Gowon régime has not deviated one iota from its policy totally to crush Biafra and her people, and no serious British attempt appears to have been made to persuade them to change their course.

On 23 August 1968 a final assault on the Ibo heartland was duly launched on all fronts and with overwhelming force. From the Imo River basin came foreigners' eye-witness reports of the wanton slaying of thousands of Ibo villagers in pursuance of Colonel Adekunle's shoot-anything-that-moves orders. There was no 'reconsideration' of policy. A supine Commons was offered yet another disdainful snub by a government that by this time had seemingly come to the view that Lords and Commons only existed to be deceived.

This was the situation as regards the arms traffic as it existed up to the debate of 27 August 1968. That debate changed things to a certain point, inasmuch as it was on that day that

* *Hansard*, 27 August 1968, cols. 754–5.

the Wilson Government finally threw aside what remained of its mask of concern and revealed what had in fact been its true policy all along.

But even by that date it had become clear that the British Government had no intention whatever of discouraging the war policy of the Gowon régime. The consequences of this policy had by the end of December 1968 become so serious that in terms of human lives, whatever the examination of history may reveal to have been the offence of the Nigerian régime, the British Government must now stand as equally co-responsible in a state of total complicity.

Arms shipments were only one of the ways in which the British Government showed its unalloyed support for the Gowon régime. As a sideline the offices of the Government became a powerful public-relations organization for Nigeria. Foreign diplomats were given the most biased briefings, and many believed them to be factually accurate and impartially composed. Correspondents were daily briefed to the Nigerian point of view, and selected untruths were sedulously implanted. Inspired leaks of such myths as the 'massive French aid' to Biafra were slipped to pressmen who had shown themselves to be suitably unlikely to check the facts independently.

Members of Parliament and other notables who wished to go down to Biafra and see for themselves were discouraged, while those wishing to go to Nigeria were given every assistance. In bars and clubs, committee rooms and cocktail parties the 'Lagos line' was enthusiastically pushed, and on orders. No effort was spared to explain the Nigerian case as being the solely valid one, and to denigrate the Biafran version in every possible way, character assassination not excluded. The campaign was not without effect. Quite a lot of influential but (on this topic) uninformed people were persuaded to accept the Lagos propaganda at its face value, to seek to inquire no further into the background to the affair, and themselves to propagate what they possibly believed to be true.

In terms of technical assistance offered to the Nigerians the British Government was neither less accommodating nor more candid than over the question of arms. Though repeated denials were issued that any British military personnel were fighting for the Nigerians, it soon became known that British technical personnel were attached to the Nigerian Government 'for training purposes'. It may be that these men were not serving in H.M. Forces at the time of their attachment, having previously retired from active service, but the hiring of these men under contract was done with the full knowledge and approval of the British Government. While the attachment of ex-army or ex-navy experts to foreign and Commonwealth governments for training purposes in time of peace is standard practice, it is habitual to review the arrangements in time of war.

It is known, and no attempt at denial has been made, that former Royal Navy officers are and have been consistently directing the blockading operations of the Nigerian Navy. They act with the full support of the British Government. It is the blockade which has resulted in the widespread starvation in Biafra, causing an estimated one million deaths from famine in the twelve months of 1968. The blockade is total, but need not have been. A selective blockade to exclude neutrally inspected shiploads of relief foods for young children would have served Nigeria's military aims just as well. However the total blockade and its resultant famine are not being used as an unavoidable by-product of war but as a deliberate weapon against civilians.

Sir David Hunt, among many statements that confirm his total and unquestioning support for the cause of the Gowon régime, and his undisguised personal hostility towards Biafra and her leader, has admitted that since the start of the war 'the close relations between the British and Nigerian Army and Navy have been maintained and strengthened'.*

Despite this the chief support that the Wilson Government has brought to Gowon has been in the political and diplomatic field. At the time of Biafra's self-declared independence, there were three options open to Britain. One was to recognize the new state; this in fact would have meant formalizing the *de facto* partition that had existed since 1 August 1966 when Gowon took the lead of a group of partially successful

* Speech at Kaduna, 24 November 1967; B.B.C. Summary of World Broadcasts, Non-Arab Africa, ME/2631/B/2.

army mutineers and Ojukwu refused to acknowledge his sovereignty. But as a policy it was not considered, and there is no reason to attach blame for that.

The second option was to announce and stick by an attitude of neutrality in thought, word and deed. This would not at the time have antagonized either party to the forthcoming conflict, because Ojukwu would have accepted the impartiality as honest (in the event he did try to cling to the myth of Britain's announced neutrality for as long as he could because he wanted to believe it) and because Gowon was confident of a quick victory.

The third option was to announce and adopt total moral, political and military support for Gowon. Here again, Ojukwu would have regretted the decision but have known that at least Britain was sailing under her true colours.

What the Wilson Government did was to adopt the last option and announce the second. In doing so and maintaining the fable for a year, it made a fool of the British Parliament and people, and several other governments, notably those of Canada, the United States and the Scandinavian countries, who later became sufficiently concerned to wish to see peace brought about through the offices of a mutually acceptable and impartial mediator.

It is still difficult to discern the precise reasons for the British Government's decision of total support for Lagos. The background to the conflict must have been known; in the most pro-Federal sense the whys and wherefores of the affair indicated that morally it was very much six of one and half a dozen of the other; civil wars are notably confused, bloody, and seldom soluble by military means.

The reasons given later were varied, and none stands up to objective assessment. One was that Britain must under all circumstances support a Commonwealth government faced with a revolt, rebellion or secession. This is not true. Britain has every right to consider every case on its merits. Even at the time South Africa was a member of the Commonwealth, it is unlikely Britain would have supported the South African Government in any way at all if that Government had been faced with a revolt by the Bantu population after having condoned a racial massacre in which 30,000 Bantu had died.

Another reason, taken straight from Nigerian propaganda, was that the Ibos of Biafra had forced the unwilling minority non-Ibos into partition from Nigeria against their will in order to grab the oil riches of the Eastern Region for themselves. All the on-the-spot evidence indicated that the minority groups fully participated in the decision-making process to get out of Nigeria, and were as enthusiastic as the Ibos. As regards the oil, Nigerian propaganda stated that 97.3 per cent of the oil production of Nigeria came from non-Ibo areas. Fortunately the oil statistics both of the major oil companies and of the Nigerian Government are available for study.* For the month of December 1966 out of total production in Nigeria 36.5 per cent came from the Midwest, which was not part of Biafra. Of the Biafran production for that month, Lagos' own figures show that 50 per cent came from Aba Province (pure Ibo area), 20 per cent from Ahoada Division (majority Ibo area), and 30 per cent from Ogoni Division and Oloibiri (Ogoni/Ijaw area). Besides which, every eye-witness present during the months before the decision to break away from Nigeria was made said later that oil was not the chief motive.

The most commonly quoted reason, and the one which has the most widespread support, is that any secession is in itself bad, since it would inevitably spark off a chain of other secessionist movements all over Africa. The spectres of 'balkanization', 'disintegration' and 'reversion to tribalism' are dutifully held up and even habitually cogent thinkers are overawed.

Mr David Williams, editor of *West Africa* magazine and one of the best known writers on the subject, wrote on 27 October 1968 in the *Sunday Mirror*: 'Yet in the end the Federal forces will win, and if this whole part of the world is not to become a mosaic of tiny, bankrupt, warring states, they must win.'

Although this has often been stated, and represents the Wilson Government's view, it has never apparently been questioned. Neither has it ever been justified. The assumption is baldly made, and presumed to be true. The evidence does not support the thesis.

* George Knapp, *Aspects of the Biafran Affair*, London, 1968, pp. 27, 28, 53 and 54.

For one thing the case of Biafra is quite exceptional. Even President Mobutu of the Congo has said categorically there is no similarity between the case of Biafra and that of Katanga, a view mirrored by United Nations diplomat Dr Conor Cruise O'Brien, who could scarcely be described as being in favour of secession.

For another thing, Mr Wilson when advocating against the use of force in Rhodesia suggested that violence in Southern Africa could spark off a chain of violence across the continent. Indeed the danger of contagious violence is considerably greater than the danger of contagious partition; yet the war goes on without any serious attempt to stop it.

Thirdly, partition on the basis of incompatibility is an acknowledged political solution to situations where two peoples have shown there is little likelihood of their ever living together in peace. It was used in the case of the partition of Ireland from the United Kingdom. More recently the British Government accepted the secession of Nyasaland from the Central African Federation, the Western Cameroons from Nigeria (on U.N. supervised plebiscite), the Cayman Islands from the West Indian Federation, Jamaica from the West Indian Federation (after Jamaica's Premier had admitted there was no legal right to secede); and they accepted the demand of the Muslim League for partition from India in 1947 when it became clear that Indian unity could only be bought at the price of a bloody civil war.

The British Government has in the past accepted the 'balkanization' of the West Indies Federation, the Central African Federation and the Malaysia Federation without a murmur. In each case there has been no consequent rash of secessions across those parts of the world. Some of the independent states of the West Indies are so tiny as to be almost completely unviable; yet independent Biafra would have the third largest population and the highest prosperity potential in Africa.

For the real reasons, one must look elsewhere. Only two seem discernible. One is that Whitehall received information at the start of the war from its High Commissioner in Lagos that the war would be short, sharp and sweet, and that one should certainly back the winner. Politically, this is not exceptionable. One does not back causes that are going to vanish from the map within a week or two. However, when it became quite clear that the whole situation had been misunderstood by Her Majesty's plenipotentiary and his staff, that their information had been bad, that 'Ojukwu's revolt' was in fact a strongly and widely supported popular movement, that the war would drag on for months and maybe years with a steadily escalating death-toll, that the behaviour of the Nigerian forces towards the Biafran civilians of all racial groups was giving cause for considerable alarm, the British Government deserves to be severely censured in that its policy was not only not reconsidered, but was escalated.

One might have been able to say that up to the end of 1967 the British Government did not know to what use its weapons and diplomatic support were being put. But throughout 1968 there was too much evidence, too much eye-witness testimony, too many photographs, too many reliable accounts, too many news and television films, for anyone to entertain a justifiable doubt.

The other discernible reason for the Wilson Government having continued to comfort and support, politically, diplomatically, and militarily the Gowon régime after the facts became known is that Britain has decided, though on the basis of what reasoning no one has explained, that the Nigerian market shall remain intact no matter what the price.

But all this became known only after repeated inquiry by the few who were sufficiently interested to ask. For twelve months the mask of neutrality was kept up, only slipping on occasion and revealing the partisanship behind.

On 20 June 1967, sixteen days before the war started, Lord Walston told the House of Lords that the Government had no intention whatsoever of intervening in the internal affairs of Nigeria and had made this 'very plain to all the Nigerian leaders'.*

Eight weeks later, correspondents asking about the arms shipments through Gatwick Airport were told they were just 'tail-end' orders being fulfilled. The 'neutrality' deception con-

* *Hansard*, 20 June 1967, col. 1376.

tinued unquestioned until murmurs of puzzlement started in January 1968. On 25 January Lord Shepherd, asked by Lord Conesford to clarify the position, replied: 'We are neutral to both sides, but there is clearly a recognized Government in Nigeria ... we certainly are not helping one side or the other.'*

Four days later he was admitting Britain supplied 'pretty well all its military equipment' to Nigeria. By 13 February Lord Shepherd was still maintaining the charade, but had modified it slightly. He told the Lords, 'To cut off all supplies [of arms] would be seen by them [Lagos] as an un-neutral and one-sided act against them, and against our own declared policy of support for a single Nigeria.'†

The questions persisted and the maintenance of the deception became increasingly difficult. On 21 May Mr George Thomson developed Shepherd's theme; replying to a question in the Commons he claimed that neutrality would mean supporting the rebellion.‡ The charade was maintained until the momentous debate of 27 August when the Wilson Government finally came out and revealed it had never done other than support Gowon with everything it had got.

On the international diplomatic scene the full enormity of the consequences of this misrepresentation did not become apparent until later. Throughout 1968 most foreign governments accepted that Britain was at least politically neutral, and therefore available as an impartial mediator if such should be required. In fact Britain was simultaneously assuring Lagos that arms shipments would continue, and thus encouraging the Federal Government to fight to a bitter and bloody finish; claiming before world opinion that it was doing everything in its power through secret diplomacy to bring about a ceasefire and meaningful peace talks; using the full persuasiveness of its diplomacy to urge deeply concerned governments not to follow the lead of Tanzania, Zambia, Ivory Coast and Gabon in recognizing Biafra; and when peace talks were finally forced on Nigeria by mounting world opinion, becoming the behind-

* *Hansard*, 25 January 1968, cols. 437–8.
† ibid., 13 February 1968, cols. 90–91.
‡ ibid., 21 May 1968, col. 266.

the-scenes spokesman and advocate for the Nigerian cause. It was a twelve-month hoax. When other governments grew restive and wished to take some initiative, they were warned off with the argument, 'We are in the best position to bring about peace moves in this situation; outside interference, however well-intentioned, could only cloud the issue; leave it to us, we are doing all we can.'

In fact Britain was doing all it could – to ensure Nigeria's total military victory in crushing the life out of Biafra. Colonel Ojukwu's refusal to accept the Wilson Government as a mediator so long as it remained the chief arms supplier to his enemies was castigated as another incidence of that callous intransigence that was always laid at his door when he refused to fall in with Nigeria's or Britain's more obvious ruses.

Nevertheless, the 'neutrality' mask almost worked even with the Biafrans. Many senior people in the Biafran régime wanted to believe in it, even though the evidence reaching their desks told them otherwise. Sir Louis Mbanefo, the Biafran Chief Justice and senior negotiator at Kampala, later talked for weeks with British Government officials and Lord Shepherd in the hopes that their assurances of neutrality and desire for peace were sincere.

If the charade almost fooled the Biafrans who were taking a deep interest in the situation, it certainly fooled other governments whose interest, though concerned, was less profound. On 9 September 1968 Mr Richard Nixon, then conducting his Presidential campaign, gave an unwitting indication of the world's attitude of hesitancy towards facing the Nigeria–Biafra situation head-on. He said:

Until now efforts to relieve the Biafran people have been thwarted by the desire of the central government of Nigeria to pursue total and unconditional victory and by the fear of the Ibo people that surrender means wholesale atrocities and genocide. But genocide is what is taking place right now – and starvation is the grim reaper. This is not the time to stand on ceremony, or to 'go through channels' or to observe the diplomatic niceties. The destruction of an entire people is an immoral objective even in the most moral of wars. It can never be justified; it can never be condoned.

And yet what the world did throughout 1968 was to stand on

ceremony, to try to go through channels, and to observe all the diplomatic niceties. This is not to say that a frank declaration of factional interest by Britain would have brought forward initiatives from other world leaders, or that any such initiatives would inevitably have succeeded in bringing peace. But it is fair to say that Britain's 'Hands Off' warning and her own self-appointed monopoly of the mediator's role ensured that no such other initiatives ever stood a real chance of getting off the ground.

The debate in the House of Commons on 27 August is worth a brief description inasmuch as it provided what correspondents the next day described as 'one of the most extraordinary demonstrations of hostility [against the Government] seen for many years in the Commons' (*Financial Times*); 'a shoddy day's work' (*Guardian*); and 'fantastic disorder' (*The Times*).

There were two debates that day – one in the Commons and one in the Lords. Both were on Nigeria–Biafra. A few hours after the Earl of Cork and Orrery described the use to which British arms were being put in Nigeria, Mr Thomson placed the British Government squarely in its true role. Referring to the outbreak of the war thirteen months previously, he told the House: 'Neutrality was not a possible option for Her Majesty's Government at that time.'*

What followed was that he and his colleagues made the Nigerian case more devotedly, more passionately, more partially and on occasions more violently than even the Nigerians could have done themselves.

Mr Thomson started by making it clear that Britain had unequivocally taken sides in the bloodiest local war in decades; that it had adopted this course thirteen months previously. He went on to opine that the Lagos Government were prepared to be accommodating on the constitutional form through which unity was to be interpreted, and even mentioned confederation. (This was never confirmed by Lagos, who indeed have maintained just the contrary.) But throughout Mr Thomson's description to the House of the exchanges between the régimes of Gowon and Ojukwu which preceded the war, he never once mentioned that Colonel Ojukwu had consistently pressed for

* *Hansard*, 27 August 1968, col. 1446.

179

confederation as a way of preserving unity without recourse to war.

If there were any doubts left in Members' minds about the total partisanship of the British Government they were dispelled by the Minister of State, Mr William Whitlock. Reading word by word from his notes prepared in the Commonwealth Office by a civil servant, this Minister gave what witnesses later described as the most biased version of a foreign government's propaganda output that the Commons had ever heard.

He launched into a slashing attack on Biafra, denigrated its case, and picked as his especial target its Overseas Press Service and the small Geneva-based firm of public relations agents who disseminate the Biafran news to the international Press. He accused Members who believed anything from Biafra of being gullible. By some freak of reasoning he assured the House that the Nigerian final offensive against the Ibo heartland, which had been personally announced by General Gowon on British television screens the night before, was not, despite what Gowon had said, the final push, but the continuing preparations for a final push.

He followed this by reading from his notes almost verbatim most of the Nigerian war propaganda claims, which had long since been proved by independent investigation to be misleading or totally untrue.

Whitlock's job was to 'talk out' the last thirty-two minutes of the debate so that the House could rise at ten p.m. without a vote. The rules of the debate had been agreed the previous day. But as the true position of the Government became clearer and clearer to an at first bemused and later outraged House, pandemonium broke loose. Nineteen times Whitlock was interrupted by Members who wished to express their indignation. Dame Joan Vickers, not normally given to outbursts, interjected: 'In his opening remarks the Secretary of State [Thomson] said that the British Government would be neutral. Does the Honourable Gentleman think that his speech is following the lead given by his Right Honourable friend?'*

Whitlock put the matter straight. He reminded Dame Joan

* *Hansard*, 27 August 1968, col. 1527.

that Mr Thomson had said the Government in this situation could not be neutral. With that he carried on.

By this time the House wanted a chance to vote. It was too late. It was no use Sir Douglas Glover protesting that when the Members had agreed the previous day not to have a vote they had no idea of the line of argument the Government would take. The debate was talked out and while the estimated death-rate in Biafra continued at between 6,000 and 10,000 a day the Members went home to resume their holidays. Ironically the issue that occasioned the recall of Parliament from summer recess was not Biafra but the Soviet move into Czechoslovakia, an aggression in which less than one hundred people died.

After 27 August the position became clearer. The mask was off and the lines were drawn. For the partisans of Nigeria, inside and outside Whitehall, the rein of pretence could be discarded. Not dissimulation but justification was the order of the day. The pro-Gowon campaign hotted up. Leaders of opinion in and out of Parliament were taken aside in bars and clubs, and carefully primed with the weary arguments of impending balkanization of Africa, the absolute necessity of preserving not only Nigeria but Gowon's Nigeria, the latent evil of the scheming Ibo and the personal frightfulness of Colonel Ojukwu.

Correspondents attending the daily briefing at the Commonwealth Office were primed with 'authoritative' reports of massive French aid moving towards Biafra from Gabon, which obviously made more guns, bullets and Saladins from Britain a necessity. The latent anti-French or at least anti-de Gaulle sentiment in some sections of the Press, the Conservative Right and the Labour Left were vigorously titillated.

Back in the House of Commons on 22 October Mr Michael Stewart, the Foreign Secretary now also in charge of the Commonwealth since the merger of the two departments, was once again blaming Colonel Ojukwu for the impending death of his own people, 'confirming' that no genocide had ever taken place, and insisting that Britain must continue to supply arms.[*]

A vigorous campaign at all levels was launched to discredit

[*] 'Yesterday in Parliament', *Daily Telegraph*, 23 October 1968.

not only Biafran propaganda, but even reports from Red Cross and Press sources about the death toll through starvation, the killing of civilians by the Nigerian Army and the fate of the Biafrans in the event of their being conquered.

A thorough study of this campaign rings a sinister bell in the minds of those who remember the small but noisy caucus of rather creepy gentlemen who in 1938 took it upon themselves to play devil's advocate for Nazi Germany, partly by seeking to persuade their listeners that any talk of German ill-treatment of the Jews was motivated propaganda that could safely be discounted. The tactics evolved, the arguments put forward, the bland assumption of congenital bias in anyone who claimed to have seen with their own eyes what was going on, and the almost personal fervour brought to the vilification of the best-informed, strike a note of remarkable similarity in the two instances.

Not only are the arguments rather similar but so are the sources and those who permit themselves to become sources by passing on the message. In the main they are either rather stupid parliamentarians and other men in public life who are susceptible to the inoculation of ideas passed on through the 'old boy' network; or people with vested personal, political, financial or reputation interests; or people who have spent happy years in a country and cannot abide to hear ill alleged of it; or journalists of the not-too-astute variety whose typewriters can be bought for the price of a Government-paid tour with a charming young Information Ministry escort and lavish hospitality. Most of these allow themselves to be used as vehicles for propaganda quite unintentionally, although a few days spent checking the reliability of what they are told would probably pay dividends.

But as in the case of the pro-German apologists of pre-war days there is always a small group whose orientation is based on a purely personal and sometimes passionate loathing of a racial minority and in the desire to see that minority suffer. In the present instance it is unfortunate that the spiritual headquarters of that kernel is to be found inside the British High Commission in Lagos and in the Commonwealth Office in London.

Not being required to explain its policy at Question Time, big business has been able to keep much quieter over its true attitude towards the Nigeria–Biafra affair and participation in it than Government. To this day the role played by business interests and particularly oil remains something of a mystery and open to widely varying interpretations.

In pre-war Nigeria foreign investment was preponderantly British. The total sum has been estimated at £600 million of which a third was in the Eastern Region. Of investment in that Region the bulk was in oil.

There was one significant difference between the oil interests and all other financial and commercial interests held by Britain in Nigeria. The bulk of the oil investments were in the East, with a minority in the rest of Nigeria. But for all other business the bulk was in the rest of the Federation and the minor share in the East. Of the total investment, about £200 million has been estimated to have been in oil.

Although subsequently accused by the Biafrans of having backed Lagos from the start, it seems likely that in their own interest business houses and oil companies were genuinely un-involved at the start and wished to remain so. Ironically, with their opportunities for making money damaged *on both sides* by the protracted war, and with much of their plant and machinery damaged, destroyed or commandeered *by both sides*, the commercial interests have suffered and still been blamed by each party far more than the diplomats who were the architects of the 'support Gowon' policy which the British Government elected to follow.

Any participation which business firms, directly or in-directly, may since have been involved in on the side of Nigeria remains something of a mystery. However, the trade union of all British business interests in West Africa is the influential West Africa Committee, based in London, and it is axiomatic that the West Africa Committee will always follow British Government policy in West Africa, *once that policy has been firmly decided upon*.

Basically the interests of big business are to exploit, trade, and make a profit, and for this reason it was in its interest that the war be short. But to say it was in the interests of either oil or other business that Biafra should be crushed is not strictly true. Businessmen interviewed at the start of the war said privately they did not care much either way; it would have involved little extra expenditure on their part to have run two separate commercial operations, one in Nigeria and the other in Biafra, and so long as the two countries were living at peace side by side, business could have continued as normal. What they did not want was a protracted war.

For oil interests this was of particular importance. The oil from the Midwest of Nigeria is not exported through the coast of the Midwest, but is piped across the Niger Delta to Port Harcourt in Biafra, where it joins the oil flowing out of the Biafran wells and proceeds through another pipeline to the tanker-loading terminal on Bonny Island. When Biafra pulled out of Nigeria and was blockaded, both Biafran and Midwestern oil was cut off. The major firm affected was Shell–BP, an Anglo-Dutch consortium which held the majority of concessions in both Regions.

In August 1967 the Biafrans sent a strong lobby to London consisting of Chief Justice Sir Louis Mbanefo and Professor Eni Njoku to try to persuade the British Government to reverse its existing policy of favouring Nigeria. For three weeks the pair sat in the Royal Garden Hotel and talked with a stream of civil servants and businessmen of the West Africa Committee. As a result there was a definite wavering in the Commonwealth Office, and the business interests on the Committee were known to be pressuring the Commonwealth Office towards at least a strict neutrality. In the first ten days of September all this changed with a surprising suddenness. It was later learned that this was the period when Banjo's plot to kill Ojukwu was coming to fruition. In the first week of September, according to one of the Englishmen involved, some information arrived from Lagos which caused Whitehall to swing quickly back to the former policy of backing General Gowon, and the businessmen were informed accordingly. The two Biafrans found themselves talking to a void, and left. From then on the Commonwealth Office and the City seem to have marched hand in hand, although business firms had increasing misgivings in the latter half of 1968. Nevertheless shortly after September 1967 the sum of about £7,000,000 owing for oil royalties earned prior to the start of the war was paid to General Gowon's government, despite Biafra's protests that it was rightfully theirs.

Long before the end of 1968 all commercial interests had become sick and tired of the war, and highly sceptical of the Government's assurances that it would all be over in a few more weeks. A number of individual businessmen employed by major operators in West Africa, who had served for years in the East and who, like Mr Parker, warned that the situation should not be pre-judged, are being listened to again. In the early days their forebodings were discounted in London as stemming from their personal liking for the Eastern people. Moreover, it is becoming steadily clearer that even in the event of a Nigerian military victory, the chances of a return to economic normality in Biafra are slim, in the face of the bloodshed, the bitterness, the certain flight into the bush of the Biafran technicians and senior staff, the wrecking of the economy and the escalating guerrilla war.

Except possibly for oil: this product needs comparatively little supervision to export in its crude form, and some production had already started by the end of 1968 from wells firmly in Nigerian hands. But whether the oil companies believe it or not, the chances of uninterrupted flow in the face of a bitter guerrilla war are as slim as those of a flourishing trade in other commodities.

But oil is different from other commodities. It has strategic value. With the Middle East apparently destined to a period of instability to which no end can be seen, alternative oil sources excite interest. Biafra provides a big alternative source. For France, Portugal and South Africa (to name but three) oil is a major strategic factor. Apart from the fact that not all the oil concessions in Biafra are bespoke, the Biafrans have repeatedly warned that the price of the British Government's policies towards them over the duration of the war could lead to a re-negotiation of the existing oil concessions to other takers.

There is reason to believe that, like the British Government, British business, having backed one horse on the assurance that it would win with ease, has now gone so far that it must continue backing that horse to win no matter what the price; that it is committed to a policy which it might privately like to reverse, but cannot see how to do so. If that is so, the oil companies and other business firms have the added irritation of knowing that it was not their policy in the first place.

THE BRITISH PUBLIC

It took the British public a full year from the outbreak of the Nigeria–Biafra war to acquire even a hazy and largely uninformed outline of what was going on. But seeing through press and television that people were suffering appallingly, the British public reacted. In the next six months it did everything it could within constitutional limits to change the Government's policy over arms to Nigeria and to donate assistance to Biafra.

There were meetings, committees, protests, demonstrations, riots, lobbies, sit-ins, fasts, vigils, collections, banners, public meetings, marches, letters sent to everybody in public life capable of influencing other opinion, sermons, lectures, films and donations. Young people volunteered to go out and try to help, doctors and nurses did go out to offer their services in an attempt to relieve the suffering. Others offered to take Biafran babies into their homes for the duration of the war; some volunteered to fly or fight for Biafra. The donors are known to have ranged from old age pensioners to the boys at Eton College. Some of the offers were impractical, others hare-brained, but all were well-intentioned.

While considerably less mobilization of parliamentary, press and public opinion in Belgium and Holland managed to bring the governments of those countries to modify their policy of shipping arms to Lagos, the efforts of British popular opinion have failed to budge the Government by one iota. This is not an indictment of the British public but of the Wilson Government.

Normally such an enormous and broadly based expression

of the popular will has an effect on Government, for although Britain has no written constitution it is generally accepted that when a British Government's policy, other than a cornerstone of defence or foreign commitment, has been condemned and opposed by the Parliamentary Party and the Opposition, the Party Executive, the Churches and the Trade Unions, the Press and the public at large, then a Prime Minister will normally heed the wishes of the great majority of his electorate and reconsider the policy.

It takes a government of unprecedented and unique arrogance first to deceive the people's representatives for a year, then to snub the expressed will of Parliament and people, and their institutions. But a government of unprecedented and unique arrogance, coupled with a flabby and gutless Opposition, is precisely what Britain has had since October 1964.

THE RUSSIAN INVOLVEMENT

From December 1968 the steadily increasing Soviet build-up inside Nigeria became of increasing concern to observers outside the conflict. Although the first shipment of Russian MiG fighters and Ilyushin bombers arrived in Northern Nigeria in late August 1967, and further shipments, accompanied by two or three hundred Soviet technicians, continued to arrive over the next fifteen months to replace losses, it was not until the signing of the Soviet–Nigerian pact of November 1968 that the door opened wide to Russian infiltration.

The pact had already incurred the disquiet of Western diplomats while it was still in the discussion stage between the two sides, and the British made three attempts to dissuade the Nigerians from signing it. Each effort managed to bring about a delay, but the pact was finally signed on 21 November in the presence of an unusually strong delegation from Moscow.

In the following weeks the Russian presence became increasingly noticeable to the disquiet not only of the British and Americans but also of many Nigerian moderates.

The pact specified certain fields of assistance for Nigeria from Russia, such as the construction of an iron and steel industry. But it seems that the signing was linked to other activities. Shortly after the signing, reports began to come through from Northern Nigeria of a nightly airlift of Soviet infantry weapons in large quantities being ferried through airfields in the Southern Sahara to Kaduna, and thence to the Nigerian First Division at Enugu. Previous presence of Russian military equipment had been in fighters, bombers, bombs, rockets, naval patrol boats and, for the infantry, bazookas and hand-grenades. In the latter half of 1968 lorries, jeeps, trenching tools and Soviet N.C.O.s operating the support weapons began to make their appearance. Of the equipment, identification was easy from captured examples, and the presence of Soviet advisers was given away by prisoners, notably a Yoruba company commander who claimed the Russians made no secret of their nationality and ordered junior officers to attend lectures extolling the virtues of the Soviet way of life.

But towards the end of the war, after the signing of the pact, the First Division was re-equipped for the January 1969 push against the Biafrans largely with Soviet ground weaponry, including thousands of RK 49 sub-machine guns, the standard Warsaw Pact infantry gun, and Kalashnikov machine guns.

Elsewhere in Nigeria, correspondents began to notice teams of Russian advisers in various fields. Some were introduced as mineralogists, geologists, agricultural experts and the like. Fears were expressed that the Nigerian extreme Left, already strongly impregnating the Trade Union movement, would become stronger than ever, and anti-Western demonstrations were seen at the end of the year. In Ibadan the American and British flags were torn down, burnt and trampled on by a chanting mob of students and labour organizers.

By the end of the year 1968 the long-term Soviet aim in Nigeria was still a subject for speculation. Some saw the Soviet aim not as being towards a quick end to the war, but towards an extension of it until such time as Nigeria should be so hopelessly in debt as to become sufficiently pliable to accede to Russian wishes for concessions far removed from mutual assistance. Others saw the aim as being to acquire a long-term monopoly of Nigeria's cash-crop produce, like ground-nuts, cotton, cocoa and palm oil, taken in lieu of cash payments for weapons and other aid, which would have the same effect on

Nigerian independence from Soviet pressure in the 1970s. Yet others saw the final aim as being strategic – the obtaining of air bases in Northern Nigeria and perhaps a sea base along the south coast. These observers recalled Britain's chain of air bases from England through Gibraltar, Malta, Libya, Cyprus, Aden, the Maldives and Singapore which gave Britain in the 1960s the option of fast intervention East of Suez. The reasoning was that Russia, with access from the Crimea to Damascus, Port Said, Upper Egypt and the Sudan, needed only Kaduna and Calabar to have a chain of air bases straight into Southern Africa. In fact by the end of 1968 Russian technicians had set up a base at Kaduna, and had improved both Kaduna and Calabar from small municipal airstrips to full-length runways capable of taking Ilyushin bombers and Antonov freighters with all facilities for bad-weather and night landings.

To quote at length, with all the minutiae of dates, names, places and references, the actions and utterances of the British Government during 1969 in pursuing its avowed policy of support for Nigeria in the war, would be repetitious in view of what has already been written in this chapter.

It suffices to say that despite ever mounting evidence of the appalling sufferings to which the British Government's policy continued to give rise, and on the basis of the realities of the situation, the policy was ill-starred and incompetent. However, that policy continued unchanged. Throughout the year ministerial and official statements continued to twist and distort the facts of the situation, even though in most cases the facts were available for checking in well-founded contemporary records. On several occasions Press, Parliament and public were fed deliberate lies in an effort to secure popular support for the Government's policy of support for the Nigerian régime's war and starvation policy.

On those occasions when an effort towards peace appeared at the time to be made by the British Government, it was inevitably and only when popular and editorial opinion in Britain made advisable some sop to conscience. Seen and examined in retrospect, each apparent initiative turned out to be no more than a propaganda exercise, commending itself to the gullible but deliberately achieving no concrete results.

The first of these initiatives occurred in the wake of the storm of protest in Press and Parliament occasioned by Mr Winston Churchill's articles in *The Times* in March. One of the upshots of the concern in Britain over Mr Churchill's reports was increased pressure inside Parliament, which culminated in yet another debate, this time on 20 March. It was another exercise in futility. The major argument against Government policy of shipping arms to support a war resulting in human suffering on the Biafran scale was avoided. The Conservative Party, to judge from the uninformed nature of its spokesmen, did not appear to have any constructive policy, or be prepared to oppose intelligently the Government on the one major issue on which it could command the united support of the Liberal Party and some measure of support from Mr Wilson's own back benches.

But in the wake of the debate Mr Wilson announced that he himself would go to Nigeria. Scepticism about the value of such a personal appearance, and of its practical usefulness, was manifest in Press and Commons. It looked at the start, and turned out to be, another example of the personal gimmickry that the public had come to expect from the Labour Prime Minister. But since the Foreign Secretary, Mr Michael Stewart, told the House on the eve of Mr Wilson's departure that 'the Prime Minister would not rule out the possibility of a visit to Biafra', and since political correspondents were hinting that moves to enable such a visit to take place were already afoot, optimists began to hope that perhaps at last the British Government might be prepared to examine both sides of the question and not simply those parts that suited its own preconceptions.

Apparently in this hope General Ojukwu issued an invitation to Mr Wilson to visit Biafra, an offer that cost him great effort in overcoming internal opposition to the idea of entertaining a man whom the Biafran populace loathes so heartily.

The optimism was as premature as Ojukwu's offer had been disconcerting to British officialdom. It was known that Mr Wilson wished to return to London and report to the Commons his eye-witness impressions. Following Ojukwu's invitation it became difficult to imagine how Mr Wilson could go to Biafra, see what he would see, and report what he had seen, while at the same time keeping what he had to say commensurate with his own previous policy and his colleagues' utterances. The problem was knotty, but soon solved.

In the *Sunday Telegraph* of 30 March Mr H. B. Boyne, accompanying the Premier's party through Nigeria, set puzzled readers' minds at rest. 'Incidentally,' he wrote, 'Mr Wilson never had any intention of going into secessionist territory now.'

In the *Sunday Times* of the same date Mr Nicholas Carroll gave his readers what could be construed as the explanation for his colleague's brief aside. 'Still, superficial though Mr Wilson's visits have had to be, he did see quite enough to confirm what he had already heard from both his hosts and from his own advisers.'

But nothing more. Which, presumably, was the object of the exercise.

One strange but revealing sidelight on this visit was cast months later, when Group Captain Leonard Cheshire, V.C., who had been touring Biafra and speaking with General Ojukwu in the week prior to Mr Wilson's visit to Lagos, revealed why he had gone there. In an article in the *Guardian* Weekly Magazine of 22 November, the former bomber pilot and war hero revealed for the first time that he had gone to Biafra as an emissary of the Foreign Office, albeit an amateur one.

This had been no surprise to the Biafrans at the time, in the last ten days of March, nor to some others inside Biafra, but the secret had been well enough kept for British readers to have heard it for the first time in November.

Group Captain Cheshire revealed that he had been asked by a personal friend at the Foreign Office to go to Biafra and try to speak to General Ojukwu to see what his feelings were about the prospects of peace. He was also asked to make his own evaluations and report back to Mr Wilson personally in Lagos.

This he did. Disconcertingly for those who sent him, his findings were:

I shall always remember my interview with Ojukwu for the impression of utter sincerity ... In Lagos where I arrived the day before the Prime Minister's visit, I made a full report to a senior member of the British delegation and was then given fifteen minutes or so with Mr Wilson. I told him that Biafra was a country fighting for a passionately held belief, not one duped by its political leaders ... I stressed my conviction of Ojukwu's good faith and pleaded with him to visit Biafra on the grounds that this was the only hope of peace. He replied that a visit was out of the question ...

At the end of the article Group Captain Cheshire related how he was debriefed in the Foreign Office in London by a plainly sceptical official, who remarked when he had finished his description of his findings, 'Curious how every single person who goes to Biafra seems to fall for it.'

The patronizing condescension that greeted Group Captain Cheshire, who, it should be recalled, was chosen by the Foreign Office in the first place to undertake the mission, is typical of the attitude accorded by the Foreign Office advisers on Nigeria policy to every single person returning from an on-the-spot assessment of the situation. The list of those so treated is long, ranging from Lords and M.P.s through clerics and professional men to reporters and photographers. For this group of advisers everyone is wrong but themselves, who have rarely been to Nigeria and never to Biafra at all.

And so it continued throughout 1969 until the end of that year. In October 1968 an amalgamation had taken place between the Commonwealth Office, whose advisers had got Britain into the Nigeria–Biafra mess in the first place, and the Foreign Office, traditionally regarded by political observers in London as a more professional institution than the Commonwealth Office. It could hardly have been less so.

Some hopes were therefore entertained that with the Foreign Office now firmly on top and some of the deadwood from the Commonwealth Office being quietly retired in the merger, a more realistic attitude to the whole Nigeria–Biafra question might be adopted during 1969. This was not to be so.

The fact that no change, even on the basis of pragmatism, took place in British policy during 1969 was very largely due to the Foreign Secretary Mr Michael Stewart, a politician whose mental flexibility is reminiscent of the laws of the Medes and Persians. Before he had long been in sole charge of all Britain's foreign affairs, he had made quite clear through public and private utterances that he was a man who did not like to be confused with facts once his mind was made up. And on Nigeria his mind was well and truly made up, unchangeable by anything short of the use of explosives, even before the merger of the Foreign Office and the Commonwealth Relations Office took place. Thus on the question of relief to the starving inside Biafra he made plain on many occasions in the House and elsewhere that so far as he was concerned the failure to reach an agreement for the transshipment of relief food by the International Red Cross after it had been forced to stop night-flying in June was the fault of General Ojukwu and no one else. No recital of the step-by-step sequence of events, revealing that the Federal offer of daylight flights was a cynical sham, will ever shake Mr Stewart's belief that the members of the Federal régime in Lagos may be likened to angels of mercy.

In order to try and persuade his colleagues in the Commons, the Press and the public, Mr Stewart nevertheless went to some remarkable lengths, even for a politician. When the International Red Cross, under pressure from Lagos, handed over its multi-million-dollar relief operation to the Nigerian Rehabilitation Commission and suspended its night flights to Biafra, cutting as it did relief supplies to Biafra by fifty per cent, the move was openly backed by Britain. Defending the move in the House during June, Mr Stewart said the I.R.C. action had the support of the combined relief operations. This was a blatant untruth and was promptly and vigorously denied by the churches concerned under the umbrella of Joint Church Aid.* On 17 November in the Commons, after the failure of an attempt to reach agreement between Lagos and Biafra on daylight relief flights, Mr Stewart made much effort to belittle General Ojukwu's military reasons for declining to open the Uli Air-port during daylight hours. During the course of this he stated that if there were such daylight flights the Americans would be ready to guarantee that there would be no military advan-

* Walter Schwarz, 'Mr Wilson and Biafran Starvation', *Guardian* Weekly Magazine, 22 November 1969.

tage to the Federal side. In fact no such American guarantee is or ever was available. Indeed, it was significant that no Power at all was prepared itself to guarantee that the Nigerian Air Force would respect the inviolability of the airplanes and the airport during a daylight flights agreement.*

Commenting about this particular performance of the Foreign Secretary in the Commons, the *Guardian* Weekly Magazine the following Saturday observed: 'Once again Mr Stewart has been disgracefully misleading about Britain's role in the Nigerian war.'†

It is lamentable to have to state that during Mr Stewart's term of office as Her Majesty's Secretary for Foreign Affairs, distortions and untruths, which it is extremely hard to believe were the result simply of bad briefing, became so frequent, at least on this issue, that they no longer continued to arouse much editorial comment at all.

* 'Britain's Role in Nigeria', editorial comment, ibid.
† ibid.

11. Refugees, Hunger and Help

IT was the starvation in Biafra that really woke up the consciousness of the world to what was going on. The general public, not only of Britain, but of all western Europe and America, though usually unable to fathom the political complexities behind the war news, could nevertheless realize the wrong in the picture of a starving child. It was on this image that a press campaign was launched which swept the western world, caused governments to change their policy, and gave Biafra the chance to survive, or at least not to die unchronicled.

But even this issue was fogged by propaganda suggesting the Biafrans themselves were 'playing up the issue' and using the hunger of their own people to solicit world sympathy for their political aspirations. There is not one priest, doctor, relief worker or administrator from the dozen European countries who worked in Biafra throughout the last half of 1968 and watched several hundred thousand children die miserably, who could be found to suggest the issue needed any 'playing up'. The facts were there, the pressmen's cameras popped, and the starvation of the children of Biafra became a world scandal.

The graver charge is that the Biafrans, and notably Colonel Ojukwu, used the situation and even prevented its amelioration in order to curry support and sympathy. It is so serious, and so much of the mud has stuck, that it would not be possible to write the Biafra story without explaining what really happened.

It has been explained elsewhere in this book that the starvation of the Biafrans was not an accident, or a mischance, or even a necessary but regrettable by-product of the war. It was a deliberately executed and integral part of the Nigerian war policy. The Nigerian leaders, with commendably greater frankness than the British ever got from their leaders, made few bones about it.

In view of this the conclusion becomes inevitable that there was no concession Colonel Ojukwu *could* have made which would have enabled the relief food to come into Biafra faster and in greater quantities than it did, other than those concessions which Nigeria and Britain wanted him to make, which would have entailed the complete demise of his country.

All the 'offers' put forward by the Nigerian Government, often after joint consultation with the British High Commission, and usually accepted and welcomed in good faith by the ingenuous British Parliament, press and public, were revealed on examination to contain the largest tactical and strategic perspectives in favour of the Nigerian Army.

All proposals put forward by Colonel Ojukwu and other concerned parties like the International Red Cross, the Roman Catholic Church, and some newspapers, which contained no built-in military advantage to either side, were flatly turned down by the Nigerians with the full blessing of Whitehall.

This then is the story. Biafra is roughly square in shape. Running down the Eastern edge about a third of the way in is the Cross River, with its fertile valleys and meadows. Along the southern edge just above the creeks and marshes runs another strip of land watered by numerous small rivers which rise in the highlands and flow to the sea. The rest of the country, representing the top left-hand corner of the square, is a plateau, which is also the home of the Ibo.

In pre-war days this plateau had the bulk of the population of the Eastern Region, but it was the minority areas to the east and south that grew most of the food. The area as a whole was more or less self-supporting in food, being able to provide all of its carbohydrates and fruit, but importing quantities of meat from the cattle-breeding north of Nigeria, and bringing in by sea dried stockfish from Scandinavia, and salt. The meat and fish represented the protein part of the diet, and although there were goats and chickens inside the country, there were not enough to supply the protein necessary to keep over thirteen million people in good health.

With the blockade and the war the supply of imported protein was cut off. While adults can stay in good health for a long time without adequate protein, children require a constant supply of it.

The Biafrans set up intensive chicken and egg-rearing farms to boost production of the available protein-rich foods. They might have beaten the problem, at least for two years, had it not been compounded by the shrinking of their territorial area, the loss of the food-rich peripheral provinces, and the influx of up to five million refugees from those provinces.

By mid-April they had lost the Cross River valley along most of its length and part of the south, the Ibibio homeland in the provinces of Uyo, Annang and Eket, and land containing the richest earth in the country. At about this time reports from the International Red Cross representative in Biafra, Swiss businessman Mr Heinrich Jaggi, from the Catholic Caritas leaders, from the World Council of Churches, the Biafran Red Cross, and the doctors of several nationalities who had stayed on, showed that the problem was getting serious. The experts were noticing an increasing incidence of kwashiokor, a disease which stems from protein deficiency and which mainly affects children. The symptoms are a reddening of the hair, paling of the skin, swelling of the joints and bloating of the flesh as it distends with water. Besides kwashiokor there was anaemia, pellagra, and just plain starvation, the symptoms of the last named being a wasting away to skin and bone. The effects of kwashiokor, which was the biggest scourge, are damage to the brain tissues, lethargy, coma and finally death.

At the end of January Mr Jaggi had appealed to the Red Cross in Geneva to seek permission from both sides for a limited international appeal for medicine, food and clothing. The agreement came from Colonel Ojukwu as soon as he was asked, on 10 February, from Lagos at the end of April. In the meantime the refugee problem had been increasing, though it should be said that a refugee problem is the almost inevitable outcome of any hostilities and no blame can necessarily be attached to governments involved, provided they take reasonable measures to alleviate the sufferings of the displaced until the latter feel safe enough to return home.

However, in the case of the Nigerian Government and military authorities, journalists and relief workers operating in areas far behind the fighting line on the Nigerian side later reported that these authorities consistently frustrated the operations mounted on foreign-donated money to alleviate the suffering, hampered the transport of the relief materials, appropriated transport paid for by foreign donation, and forbade access to areas where suffering was great and risks minimal. The Commander of the Third Nigerian Division, Brigadier Benjamin Adekunle, left no doubt in the minds of the many reporters who visited him and listened to his speeches that he had no intention of even letting relief workers operate at all to save lives, let alone assisting them. This attitude, which was noticed and reported at all levels, was all the more odd since from the Nigerian standpoint the suffering civilians were their fellow-Nigerians.

The great majority of the civilian population fled from the fighting zone into rather than out of unoccupied Biafra. By the end of February 1968 there was an estimated one million refugees inside the unoccupied zone. In the main these were not Ibos but minority peoples. The extended family system which had assisted the Easterners to absorb their refugees from the North and East eighteen months previously could not operate, since most of the refugees had no relatives with whom to stay. Most therefore huddled in shelters built in the bush on the outskirts of villages, while the Biafran authorities with the assistance of the Red Cross and the Churches set up a chain of refugee camps where the homeless could at least have a share of a roof and a meal a day. Many of these camps were set up in the empty schools, where most of the housing facilities were already *in situ*, and later provided targets for the Egyptian pilots of the MiGs and Ilyushins.

By the end of April, for military reasons explained earlier, the refugee wave had increased alarmingly, to an estimated three and a half million.

Caritas and the World Council of Churches, being organizations not operating on the Nigerian side of the fighting line, and not being required by Mr Jaggi's charter to go through procedural channels before bringing relief, had decided to go it alone. From early in the year onwards they were purchasing abroad various quantities of food and medicines to fly into

Biafra. They had no aircraft or pilots, and therefore came to an arrangement with Mr Hank Wharton, an American freelance who flew in Biafra's arms shipments from Lisbon twice a week, to buy space on his aircraft. But the quantities that could be brought in in this way were tiny.

From 8 April the Red Cross also started to send in small quantities of relief on Wharton's aircraft, and wishing to ask for or buy their own aircraft and hire their own pilots, sent in repeated appeals from Geneva to the Nigerian Government asking for safe conduct for clearly marked Red Cross aircraft to fly in by day without getting shot down. These appeals were consistently refused.

Attempts were made to overcome the Nigerian fear that Wharton might fly in arms under cover of such daylight flights. First it was proposed that a team of Swiss Red Cross personnel guarantee that Wharton's planes remained on the ground during daylight hours. No. It was feared the relief aircraft might carry weapons. Then it was suggested that Red Cross staff supervise the loading. No. Then that Nigerian Red Cross staff supervise the loading. No. Ojukwu agreed that Nigerian Red Cross staff should accompany each relief flight right into the airport in Biafra. No.

At that time it was still not realized even by the Biafrans that there never was and never would be any intention of letting relief flights in. While all this was going on the Churches just plodded on regardless, sending in what they could whenever there was space available.

Colonel Ojukwu realized when he had studied the joint reports on the protein deficiency situation in mid-April that time was running short if a major disaster was to be avoided. The problem, so the relief agency representatives told him, was not to buy the food (which they felt sure they could do without much trouble) but to get it into Biafra through the blockade. This was obviously a technical rather than a medical problem and Colonel Ojukwu asked a technical committee to report back to him in the shortest possible time on the various ways in which food could be brought in.

Early in May these technicians brought him their findings. There were three ways of getting food into Biafra; air, sea and land. The air bridge, if it were to carry sufficient quantities to cope with the problem, would have to be bigger than Wharton's three aircraft could manage, and it would be expensive. But it was the quickest by far. The sea route, through Port Harcourt or up the Niger River, would be slower, but once under way would carry more tonnage of food for less money. The land route, bearing in mind the food would have to come into Nigeria by ship in the first place, cross hundreds of miles of Nigeria to get to Nigerian-occupied Biafra, then be carried down roads made unusable by broken bridges and clogged with Nigerian military traffic, would be slow, arduous and expensive. It offered neither the speed advantages of the air bridge nor the cost/efficiency advantages of the sea corridor.

Impressed by the medical men's cry for urgency, Ojukwu opted for an air bridge as a temporary stopgap, and a sea route if possible later to bring in the bulk supplies. Mr Jaggi and the other relief organization leaders were made aware of the findings of the technical experts and did not demur.

In the middle of May Biafra lost Port Harcourt and another estimated million refugees poured into the heartland, some being indigenes from the city and its environs, others being previous refugees from areas earlier overrun. But the loss of the port did not change the relief options. Uli airport, nicknamed Annabelle, opened up to replace the loss of Port Harcourt airport, and from the sea the access to the Niger River and the port of Oguta was still open, if the Nigerians would agree to order their navy to let Red Cross vessels through.

At the end of May the International Red Cross in Geneva had launched its second appeal, this time specifically for Biafra, since Nigeria would not agree.

But all this time the problem had remained unknown to the world public. The story had still not broken. In the middle of June Mr Leslie Kirkley, Director of Oxfam, visited Biafra for a fifteen-day fact-finding tour. What he saw disquieted him badly. Simultaneously Michael Leapman of the *Sun* and Brian Dixon of the *Daily Sketch* were reporting from inside Biafra, and it was these two men who, with their cameramen, saw the story for what it was. In the last days of June the first pictures of small children reduced to living skeletons hit the pages of the London newspapers.

Throughout this month the only food that came in from outside was the small amount that could be fitted into the spare space on Wharton's Super Constellations flying down from Lisbon. But with three organizations now jockeying for space on his aircraft, there was more food to be shipped than aircraft to carry it. In the ensuing weeks all three organizations bought their own planes, but Wharton insisted that he should run them, maintain them, and that his pilots should fly them. During these weeks food started to come by ship to the Portuguese offshore island of São Tomé, which had hitherto only been used as a re-fuelling stop, so that a shorter shuttle service could be set up from the island to Biafra for food, while the arms shipments came the different route from Lisbon to Biafra direct. Thus cargoes of dried milk and bullets once again became separated into different compartments of the Wharton operation.

Before leaving Biafra Mr Kirkley gave a press conference in which he estimated that unless substantially larger quantities of relief food came into Biafra within six weeks, up to 400,000 children would pass into the 'no-hope' period and die of kwashiokor. When asked for a figure of the tonnage required in a hurry to avert this prospect, he named the figure of 300 tons a day (or night).

Back in London this was reported on 2 July in the *Evening Standard*, but was widely believed to be more 'Biafran propaganda' until on 3 July Mr Kirkley himself went on the B.B.C. current affairs television programme 'Twenty-Four Hours' and repeated his estimates. Meanwhile public opinion was slowly being awakened by the photographs appearing in the British press. Before leaving Biafra Mr Kirkley had had a joint meeting with Mr Jaggi and Colonel Ojukwu, during which the Biafran leader had offered to put not any one, but his best airfield exclusively at the disposal of the relief organizations. This would separate the arms airlift from the food airlift and enhance the chances of Nigeria granting daylight access for the mercy planes. Mr Jaggi and Mr Kirkley accepted the offer.

On 1 July in London Mr Kirkley met Lord Shepherd, and

on 3 July Mr George Thomson. During these meetings he gave both ministers the fullest briefing on the size and scope of the problem, the necessity for urgency, the relative merits of the three possible avenues of transit for relief foods, and the offer of an exclusive airfield. As Mr Kirkley had both landed and taken off at Annabelle airport he was able to inform both ministers that it was capable of taking heavy aircraft like the Super Constellation, and had been doing so for several weeks. Here, observers thought, was an excellent opportunity for Britain to use the influence for good which her arms sales to Lagos had (in the view of the Labour Government) given her in the Nigerian capital. A request was duly sent to General Gowon asking him to permit daylight flights of Red Cross planes into Biafra. His reply, which came on the afternoon of 5 July and was published in the evening newspapers, was brief and to the point. He would order any Red Cross planes flying in to be shot down.

Mr Harold Wilson apparently had his moral sun-ray lamp handy. In a telegram reply to Mr Leslie Kirkley who had headed a delegation to him asking him to use his influence on Lagos, he replied that General Gowon had only meant that he would shoot down unauthorized planes flying into Biafra. As there were no Gowon-authorized planes, the point became academic and has remained so ever since.

The British Government had taken a slap in the face from Nigeria, and something had to be done to restore harmony to the partnership. It was. On 8 July the Nigerian Foreign Minister, Mr Okoi Arikpo, held a press conference in Lagos in which he proposed a land corridor. Food would be brought by ship into Lagos. From there it would be airlifted to Enugu, safely in Nigerian hands, and then convoyed by road to a point south of Awgu, captured the previous month by Federal forces. There the food would be left on the road, in the hopes that the 'rebels' would come and take it.

The proposal was hailed by the British Government and Press as a most magnanimous gesture. No one bothered to point out that it was as expensive to bring a ship into Lagos as into São Tomé, or Fernando Póo, or the Niger River; or that an airlift from Lagos to Enugu was as expensive as an airlift from São Tomé to Annabelle; or that the Nigerians had said an airlift could not work due to weather conditions, lack of planes and pilots; or that they did not have the trucks to run a shuttle of 300 tons a day from Enugu to Awgu; or that bitter fighting was going on around Awgu still.

In point of fact, agreement to the idea as elaborated by Mr Arikpo was not necessary, since the cooperation of the Biafrans in the plan was not required. Actually, not one packet of dried milk powder was ever taken to Awgu for use inside unoccupied Biafra, or laid on the road for the rebels to pick up. So far as one can discern this was never even intended.

From the Biafran standpoint it was not in any case any longer simply a technical problem. There was enormous antagonism inside the country, not from Colonel Ojukwu but from the ordinary people, to the idea of taking any food at all by courtesy of the Nigerian Army. Many expressed the wish that they would prefer to do without than take food handouts from their persecutors. Then there was the question of poison. There had recently been incidents of people dying mysteriously after eating foodstuffs bought across the Niger in the Midwest by bona fide contrabandiers. An analysis of samples made at Ihiala hospital laboratory revealed that white arsenic and other toxic substances had been present in the food.

This was ridiculed abroad, but non-involved foreigners inside Biafra, notably the journalist Mr Anthony Hayden-Guest, also investigated and came to the view that the reports were not propaganda.* The damage done in physical terms was small, but in psychological terms enormous. For many people food from Nigeria meant poisoned food, and these people were not all Biafrans. An Irish priest said, 'I cannot give a cup of milk I know has come from Nigeria to a small baby. However small the chance, it's too big.'†

The overriding question was the military one. Colonel Ojukwu's military chiefs reported there was a big build-up of Nigerian military equipment going on from Enugu to Awgu, and for them to lower their defences to let through relief sup-

* *Daily Telegraph*, 8 July 1968.

† Father Kevin Doheny, of the Order of the Holy Ghost, at Okpuala Mission, August 1968, to the author.

plies would simply open up a defenceless avenue into the heart of Biafra. Could they trust the Nigerian Army not to use it to run through armoured cars, men and guns? On previous experience the answer was no.

At a press conference at Aba on 17 July Colonel Ojukwu made his position plain. He wanted an airlift in the short term as the quickest means of getting the job done. He proposed either a neutral river route up the Niger, or a demilitarized land corridor from Port Harcourt to the front line, to bring in the bulk supplies. He could not agree to food supplies that passed through Nigerian hands unobserved and unescorted by neutral foreign personnel, nor to a corridor that was uniquely under the control of the Nigerian Army. That night he flew off to Niamey, capital of Niger Republic, at the invitation of the Organization for African Unity's Committee on Nigeria. Here again he elaborated the choices open, if it was intended to solve the problem rather than play politics.

In Britain the Enugu–Awgu plan was strongly supported by the Government with everything it could muster. Alternative proposals were impatiently brushed away. The Government, increasingly aware of public outcry, offered £250,000 to Nigeria to help with the problem. Although the issues at stake, the options open, and the technical eyewitness evidence were either known or available, the Government decided to send Lord Hunt out to tour Nigeria and Biafra to decide how best the British donation could be administered.

Colonel Ojukwu replied by saying his people did not wish to accept money or aid from Mr Wilson's Government, alleging that the sum involved was less than one per cent of the sales of the arms which had caused the disaster in the first place, and that so long as arms shipments went on they found donations of milk from the British Government unpalatable. At the same time he made clear that assistance from the British people would be received with genuine gratitude. However as Lord Hunt's mission was concerned with the modalities of administering the Government gift, there was no point in his coming to Biafra.

Some observers in Biafra felt this decision was hasty, since Lord Hunt and his companions could have seen, had they visited Biafra, the practicability of an airlift into Annabelle. But Colonel Ojukwu knew that his people were massively against the Hunt visit. He came within an ace of changing his mind, but an injudicious statement by Mr Thomson to the effect that world opinion would condemn him utterly unless he accepted the Awgu corridor made it impossible for Ojukwu to do other than stick by his original decision.

So for two weeks Lord Hunt visited various war-fronts on the Nigerian side of the fighting line, but had no opportunity to hear arguments other than those advocating the Awgu corridor, which the British Government had said during Hunt's absence it intended to support. The usefulness of Lord Hunt's subsequent report has yet to be proved. In later weeks and months it became somewhat doubtful if £250,000 worth of food would ever get delivered to the suffering behind the Nigerian lines, let alone through them.

Some in Britain did see the Biafrans' anxieties. On 22 July in the House of Commons, protesting against the continuing supply of arms, Mr Hugh Fraser said: 'In the name of humanity it would be foolish to ship instruments of war which would convert corridors of mercy into avenues of massacre.'*

To make the case for the Awgu corridor more plausible it was necessary to deal with the question of an airlift, notably by denigrating the suitability of Annabelle airport, by now being referred to by its real name of Uli. This was duly done. Mr George Thomson referred to Uli as 'a rough grass strip', and said it could not take an airlift. There were, apart from Mr Kirkley, at least a score of journalists within a mile of White-hall who could have testified that it was not a rough grass strip and could take heavy aircraft. Their experience was not sought, and when the precise specifications of Uli were provided to the Commonwealth Office, they were smoothly and hurriedly brushed aside.

The runway of Uli is 6,000 feet long, that is, twice as long as Enugu runway and half as long again as Port Harcourt. It is 75 feet wide, slightly less than a pilot would like, but wide enough for most undercarriages with room to spare, and it has

* Hansard, 22 July 1968, col. 68.

an all-up load capacity of 75 tons. It was built by the same Biafran who before independence was the project engineer for the construction of the main runways at Lagos and Kano international airports in Nigeria.

Nevertheless, the British Government's campaign stuck, and millions in Britain were duped into thinking that Colonel Ojukwu was refusing a land corridor under any circumstances, and that in this way he was responsible for any deaths that might occur among the Biafran people.

In point of fact, he never received from the Nigerians directly or indirectly, a formal proposal for the Awgu corridor. After Mr Arikpo's press conference, the red herring by then swimming nicely, the matter was dropped. It was briefly raised again by the Biafrans when they met the Nigerians at Niamey, but when the respective arguments were examined for the various alternative proposals, the Nigerians realized that on feasibility alone the Biafran proposals were better, and they then backtracked on everything and told the Biafrans they intended to starve them out. This is described more fully in a later chapter.

However, when he left Niamey to return to Lagos the chief negotiator for the Nigerian side, Mr Allison Ayida, was interviewed by the *Observer* which published on 28 July 1968 the following:

According to Mr Ayida the Biafrans were prepared to accept a land corridor even without winning their own demand for a day-time air corridor into Biafra, provided the land corridor was patrolled by an armed international police force.

After the Nigerian spokesman at Niamey, Mr Allison Ayida had made the Nigerian intention plain once and for all, any real hope of getting an agreement to fly, drive or ship food into Biafra went out of the window. It is difficult to see why in this case such a fuss was made about negotiating a corridor at all. The only way to get food in was to fly at night and thus technically at any rate break the blockade. Only the churches realized this, and without clamour or publicity quietly flew in as much food as they could. By this time each of the two church bodies had bought planes of their own, but Wharton still controlled them, and the churches wanted to set up their own operations.

The difficulty was the opposition of Wharton himself to the idea of losing his monopoly of flights into and out of the country. The churches could not hire their own pilots and servicing crews and fly in independently because Wharton's pilots alone knew the vital landing codes by which a friendly aircraft identified itself to the control tower at Uli.

Apart from the churches, even the Biafrans hesitated to affront Wharton by breaking his monopoly; for one thing they depended on him for their arms flights. But at last they decided to give the codes to the Red Cross and the Churches. This was not so easy. One Biafran emissary flying to São Tomé was refused access to the aircraft at Uli by a Wharton pilot because the pilot suspected (quite rightly) that he had the codes in his pocket. It was eventually through a delegate of the Biafrans going via Gabon to Addis Ababa for the Peace Conference that the codes were smuggled out, and in the Ethiopian capital that they were handed over to a representative of the Red Cross, who later passed them on to the churches.

Whether this breaking of his monopoly had anything to do with Wharton's later activities over the non-arrival of Biafran desperately needed ammunition supplies towards the end of August when the Nigerian 'final offensive' was on, is something that only Wharton can answer.

On 15 July Nigerian anti-aircraft fire started from flak-ships in the creeks to the south of Biafra, and Wharton's pilots decided the pace was getting too hot. They quit and for ten days no planes came into Uli. They eventually started again on 25 July after certain reassurances not entirely uninvolved with hard cash.

On 31 July the Red Cross at last started its own operation from Fernando Póo, an island then a Spanish Colony and much nearer to Biafra than São Tomé, being only forty miles off the coast as opposed to the 180 miles to the Portuguese island. But Fernando Póo was due for independence on 12 October, and the mood of the future government of Africans was not known. In the event the party that won the elections was not the expected one, and subsequently proved thoroughly unhelpful, a state of affairs for which the constant pressure brought by the Nigerian Consul on the island was largely responsible.

Many criticisms have been levelled at the International Red Cross from both sides, and from journalists. They are accused of not doing enough, of spending more money on administrative gallivanting than on getting the job done, of being too concerned with not treading on political toes and not concerned enough in passing out relief.

But their position has not been easy. By the nature of their charter they have to remain totally neutral. Their neutrality must not only be kept, it must be seen to be kept. They had to operate on both sides of the fighting line. Certainly they could have been more efficient and made fewer mistakes. But it was the first time any operation of this size and scope had ever been undertaken anywhere. There were teams from various nations attached to the International Red Cross, and other teams from the same nations working under the flag of their own national Red Cross. Thus in Biafra there were two French teams, one attached to the IRC, the other sent by the French Red Cross. The effort was often disparate and uncoordinated. It was to bring some order into the state of affairs that Mr August Lindt, Swiss ambassador to Moscow and a former United Nations senior servant in refugee and famine matters, was asked by the IRC to come and head the whole operation.

Of the accusations usually made that the IRC was not tough enough in brushing aside the obstacles, one weary spokesman said: 'Look, here in Biafra we get all the cooperation we need. But on the other side they've made it quite plain they don't want us. They don't like what we are doing, which is saving lives a lot of them would privately like to see waste away, and they don't like our presence because it prevents them doing certain things we think they would like to do to the civilian population.

'If we get too stroppy with them they can just as easily order us to leave. O.K., fine, so we get a day in the headlines. But what about the million people our supplies are maintaining in life behind the Nigerian lines? What happens to them?'

208

But one criticism that can reasonably be made is that the International Red Cross in Geneva took a disastrously long time to wake up and get moving. Although they were kept informed from the very earliest days by Mr Jaggi of the urgency of the situation, and although the money that came in from all sources during July ran into millions of dollars, it was not until the last day of the month that the first all-Red Cross plane flew into Uli. Even throughout the month of August, with their own air operation, the Red Cross only brought in 219 tons of food while the churches with less money and still relying on Wharton for transport shifted over 1,000 tons. But as the generally accepted required tonnage of 300 tons a night would have meant that this combined quantity should have come in every four days, Mr Kirkley's gloomy prediction came true.

It is not the intent of this chapter to paint gaudy pictures of human suffering; it is rather a chronicle of events to explain to the puzzled reader what really happened. Besides, the pictures have been seen, in newspapers and on television, and highly emotional word-portraits have been painted by scores of journalists and writers about what they saw. A brief résumé will suffice.

By July, 650 refugee camps had been set up and they contained about 700,000 haggard bundles of human flotsam waiting hopelessly for a meal. Outside the camps, squatting in the bush, was the remainder of an estimated four and a half to five million displaced persons. As the price of the available foodstuffs went up, not only the refugees but also those indigenous to the unoccupied zone suffered.

Wildly varying figures have been hazarded to describe the death toll. The author has tried to achieve a consensus of estimates from the best-informed sources within the International Red Cross, the World Council of Churches, the Caritas International and the orders of nuns and priests who did much of the field work of food distribution in the bush villages.

Throughout July and August, the politicians postured and the diplomats prevaricated. A land corridor, even if it had been set up at that period, could not conceivably have been in operation in time. The donations from British and West

European private citizens were pouring in; several Governments, notably in Scandinavia, indicated privately that they would not be unsympathetic to a request from the Red Cross for the loan of a freighter and aircrew, if asked. The Red Cross in Geneva preferred to negotiate with a private firm whose pilots said they would only fly into Biafra if Nigeria accorded them a safe-conduct guarantee; and to ask Lagos for that guarantee. As ever it was refused.

The death-toll spiralled as predicted. Starting at an estimated 400 a day, by its peak it had reached what the four main foreign-staffed bodies of relief workers in Biafra reckoned to be 10,000 a day. The food imports throughout July and August were pitifully small. While some of the deaths occurred in the camps, and could be noted, far more occurred in the villages where no relief percolated at all. As so often, the most heartbreaking tasks and the dirtiest work were undertaken by the Roman Catholics.

There are no words to express nor phrases in this language to convey the heroism of the priests of the Order of the Holy Ghost and the nuns of the Order of the Holy Rosary, both from Ireland. To have to see twenty tiny children brought in in a state of advanced kwashiokor, to know that you have enough relief food to give ten a chance of living while the others are completely beyond hope; to have to face this sort of thing day in and day out; to age ten years in as many months under the strain; to be bombed and strafed, dirty, tired and hungry and to keep on working, requires the kind of courage that is not given to most men who wear a chestful of war ribbons.

By the end of 1968 the consensus estimate of deaths within unoccupied Biafra was three quarters of a million, and the most conservative estimate to be found was half a million. The Red Cross, whose colleagues were working on the other side of the fighting line, reported an estimated half a million dead in the Nigerian-occupied areas.

It must be stated that much of the food bought with the money donated by the people of Britain, Western Europe and North America that did not go to Biafra direct did not reach the hungry at all. While reporters like Mr Stanford and Mr Noyes Thomas of the *News of the World* were reporting in

June and July the scenes of human degradation they witnessed at Ikot Ekpene, an Ibibio town which Lagos had quite correctly been claiming for twelve weeks to be firmly in their hands, other journalists in Lagos were uncomfortably reporting that piles of donated food were rotting on the docks. Red Cross workers there were complaining of being deliberately frustrated at all official levels.

Despite this, Red Cross sources also later reported quiet efforts by British diplomacy in August and September to persuade the IRC to discontinue their aid to Biafra direct, on the grounds that Biafra was finished anyway, and to hand over the problem on the Nigerian side to the Nigerian Red Cross who, they said, were 'more efficient'.

In the first week of August 1968 the two church relief organizations, having got the vital landing codes from the Red Cross, also broke away from Wharton and set up their own operations, but still from São Tomé. On 10 August, against all advice, Count Carl Gustav von Rosen, a veteran Swedish pilot from Transair, flew in a hedgehopping daylight relief flight to show it could be done. This was the first flight of yet another relief organization, Nord Church Aid, an association of the Scandinavian and West German Protestant churches. Later the three church organizations merged at São Tomé under the title Joint Church Aid.

Meanwhile the Biafran idea for a separate airport had been resuscitated as hopes to get Nigerian permission for daylight flights into Uli faded. An airport and runway was available at Obilagu, but there were no electrical installations, nor a fully fitted control tower. The Red Cross agreed to fit these off its own account, and work started on 4 August. On 13 August an agreement was signed between Colonel Ojukwu for the Biafran Government and Mr Jaggi for the Red Cross. It provided that either side could rescind the agreement on demand, but that so long as it operated the airport should be demilitarized.

M. Jean Kriller, a Geneva architect, became the Red Cross commandant of the airport. His first act was to insist on the removal of all troops and military equipment, including anti-aircraft guns, to outside a five-mile radius of the centre of the runway. The Biafran Army protested that with the advance

211

positions of the Nigerian Army only thirteen miles away, this would affect the defensive position. Colonel Ojukwu backed Kriller, and move they did. Kriller's next act was to paint three 60-foot wide white discs at equidistant intervals down the runway with a big red cross painted into each. Thus protected he took up residence in a tent on the side of the runway. On 20, 24 and 31 August the airport was bombed and rocketed, smack on the target. Half a dozen local food-porters were killed and another score injured.

On 1 September 1968 the first token flight into the new airport was made from Fernando Póo. The Red Cross was still trying to get permission from Lagos for daylight flights, and felt its case to be enormously strengthened now that it had its own airport. But the answer was still No. Then on 3 September Lagos changed its mind, or seemed to. Daylight flights would be permissible, but not for Obilagu, only for Uli.

While the Red Cross politely pointed out that it was not at Uli that the relief food flights were coming in any more, but at Obilagu, and argued that if the aim was to bring in the maximum amount of food to save lives, then it was at Obilagu that the daylight flights should take place, Colonel Ojukwu's advisers considered this sudden and to them surprising decision from Nigeria in another light.

Why Uli, and only Uli, they wondered. After thinking it over they could only come up with one answer. Although Uli had been frequently raided by day, that is, when it was out of use, the Biafran anti-aircraft fire, although not terribly accurate, was good enough to force the Nigerian bombers to fly high and to put them off their aim. As a result the actual runway had not been hit with a big bomb. Small rocket craters from diving MiG fighters could be easily filled in. But if the ack-ack were silenced by day to allow the big DC-7s from Fernando Póo and São Tomé to bring in food, it would only need one Nigerian Soviet-built freighter like the Antonovs sometimes seen passing high overhead to sneak into the circuit with a 5,000-lb bomb slung under it to blow a hole in the runway that would close the airport for a fortnight. With the Nigerians sweeping into Aba and preparing for a big push to Owerri, and with the Biafrans desperately short of ammunition and almost scanning the skies for the next arms shipment, Colonel Ojukwu could not risk the destruction of his weapons airport.

On 10 September the Nigerians made a dash for Oguta and secured the town. Although they were pushed out forty-eight hours later, Ojukwu had to rescind his agreement on Obilagu's exclusivity. When Oguta was occupied, being uncomfortably close to the Uli airfield, Uli was evacuated. It opened again on 14 September, but for three days, with ammunition planes at last beginning to come in, Ojukwu had to give them landing permission at Obilagu. From then on both arms and relief flights came into both airports without discrimination. Not that it mattered much, since there was at that time no Nigerian bomber activity at night and no apparent chance of getting permission for daylight flights to the relief airport. On 23 September Obilagu fell to a big push by the Nigerian First Division, and Uli once again became the only operational airport.

Since that time Lagos has again offered to permit daylight flights for relief planes. Ojukwu has again been widely accused of having refused this, and in consequence of being wholly responsible for the famine. What he said was that he would agree to daylight flights to any airport other than Uli, on which he dare not risk an accurate daylight attack with heavy-weight bombs.

For the rest of the year, from 1 October to 31 December, the flights continued by night into Uli. During October Canada lent the Red Cross a Hercules freighter with a carrying capacity of twenty-eight tons per flight. Basing their estimates on two flights per night for this aircraft, the Red Cross prepared a hopeful plan for November. But after eleven flights the Hercules was grounded on orders from Ottawa, and later withdrawn. In December the American Government offered eight Globemaster transports, each with a capacity of over thirty tons, four to the Red Cross and four to the churches. Great hopes were placed on these aircraft, which were due to go into operation after the New Year.

But also in December the Government of Equatorial Guinea, which now ran Fernando Póo, informed the Red Cross that it could no longer carry diesel oil for its distribution trucks

213

or oxygen bottles for its surgical operations. This change of policy originated, apparently, on the night the Guinean Interior Minister turned up drunk at the airport with the Nigerian Consul and created a disturbance in which one of the freighter pilots spoke his mind.

In October, night bombing of Uli airport started. The bombing was done by a piston-engined transport plane from the Nigerian Air Force which droned around overhead for two or three hours each night dropping large-sized bombs at odd intervals. They were not particularly dangerous as with all the airport lights extinguished the plane could not find the airfield in the darkness. But it was uncomfortable to lie face down in the passenger waiting lounge for hours waiting for the next shriek as a bomb plummeted into the forest nearby. One had the sense of unwillingly partaking in a game of Russian roulette.

By the end of November the kwashiokor scourge had been brought under control, though not entirely eradicated. Most of those surviving children who had suffered from it, although on the way to recovery, could relapse at any time if the tenuous supply line broke completely. By December a new menace threatened – measles. Along the West African coast measles epidemics among children occur regularly and usually have a mortality rate of five per cent. But a British paediatrician who had done long service in West Africa estimated that the mortality rate would be more like twenty per cent in wartime conditions.

A million and a half children were likely to suffer from it during January; that put the forecast death toll at another 300,000 children. In the nick of time, with the aid of UNICEF and other children's organizations, the necessary vaccine was flown in, packed in the special cases needed to keep the vaccine at the required low temperature, and wholesale vaccination began.

As the new year approached it became clear that the next problem would be a lack of the staple carbohydrate foods like yams, cassava and rice. The January harvest was predicted as being a small one, partly because in some areas the seed yams had been eaten the previous harvest, partly because unripe crops had been harvested prematurely and consumed. Efforts were being made to bring in supplies of these as well, but because of their greater weight the problem of transporting a far greater tonnage called for more and heavier aircraft, or vigorous efforts to persuade the Nigerians to permit food ships to pass up the Niger.

On balance, the effort to save the children of Biafra was alternately a heroic and abysmal performance. Despite all the efforts, not one packet of food ever entered Biafra 'legally'. Everything that came in entered by a process of breaking the Nigerian blockade. In the six months from the time Mr Kirkley gave his six weeks deadline and his estimate of a needed 300 tons of food a night, the Red Cross brought in 6,847 tons and the combined churches about 7,500 tons. In 180 nights of possible flying, these 14,374 tons of food worked out at an average of 80 tons a night only. But even the average is misleading; the time when the food was really needed and could have saved two or three hundred thousand children's lives was in the first fifty days after 1 July. But at that time virtually nothing came in.

More than the pogroms of 1966, more than the war casualties, more than the terror bombings, it was the experience of watching helplessly their children waste away and die that gave birth in the Biafran people to a deep and unrelenting loathing of the Nigerians, their Government and the Government of Britain. It is a feeling that will one day reap a bitter harvest unless the two peoples are kept apart by the Niger River.

The British Government, behind the façade of claiming to be doing all it could to ease the situation, fully went along with Nigeria's wishes after the snub of 5 July. Far from doing what it could to persuade Lagos to let the food go through to Biafra, the British Government did the opposite. Mr Van Walsum, the highly respected former Mayor of Rotterdam, ex-Member of Parliament and Senator, present chairman of the Dutch Ad Hoc National Committee for Biafra Relief, has already said publicly he is prepared to testify that reports that the British Government and the American State Separtment during August and September brought 'massive political pressure' on the International Red Cross in Geneva not to send any help at all to Biafra are accurate.* Checks by British journalists direct with the IRC in Geneva have confirmed Van Walsum's statement.

It may well be that later and fuller study will reveal that out of a consistently shabby policy on this issue the British Government's attempted interference with relief supplies to helpless African children was the most scabrous act of all.

The narrative of what befell the emergency relief operation to the hungry children of Biafra in the latter half of 1969 provides a classic object lesson of what a hectoring, bullying dictatorship can get away with when confronted only by a civilized world unprepared to stand up for itself or for those standards of conduct which it has decreed to be inviolable.

From January until the end of May the relief flights of both Joint Church Aid (an amalgam of Caritas, World Council of Churches and Nord Church Aid) and the International Red Cross proceeded without incident. With the addition of eight extra planes sold for a peppercorn figure by the United States Government to Joint Church Aid and the Red Cross, tonnages of relief food were steadily increased.

During the peak months of March and April the combined tonnage entering Biafra by night came to a climax of nearly 400 tons per night, substantially more than the 300 tons estimated by the relief experts to be the minimum needed to halt kwashiokor and undernourishment. With these tonnages, not only was this task achieved, but the spectre of famine and its attendant scourges began to recede.

The major part of the IRC operation was by this time flying out of Cotonou, the capital of Dahomey, Nigeria's western neighbour, while a few IRC aircraft had restarted operations from Fernando Póo with the personal permission of President Enrico Macias who had intervened to settle the earlier unpleasantness. The JCA operation still flew out of São Tomé, which it had to itself.

Inside Biafra the prospect occasioned by the increase in relief foods was a heartening one. Over two million children and

* Statement to Mr Peter Gatacre, quoted by Mr Gatacre in a letter to *The Times*, 2 December 1968.

half a million adults were getting regular access to the protein-rich food they needed. Where a few months earlier travellers through the landscape had beheld silent, deserted compounds whose inhabitants lay exhausted and dying inside their huts, there were now to be seen groups of children playing in the sun, running to the roadside to yell and wave at a passing car. The sight of endless rows of rough cots in hundreds of sickbays up and down the country, crammed with the skeletal forms of dying children, became rarer, and even those children lining up in long queues at the three thousand feeding centres administered by the two relief organizations could be seen to be on the mend. Had nothing intervened, the prospects of May 1969 were that, whatever the military outcome of the struggle, millions of children would still be alive to have a chance at whatever life had in store for them; without the relief operation they would undoubtedly have died.

Despite allegations that this relief food was going to the Biafran soldiery, the administrational chiefs of both distributing organizations, who kept a close check on all tonnages entering the country and being distributed, were satisfied that only an 'acceptable' proportion, about five per cent, of the tonnage was being lost or purloined in transit. In view of the remarkable circumstances of the airlift, the complete lack of mechanized cargo-handling devices at Uli, the fact that all was unloaded in darkness, etc., this figure was as low as human endeavour could bring it.

The Red Cross organizers, who were the only one of the two groups running a large operation among the hungry on the Nigerian side of the firing line, estimated that the loss-and-misappropriation figure was higher in Nigeria than in Biafra. This was partly due to the efficiency of the handling and distribution system in Biafra, partly because the supply lines between the point of entry and the point of consumption were so much shorter.

The JCA operation had the advantage of a comprehensive infrastructure of European missionaries already on the spot – eighty Irish priests and fifty Irish nuns working for Caritas, and twenty-seven missionaries and twenty imported volunteers working for the World Council of Churches. These Europeans, most of whom had an intimate knowledge of the country and the people, were able to provide personal supervision at every level and prevent all but the most occasional misappropriation. The Red Cross, although it had to build its own distributing organization, also imported enough volunteers to provide intensive supervision. Nord Church Aid, the third of the consortium that composed JCA, having no distributing structure on the ground, wisely did not try to compete with the Catholic and Protestant churches in setting up their own network inside Biafra, but instead ran the airlift, and did it with brilliant efficiency.

Throughout these five months the only thing to mar the importation of food was the nightly activities of a Nigerian Dakota freighter, converted into a bomber and flown by a South African mercenary. This bomber regularly overflew Uli in the hours of darkness, dropping bombs at random, while its pilot baited the relief crews over the R/T, nicknaming himself 'Genocide' and threatening them with what would befall them if they tried to land.

His bombs, however, never hit a relief plane or any of the aircrew while they were on the ground, and he had only nuisance value. As Uli was still being used as the airport by which arms were imported into Biafra, no one could fairly say that it was not a military target, and the relief agencies never claimed this.

In late May, Count von Rosen's Minicons went into operation, and in four successive raids on the Federal-held airports of Enugu, Benin, Calabar and Port Harcourt, destroyed most of the operational MiGs and Ilyushins of the Nigerian Air Force. The bomber of Mr Genocide was also destroyed on the ground. The response by Russia was rapid.

On Monday 2 June, while landing at Uli, Australian relief pilot Captain Vernon Polley, working for JCA, was strafed by two MiGs flying in close formation. They came out of the night sky ahead of him while the airport lights were on, and each let rip a short burst of cannon fire. The next second they were gone, screaming over the tail of the freighter and off into the darkness. Captain Polley's DC-6 was riddled from stem to stern, although luckily no one was hurt.

A repair crew was flown out from São Tomé the same night, and through the next day they worked on the freighter under camouflage to get it back into flying condition. On Tuesday night Captain Polley, flying alone, brought the limping DC-6 back to São Tomé. The lesson of Monday night was not slow in coming home to the relief pilots. To strafe an illuminated target while flying out of darkness does not require a fully equipped night fighter, but it does require piloting of considerable skill.

Flying a day fighter at night is standard practice, since all fighters are equipped with night-flying instruments and homing devices. But the skill of the gunnery indicated that the pilots concerned were a far cry from the useless Egyptian pilots who had flown for the Nigerians up till then, but who had never done a night mission.

When diving at night towards an illuminated target, the fighter pilot will temporarily lose some of his night vision, even with a tinted eyeshade, as he gazes into the illuminated area. To dive to within eighty feet of the ground and fire with pinpoint accuracy, to do so in tight formation with another fighter flying alongside at over 500 m.p.h., to risk having to pull out blind at a split second's notice if the lights should go out – all these require pilots of considerable skill, with an intimate knowledge of their aircraft and their squadron colleague on the wingtip. Such expertise is not learned in a few hours, nor possessed by the Egyptians. Therefore somebody new was flying for the Nigerians.

The *Sunday Telegraph* broke the story on 22 June; the new pilots were half a dozen East Germans sent down at the behest of the Russians. Ten days later the West German Government's deputy spokesman, Herr Konrad Ahlers, said that West German intelligence had confirmed that there were East Germans flying for Nigeria. Yet the fact that the so-called 'Federal Air Force' was in fact an amalgam of Russians, East Germans, Egyptians and mercenaries elicited little interest from the governments of the West, and continued to be referred to as 'the Nigerian Air Force'.

Before this, the planes themselves, flying by day, had been identified in the skies over Biafra. They were MiG 19s, considerably more modern than the previous MiG 15s and 17s hitherto flown by the Egyptians.

Despite the increasing risk of being hit on the ground, the pilots of both the International Red Cross and JCA elected to continue flying in the relief food. They stipulated that the lights of Uli should only be switched on for landing at the very last second, to shorten the time the airstrip would be illuminated, and switched off on command from the landing pilot when his speed along the runway was slow enough to enable him to come to a halt in darkness without mishap. Take-offs from then on were by aircraft headlights only.

The idea worked. Although the MiG 19s continued to strafe the airport whenever they could find it in the darkness, they never hit another relief plane. Listeners on the ground waited until the whine of the jets was heard far away, then bade the pilot begin coming down the approach glide path. At the last second the lights flashed on; high above the jets wheeled and dived, but before they could get into range the lights went off and they were forced to pull out in raking climbs to avoid a smash into the ground. They continued to spray the area where they thought the airfield was with cannon and rocket fire, but were usually wild.

On Thursday 5 June the Federal Air Force really excelled itself. A MiG 17 shot down in broad daylight a clearly marked Red Cross relief plane in cold blood. In terms both of the written laws of the Geneva Convention on War and the unwritten laws of the world of flying, this act was just about as far as an Air Force can go. The pilot of the Red Cross DC-6 was an American veteran of the Second World War and Korea, Captain David Brown.

Almost incredibly, some British journalists sought to justify or mitigate the act. One, writing in a Sunday newspaper some days later, reported that the fighter pilot in a long R/T conversation with Captain Brown had repeatedly told him to land at a Nigerian airfield and only shot him down when he persistently refused to do so. This was arrant nonsense, for three reasons:

1. A MiG 17 fighter communicates with its own ground base or other fighters in the air on a series of fixed-crystal wave-

lengths available to its own channel selector. It cannot 'sweep the bands' as can the radio operator of a freighter aircraft who has at his disposal a more versatile radio set. It was the habit of the pilots of the Red Cross, and those of the JCA, to keep changing their operating wavelengths on a daily basis, agreed beforehand with their own control tower. On not one recorded occasion did the relief pilots ever find themselves on the same channel as the Nigerian fighter pilots. There is moreover no known system of hand signals by which a pilot flying on the wingtip of another aircraft may instruct the pilot of the intercepted plane to change over to his own channel so that voice communication can take place. Even had there been such a system of hand signals, it would be extremely doubtful whether the freighter's radio operator could have found the MiG's wavelength.

2. There does exist an internationally known system of hand signals by which a pilot may signal across the intervening air to another pilot that he has been intercepted and should do what he is told. This system is occasionally used when an aircraft is sent aloft to 'shepherd' to safety a plane which has lost its radio. The system has also been used by fighters to require an intercepted transport aircraft to land at a designated airfield of the fighter pilot's choice – for example in the case of airliners that have strayed out of the Berlin air corridors and been intercepted by Soviet MiGs. A freighter who, having been intercepted and signalled to divert to another airfield, refuses to do so, particularly when his interceptor is an armed fighter, would have to be a lunatic or a suicide case. Captain Brown was neither. There is an adage in flying: 'There are old pilots and there are bold pilots, but there are no old, bold pilots.' Captain Brown was an old pilot with a quarter of a century of flying behind him. He knew the procedures and he knew the drill. Had he landed as instructed at Port Harcourt, for example, his cargo would have been proved to be a harmless ten tons of milk powder and stockfish, and after a period of detention his own government or the International Red Cross would have secured his release. He knew this.

3. It is inconceivable that a pilot of his experience should have been intercepted, and ordered to land at an airfield de-

signated by the fighter pilot, without breathing a word of what happened to his own control tower. To a pilot it is as clear as day that if such an interception took place, the first action would be to inform one's own control tower what had happened, and what action one was taking. So far as the listeners at Fernando Póo were concerned, Captain Brown never left his own frequency linking him with Fernando Póo control tower.

What really happened was this. At 5.38 p.m. on that Thursday evening Captain Brown took off from Fernando Póo with his cargo. Accompanying him were his crew of two Swedes, co-pilot and flight engineer, and a Norwegian loadmaster in the back. His aircraft was a DC-6 painted white from stem to stern. On the upper and lower surfaces of each wing were painted two large red crosses, each eight feet across. Other red crosses adorned each side of the fuselage at the mid-section, and each side of the tail fin. It would have been almost impossible to mark an aircraft more distinctively.

If he made any mistake it was in leaving too early for Biafra. The sky was a brilliant blue, without a cloud, and the sun was still well above the horizon. It was habitual for planes leaving São Tomé to depart at this hour, for with the longer journey they only came over the Biafran coast after 7 p.m., that is, after dark. Dusk is very short in Africa. The light starts fading in June around 6.30 and by 7 p.m. it is dark. But with the much shorter journey (only sixty miles) from Fernando Póo to the coast, he came over the coast about 6 o'clock in brilliant daylight.

It was an error, although it is easy to be wise after the event. His concern, like that of all the pilots, was to get as many shuttles as possible to and from Uli into one night. Three other Fernando Póo relief planes were aloft at the same time.

At 6.03 p.m. his voice was heard in the Fernando Póo control tower, and by other Red Cross pilots on the same run. He gave no call-sign, and the voice was high-pitched with alarm. He said: 'I'm being attacked . . . I'm being attacked.' His switch went dead, there was a moment's silence, then a babble on the ether, with Fernando Póo asking for the identification of the

222

caller. Thirty seconds later the voice came back on the air. 'My engine's on fire ... I'm going down ...'. Then there was silence. Nothing was ever heard from Captain Brown again.

His plane crashed in flames in the marshes outside Opobo on the coast. At first it was said that three of the four men were alive, then that they were dead. The United States Government and the Swedish Government protested about the incident and asked for the bodies of their nationals back. The matter was not pressed, neither were the protests.

To every pilot along the coast one thing was patently clear, and their own quiet investigations confirmed it: the American, the two Swedes and the Norwegian had been murdered. The next question became that of finding the identity of the man who did it. At first it was thought it might be an East German, then rumour circulated that it was a Nigerian who had flown the MiG.

The world of flying is strange. It has its own laws, its own code and its own information network. There exists a kind of brotherhood between pilots, as between seamen. Pilots who have fought against each other can sit down years later and talk over old times without animus, in a manner unlikely in any other branch of fighting. It would be perfectly possible today for the relief pilots to have a beer at the bar with the mercenary pilot who flew the Nigerian night bomber over Uli; he was doing his job and they theirs. That is all there is to it. On the fringes of the air charter world, inhabited by men who have flown many strange cargoes and passengers into bizarre airfields for the right price, there is little animus over bygone 'jobs' when they may have been competing with each other. There is also little that is unknown. It is rare to stand in a group of such pilots and mention the name of another veteran of fly-for-hire without one of the company knowing the man.

Within a fortnight the Red Cross and JCA pilots had the name of the man who shot down Captain Brown. He was an Australian mercenary, and several of Brown's colleagues swore that one day, somewhere, they would 'get' him. For the Australian had broken the last rule in a remarkably tolerant brotherhood. He had shot down a fellow pilot without giving him a chance, and that was unpardonable.

All this, of course, was going on inside the closed club of the fliers. In the outside world, observers watched and waited to see what would be the reaction to this last remarkable piece of brutality by the already heavily blood-stained Nigerian Air Force. Would the United States protest that this had gone too far, and further interference produce an American offer to give protective cover to the relief planes? This was not to be. Would the Swedes protest in similar terms? It was seriously mooted in Sweden, but the government in Stockholm was content to protest formally and let the matter drop.

None watched the world's reaction more closely than the Nigerian Government. Like all bullies, they were trying something on to see how far they could go. They are Africans, and the African, like many others, will watch with great interest to see how far a 'tough guy' can go. If he can get away with what he tries, there will be no demur. If, on the other hand, someone stands up to the tough guy and, being in a position of strength, makes it quite clear that so far as he is concerned a particular course of action has gone far enough, he will usually win his point. At that stage the African will come to respect the newcomer and repudiate the bully. In short, this is human reaction the world over, as the years 1935–39 in Europe so poignantly showed.

General Charles de Gaulle understood this, which was why he got on extremely well with Africans and was much respected by them. The British and American governments do not understand this, and that is why both are regarded with contempt throughout Africa. No amount of dollar or sterling aid will ever win the respect that the African will accord freely to a man who stands up for his own irreducible standards.

Within six days it became clear to the Nigerian Government that they had got away with the outrage of 5 June scot-free and would continue to do so. Thus emboldened they proceeded to humiliate the International Red Cross and destroy its operation. In this they were assisted by the American Embassy in Lagos.

The day after the shooting down, the IRC, on orders from the Committee in Switzerland, suspended its operations, at least temporarily. What followed was a classic example of a psychological campaign intended to undermine the morale of a group of men trying to achieve a course of action. It succeeded perfectly.

In the aftermath of the shooting incident, the Red Cross in Geneva expected, and thought they had the right to expect, the moral support of the governments of the Western world. They got none. Down in Cotonou the co-ordinator of the Red Cross operation, Dr Lindt, urged that the airlift should start again. He pointed out that there was no need to fly in daylight as Captain Brown had done, that flights in darkness could continue just as before, and that Joint Church Aid was continuing its flights.

In fact JCA had restricted its flights to three or four a night in the aftermath of 5 June and its pilots were getting restive, not because of the shooting down of Captain Brown but because of the continuing activity of the MiGs in strafing Uli at night. What won the battle of indecision for Joint Church Aid was the iron will of Pastor Vigo Mollerup, the Danish pastor of a slum parish in Copenhagen who headed the Nord Church Aid scheme, which was responsible for the actual air bridge out of São Tomé, and the remarkable personality of Danish Air Force Colonel Denis Wiechmann, the operations chief on São Tomé. Pastor Mollerup, commuting between his own people in Copenhagen and his colleagues of Caritas and the World Council of Churches in Geneva, urged and wrangled that their air bridge should not be dismantled because of this one incident: in the pilots' crew room at São Tomé, Colonel Wiechmann cajoled the pilots back into the air. By 10 June they were struggling back to their usual complement of two shuttles of eight or ten aircraft a night.

On 10 June Dr Lindt went back to Moscow, where he had formerly been Swiss ambassador, to pick up his effects and furniture which had lain there for eleven months, since his hasty departure to answer the call of the Red Cross the previous July. Behind him he left instructions with the Cotonou operations chief, Nils Wachtmeister, that after a series of proving flights by one or two aircraft, the Red Cross air bridge should be steadily built up again. He made several provisos: take-off times should be strictly after dark, even if that meant cutting out one of the shuttles, and the utmost precautions should be taken on landing and take-off from Uli to keep the lit-up period to a minimum.

On 10 June the Icelandic pilot flying for the Red Cross from Cotonou in his own aircraft, Captain Lofto Johanssen, flew two missions into Uli in one night and returned safely from both. He had two more proving flights scheduled for the 12th, after which full flights would be resumed.

On the evening of 12 June a mysterious telephone message reached the chiefs of Joint Church Aid who were conferring in Lucerne, Switzerland. It came from the American Embassy in Geneva (a check-back call was made to make quite sure the message was no hoax) urging JCA with the utmost show of concern to call off all their flights for that night. The reason for this advice, said the message, was extremely serious but could not be revealed.

After a hasty consultation the four JCA chiefs in conference agreed to send a message to São Tomé cancelling all that night's flights, but they also insisted on knowing from the Americans, within twelve hours, their reasons for this demand.

Nord Church Aid got off a top priority telex through the International Aviation Control Tower Service. Inevitably, when Colonel Wiechmann got it, it looked like a panic call. Seven aircraft were in the air, and a recall message was sent out from São Tomé to all of them. One had already landed at Uli, two others were overhead and decided it was too late to pull back, so they went in and landed. The other four turned back for base, and the second shuttle was abandoned. Few events more likely to shatter the already strained morale of the pilots could be imagined.

When the next morning the Americans vouchsafed an explanation for the previous evening's panic, it was that 'there was some political trouble in Cotonou'. Pastor Mollerup replied with some asperity that that had nothing to do with the JCA air bridge out of São Tomé.

Once again Colonel Wiechmann got the airlift re-started. Meanwhile, exactly the same panic message had been passed on the evening of 12 June by the U.S. Embassy in Geneva to the Red Cross. They too ordered their flights for that night to be cancelled, and Lofto Johanssen remained on the ground. The Red Cross never flew again, apart from a few planeloads of medicaments several months later.

In Geneva, in the wake of 12 June, more deliberations took place as to whether to restart the airlift or not. In later weeks, intrigued by the events of 12 June, both relief organizations made their own inquiries to ascertain where the phony messages of unspecified dangers for them if they continued to fly in relief had originated. Independently they tracked the messages down to the same source – the American embassy in Lagos.

Meanwhile the Red Cross had been hit by another blow. Returning to West Africa on 14 June to try and put back together the bits of the operation he had so sedulously built up over the preceding months, Dr Lindt was arrested at Lagos airport for allegedly flying into the airport in his private Beechcraft without the proper authorization. (In fact, his papers were perfectly in order.) After being held for several hours he was expelled and declared *persona non grata*.

It was the final humiliation, and it broke Geneva's will to continue. From then on they decided to try to negotiate their way back into the relief operation, a futile exercise as any who knew the situation could have told them. Speaking to the author months later, one of the senior Red Cross men involved throughout said, 'There is not a vestige of doubt in my mind that we were the butt of a deliberate conspiracy, hatched in Lagos between the Nigerians and the American embassy, and it worked perfectly.'

The same source added, however, that even without the shooting down of the Red Cross plane on 5 June, the departure of Dr Lindt alone would have seen an end to the Red Cross operation in Nigeria–Biafra. This remarkable man had built it up, nursed it, argued and cajoled it through many troubles. His stern appearance and brusque manner concealed a deep and sincere concern for the suffering he witnessed on both sides of the firing line, and despite his late middle age he put in more energy than most younger men could have mustered. He also made bitter enemies in Nigeria. Refusing to tolerate the misappropriation of relief stores by private racketeers, the commandeering of relief transport of all kinds for military use,

227

Dr Lindt cut out the rake-off specialists and the bribery boys, ensuring that the absolute maximum of relief food got through to the hungry children and refugees on the Nigerian side of the line.

What is not so certain is that the Nigerian régime would have dared to humiliate and expel the International Red Cross chief, and order the IRC to hand over the whole relief operation to their own corruption-riddled appointees, if they had not been able to get away with the shooting down of Captain Brown.

It has been said since that in packing up in Nigeria and Biafra the International Red Cross betrayed the two parties towards whom its true responsibility lay – the suffering on both sides, and the donors of the money who had hoped to see their donations help save lives rather than rotting in a warehouse. But it should be stressed that in its hour of need the International Red Cross was itself betrayed by the two Western governments from whom it had every reason to expect unswerving support as the world's foremost and wholly neutral charitable organization – the British and American Governments.

Throughout the episode, not a word of support for the IRC mission in Nigeria–Biafra emerged from Whitehall or Washington. Indeed, the British Government, which had not lifted a finger to secure the release from detention in Biafra of Miss Sally Goatcher (her release was obtained by the Churches and Red Cross), made vague and unspecified threats as to what might befall if anything should happen to her in Biafra, but was not able to issue one word of condemnation of the murder of Captain Brown and his three crewmen.

Perhaps the climax in tastelessness was left to the *Daily Telegraph*. On 8 July part of the editorial read: 'The increasingly effective Federal Air Force, trying to stop arms flights, shot down what turned out to be a relief aircraft, a misfortune which Biafran propaganda duly exploited.' One was left wondering who were the more unfortunate, the four airmen lying in their graves in the marshes or the mercenary who killed them.

On 17 June one last effort to halt the JCA air bridge was made. A very strong rumour reached Geneva from American sources that Nigeria had imported two Sukhoi-7 night fighters, fully equipped with radar, whose job was to intercept the relief planes in the darkness and shoot them down. This rumour was also widely reported in the Press. A quick check from JCA headquarters in Geneva revealed that this titbit, also, was from the American embassy in Lagos. By this time Vigo Mollerup had had enough of American rumours, and told Colonel Wiechmann to go right ahead. The rumour turned out to be false. There never were any Sukhoi night fighters in Nigeria, a fact of which the American embassy, with its enormous CIA operation in Nigeria, was certainly aware.

Inside Biafra the effect of the suspension of the airlift was quick and disastrous. The two main relief agencies had between them supplies for about ten days. They provided aid in one form or another to close on three million souls per day. At one stroke this had been cut by half with the Red Cross ceasing operations, and further reduced by the cut-back in JCA flights.

Most of the children being daily supported by relief food were already at the minimal level of subsistence, devoid of any physical reserves with which to sustain another prolonged period of starvation or protein-deficiency. Within a week the death toll started to creep back up again.

For the second time the missionaries, Catholic and Protestant, were faced with the agonizing choice: does one cut off from relief aid those children so badly diseased and debilitated that their chances of survival are remote, in order to make sure of saving the not-so-bad, or does one give first to the neediest in the knowledge that the others will soon have reached that stage as well? Both Church groups came to the same view – the food should be used curatively first, preventively second. The effect, with stocks running low and little more coming in, was to spread the available food so thin on the ground that a general and very widespread debilitation of the junior population soon set in.

From this point there was already virtually no distinction between refugees and non-refugees, such as could still be discerned during the autumn of 1968. By August 1969, almost all the children in the country were suffering from malnutrition in one form or another, and most of the adults as well. The lethargy and listlessness that accompany hunger and anaemia reappeared on a wide scale. The death toll started to climb again and by late July was estimated at over 1,000 per day. By the end of the year the resumed air bridge by JCA had helped to stem the tide again, although consensus estimates even by November put the death toll at a fairly steady 500 to 700 per day.

Slowly, it seemed, from 20 June onwards the JCA air bridge crept back to what it had been in May, although this time it was done without any publicity at all. Tonnages were never mentioned by the JCA authorities for fear of provoking yet more reprisals from the Lagos Government. It was not until October that the steady importations began to exceed in nightly total what the JCA had been bringing in during May. Compared with the combined JCA–Red Cross total, even this was just over half what the two organizations together had brought in, and well below the estimated minimum required.

Two factors, apart from Vigo Mollerup and Colonel Wiechmann, were instrumental in getting the demoralized pilots and crews flying again. One was the example set by the pilots of Africa Concern and the French Red Cross flying to Uli out of Libreville. Africa Concern, a private company founded in 1968 by Father Raymond Kennedy and based in Dublin, represented the Irish people's contribution to Biafran aid, and it flew its own lone operation with a DC-6 from the Gabonese capital. So did the French Red Cross which, although it had had a team attached to the International Red Cross, also ran its own one-plane shuttle from Libreville. Both the Belgian crew flying for Africa Concern and Commandant Morencey for the French Red Cross, kept flying unperturbed throughout the whole crisis. Seeing they were continuing, the reaction of the pilots at São Tomé was, 'If they can do it, why not we?'

The other factor was perhaps the same one that gave the Frenchman his confidence. Sitting out in the Bight of Biafra, just off the coast, were five Soviet 'trawlers', or spy-ships, blossoming radio aerials and radar scanners. It was possibly one of these that had reported the incoming flight of Captain Brown two weeks earlier in time for the MiG to 'scramble' to intercept. As the São Tomé pilots overflew this flotilla in the dusk, they observed sitting in the midst of it a French aircraft carrier with a deck-full of jet fighters.

The carrier had been on a routine courtesy call to Libreville when the trouble started. Without a word it quietly sailed from Libreville and anchored for two weeks between São Tomé and Biafra. The sight of it sitting there waiting (for what?) was immensely comforting for the relief pilots. Then on 20 June the MiGs suddenly stopped flying at night and strafing the airport. They never flew again against the JCA air bridge.

While this work of life-saving was quietly being done by the Churches, the headlines had switched to the problems of the International Red Cross. Having won hands down against the Red Cross, the Nigerian régime was in a position to dictate terms, which it did. These included the handing-over of the whole relief operation in Nigeria to the Nigerian Rehabilitation Commission. There were by this time 1,400 foreign workers under the sign of the Red Cross working among the war-stricken on the Nigerian side of the line.

The Red Cross, devoid of support from Britain or America, was forced to yield. Subsequently donations from outside for the relief work under Nigerian auspices predictably plummeted. Meanwhile the Red Cross timidly tried to negotiate for a resumption of their air bridge with Federal permission.

On Wednesday 25 June Chief Awolowo commented that starvation was a legitimate weapon and that he was opposed to the shipment of relief supplies to the secessionists.* The next day the Chief of Staff of the Army, Brigadier Hassan Usman Katsina, was reported as saying, 'Personally I would not feed somebody I am fighting.'†

It was significant that the remarks of these two men, the latter of whom particularly had more power to influence events in Nigeria than twenty General Gowons, went completely unremarked by the British Government and largely by the Press. On 6 July, after a meeting in the Foreign Office in London between Mr Maurice Foley, Minister of State for the Commonwealth, Mr Okoi Arikpo, Nigerian Foreign Affairs Commissioner, and Professor Jacques Freymond, acting President

---

* *The Times,* editorial, 28 June 1969.
† ibid.

of the ICRC, the Foreign Office issued a statement claiming that 'complete agreement' had been reached between the three for a new Red Cross airlift by day of relief food to Biafra. The plan involved Red Cross planes flying from Lagos, to which all relief foods would be imported.

It was a particularly silly piece of mischief. Professor Freymond had flown home on the evening of 6 July, and the first he learned of it was from the headlines in the British Press the next day, which reached Geneva about 9 a.m. There had been no joint communiqué the previous evening, and the Foreign Office had acted entirely on its own. From Geneva the ICRC issued a vehement denial that there had been agreement between the three of them.

What there had been in fact was an Anglo-Nigerian plan which the Red Cross had agreed to transmit to General Ojukwu and the Biafran Government. The claim that without any consultation with the Biafrans the Red Cross had agreed to it severely compromised the Red Cross in its pending negotiations with the Biafrans.

This did not stop Mr Michael Stewart, speaking on 7 July in the House, putting the whole onus of whether or not the Biafran children got fed onto General Ojukwu, a ploy which by this time had become standard practice. In fact, the Biafrans, after considering the plan transmitted to them by the Red Cross, rejected it. The plan would have put the whole relief operation under Lagos' sole control, without any proscription against taking advantage of the opening of Uli during daylight hours to mount an attack against this prime target under cover of the relief flights.

The Red Cross went back to square one, and started on its own. On 19 June Dr Lindt had formally resigned in order to give the Red Cross negotiations a better chance of success.

On 1 July the new President of the International Committee of the Red Cross took office. He was M. Marcel Naville, a banker who had been on the Committee for several years, had been elected President some months previously, but could only be inaugurated on 1 July. That day in Geneva he gave a remarkably passionate and forthright press conference. He criticized the Nigerian régime as 'insolent ... showing a humanitarian the door like an unfaithful servant'. He lambasted the gun-merchants whose supplies of weapons had kept the war going, and without naming names suggested there was not enough oil in all Nigeria to make the detergent needed to cleanse the hands of the men responsible. Observers felt he was either a very rash man, or had foreknowledge of some powerful diplomatic backing that would enable him to win a showdown with the Lagos junta once and for all.

In the event the first judgement was the correct one, and unfortunately besides his rashness M. Naville showed he had little strength of character. In subsequent debate inside the committee, the more timid spirits won the day. The result was a communiqué stating that the ICRC would pursue the path of 'strict legality', which in the circumstances meant complete inertia.

A series of protracted and laborious negotiations began, while east of the Niger the children continued to die. On 8 July M. Naville himself headed the ICRC negotiating team to Lagos, pointedly cancelling a trip to London en route. He was soon back with nothing achieved, and the talks passed into the hands of M. Enrico Beniami, the senior ICRC delegate in Lagos. For weeks the talks got nowhere.

On 4 August the Red Cross did what it should have done at the outset. It produced its own compromise plan. This plan provided for Red Cross planes to take off from Cotonou in Dahomey, overfly Nigeria down a specific air corridor, deposit the relief food at Uli and return to Cotonou over Nigeria down another air corridor. Flights would be between 9 a.m. and 6 p.m. and would be protected. Cargo content would be verified during loading and just before take-off by a mixed commission including Nigerian staff, who might if they wished even accompany each flight to ensure there were no diversions.

This business of Nigerian representatives accompanying each flight to prove there was nothing of any remote military significance on board (ostensibly the Nigerians' main complaint) was what Ojukwu had proposed in July 1968.

The plan was put to Ojukwu first. For him it contained certain risks, as his security advisers were quick to point out. Firstly, with daylight flights operating, the pressure on JCA to

233

discontinue its 'illegal' night flights would be immense. If the night air bridge was dismantled and JCA joined in the daylight run, what would happen if the Lagos Government then unilaterally rescinded the agreement? Relief would be wholly cut off. Secondly, although the agreement specified that the flights and the airstrip should be inviolable between the hours of 9 a.m. to 6 p.m., would anybody guarantee that no attack would be made by the Federal Air Force in contravention of the agreement? Such an attack, if made from a freighter with an especially heavy bomb, could wreck the airfield. Significantly no Power, least of all those who screamed loudest about the integrity of the Federal régime, was prepared to consider such a guarantee.

Nevertheless, and despite opposition from within his own cabinet, Ojukwu decided to take a risk. On 29 August Biafra finally agreed to the plan. Delighted, the Red Cross took the plan to Lagos. At this point a bit of international backing for the Red Cross could have swung the issue in favour of their own compromise plan. None was forthcoming. The Federal régime objected to the plan unless certain changes were made. This was where the Red Cross made another of its major mistakes. It should have insisted the plan remain unchanged by either party. On 5 September Lagos agreed to the plan 'in principle' providing a few technical details could be worked out. On 14 September Lagos signed the agreement, with its own changes included in the text. The agreement was then shunted back to Ojukwu.

Any consumer organization will stress to its customers the importance of the small print on a legal document. The new agreement on daylight flights contained five extra paragraphs of small print, which substantially changed the spirit and letter of the original. Three may be mentioned.

One cut the flying time back to 5 p.m., cutting the possible flights per plane per day from two to one. Another specified that Lagos control tower could at any time call down any relief plane flying over Nigerian territory for supplementary inspection, after which the plane would have to go back to Cotonou still laden. The third specified that the agreement 'should in no way prejudice military operations' against Uli.

The last two conditions virtually undid the original agreement. The first left the day-to-day continuance of the relief operation to the sole discretion of the Federal government; the second exempted the actual airfield of Uli from inviolability from attack during relief flying hours. How the relief aircraft were supposed to land with Uli under jet attack was anybody's guess.

On 11 September, however, another and more sinister document came into the hands of the ICRC in Geneva. It was a photostat copy of an order from the Commander of the Federal Air Force, Colonel Shittu Alao, instructing his base commanders at Enugu, Port Harcourt, Calabar and Benin to have their MiGs 'patrol' Uli during daylight hours, and if they were fired upon to go into the attack. This sent a shiver down the Committee's collective spine.

It needed little imagination to foresee that patrolling jets overhead were bound to be fired at by some nervous gunner. What would they see on the ground? Long, inviting columns of Red Cross trucks lined up waiting for relief supplies; parked airplanes on the aprons, scores of European Red Cross staff. One of the advisers with experience of Biafra pointed out that not only would a MiG attack on such a target in broad daylight result in a bloodbath involving European personnel, but that the enraged Biafrans could turn on the Red Cross staff and vent their bitterness on them. In that event, the adviser told the Committee, the responsibility would devolve on Geneva.

It was almost with a sigh of relief that the Committee learned in late September that, thanks to the extra clauses, the Biafrans had refused the amended draft. There the matter rested until the end of 1969. The Churches continued flights by night, and, by the end of 1969, with a steadily expanded airlift and more planes expected, had brought their tonnage up from an original 150 tons a night in July to nearly 200 tons in December.

In essence the whole daylight flight plan, its success or its abysmal and possibly bloody failure, depended not on assurances from Lagos but on the honourableness of the Federal Air Force. This was the same air force that for two years had shocked and angered the world by the brutality of its raids on markets, hospitals, clinics, refugee camps and townships; that had repeatedly broken truces called by General Gowon himself; and had finally excelled itself by shooting down an unarmed Red Cross freighter in cold blood.

General Ojukwu was once again accused of playing politics with his people's lives, a hoary chestnut but still usable in Whitehall and Washington. The accusation hardly stands up. On refusing the daylight airlift scheme General Ojukwu in person was once again the butt of bad publicity. A man concerned with playing politics would have acted in precisely the opposite way, seeking the world's favour rather than its odium. For him there were not one but two considerations that had to be borne in mind. One was Biafra's security, which was for the Biafrans primordial, and of which Uli airport was the cornerstone. Relief came second to security, and the bulk of the Biafrans agreed with this order of priorities.

The tragedy of the Red Cross during 1969 was that it failed to understand the two immutables of the Nigeria–Biafra situation. One was that Ojukwu could not compromise the national security even for relief aid; the other was that the Nigerian armed forces chiefs, who stood looking over the shoulder of the government, would never permit the transmission of relief aid to Biafra other than in conditions that offered themselves a substantial military advantage.

THE AMERICAN CONTRIBUTION

It would be difficult if not impossible to imagine a more generous-hearted or compassionate people than those of the United States of America. Thus it was no coincidence that when the plight of the suffering children on both sides of the Nigeria–Biafra war came to the notice through the American Press of the people of the United States, their contribution exceeded that of all other countries even on a *pro rata* basis of population.

And yet the Government of the United States, guided by the dead hand of State Department, remained steadfast in its support of Nigeria regardless of the cost in lives involved in the war. The reason for this strange dichotomy lies in one simple fact: almost every dime and cent brought forth by the American Government to aid the suffering on both sides had to be almost literally ground out of the authorities by public pressure.

By the time it ceased operations the International Red Cross had received cash and gift contributions of over 19 million dollars from Washington. By the end of 1969 the Joint Churches had received in the same form about 60 million dollars' worth of aid. The total contribution by the United States to relief was just over half the global total.

Much of the aid was in kind; enormous donations of Corn-Soya-Milk, known as CSM or Formula Two, a newly devised relief food in light powder form, of which the U.S. Government is the sole producer, were sent. Shipping costs across the Atlantic were paid in cash. Four C-97 Stratofreighters (they were originally announced as Globemasters, which proved too heavy) were sold to the ICRC and the Churches for a nominal 3,800 dollars each. Air shipment and running costs for these planes were also paid in dollars, and later air bridge costs for U.S. cargoes in non-U.S. planes were also reimbursed by America.

To watch this effort going on was extremely heartening to those who knew that each sack and each dollar meant another bunch of children with a chance of life who would otherwise have died. Yet throughout the operation the State Department itself dragged its feet in almost every conceivable manner.

What was sent was never on the basis of the need involved, or the size of the emergency, but simply on the basis of what would be enough to satisfy American internal domestic pressure while not going so far as to upset the régime in Lagos. Just why the immensely powerful State Department felt obliged to exert itself not to upset these tiny demagogues will presumably always remain a mystery.

Despite his brave words of September 1968, President Richard Nixon, after coming to power, was personally responsible for the square root of nothing being sent to Nigeria–Biafra. The donations resulted from pressure from Press, Congressmen and Senators, and many others in public life who were in a position to exert influence. Even the sale of the eight freighters was one of the last decrees of the outgoing Johnson administration.

Early in 1969 Dr Clarence Clyde Ferguson, Professor of Law at Rutger's University, and a Negro, was named as Special Co-ordinator of Nigeria Relief. For the rest of that year he and his team by and large wasted their own and everyone else's time, and got remarkably little done. Just after the shooting down of Captain Brown on 5 June, when an expansion of the JCA airlift (which, although not perfect, was at least getting the job done) was vital, Dr Ferguson chose to downplay the airlift. He spent his energies trying to push through his own pet project for running two landing craft laden with relief supplies up the Cross River into Biafra.

Technically the plan could have worked, and two such landing craft, the Donna Mercedes and the Donna Maria, were sent across the Atlantic to Lagos. As General Ojukwu had agreed to the plan, the Nigerians vetoed it, using as trouble-shooters the puppet government they had installed at Calabar on the south of the Cross River. The landing craft ended up on unspecified duties in Nigerian-occupied Port Harcourt. For the rest, Dr Ferguson pottered round West Africa, shuttled between Nigeria and Biafra, flew to Europe and Washington, and back again. On one occasion he tried to put through his own plan for daylight flights, but omitted to warn the Red Cross who were already negotiating this idea.

The people who really did do something were the Americans of Joint Church Aid (USA). The American government aid was sent through three main agencies: USAID of the State Department, UNICEF of the United Nations, and JCA/USA. The last-named procured and transmitted the great bulk of the aid.

Those in this organization who had to liaise with State Department over the allocations left no doubt in the minds of inquirers later that in their view the Department, if left alone, would have been happy to stop the lot. Fortunately they were not allowed to. It has been necessary earlier to deal harshly with certain servants of the American people for the things they got up to in Lagos and Geneva. There is not a shadow of doubt that these ignoble antics were not known to the American people and would not have received their support had they been known.

In the State Department itself there were eventually three separate offices dealing with the Nigeria–Biafra situation. One was the Nigeria Desk, an offshoot of the West Africa Desk, but heavily staffed with the former colleagues of ex-Assistant Secretary of State for Africa, Mr Joseph Palmer. Mr Palmer, a former ambassador to Nigeria, had long been a firm supporter of Nigeria regardless of the fact that since his day that country had deteriorated into just another dictatorship. Not surprisingly the Nigeria Desk, even in Mr Palmer's absence (he was sent off as ambassador to Libya during 1969), was strongly pro-Nigerian and anti-Biafran. This was fully in harmony with the reports flowing back from Mr Elbert Matthews, the American ambassador in Lagos, who was relieved only at the end of 1969. Down the corridor was the AID office and further on was Dr Ferguson's office. To the surprise of the JCA/USA staff who had to deal with all three, none of them seemed to know what the other was up to or what it was saying as its official 'line'. The result was a fair degree of confusion.

The brunt of the work therefore fell on JCA/USA. This was mainly composed of Catholic Relief Services, the giant relief organization that is the largest United States exporter after the U.S. Government and annually ships up to a million tons of supplies yearly to 72 countries; Church World Service, representing 30 U.S. Protestant denominations and bringing relief to 42 countries in the world; and the American Jewish Committee, representing 22 Jewish organizations. These were supported by a plethora of other and smaller bodies.

Constantly agitating, pushing, yelling, shoving, the chiefs of those organizations bullied the State Department into producing the cash and kind needed to keep the relief operation going to the children on both sides. These men included Bishop Swanstrom and Ed Kinney of CRS; James McCracken and Jan von Hoostraten of CWS; and Rabbi James Rudin in Marcus H. Tannenbaum of the AJC.

Alone they might not have been able to pull it off. But also backing them were numerous men in public life who spoke out and kept speaking out until something was done. The spectrum of support that this humanitarian cause received from pressure groups in the States was as wide as life in America is varied. Pressure came from the extreme Right, and from the Left; from liberals and conservatives, Democrats and Republicans, Labour unions and corporate management, and from all the fifty widely varying states of the Union. It also came from the American Press, which never let the issue die, the surest way to kill any idea in the modern world.

One of those who did as much if not more than anyone in using his power to get relief food on its way was Senator Edward Kennedy. As chairman of the Senate Sub-Committee on Refugees, Senator Kennedy could and did call hearings at which embarrassed and sheepish officials were forced to appear and explain why more was not being done. By this means the Senator's committee kept an unwilling State Department on the hop.

In terms of America's wealth the sums involved were not huge – about three days of the cost of taking lives in Vietnam covered the cost of eighteen months of saving them in Biafra; it was also equivalent to about twenty minutes of the Apollo Eleven flight. But its effect was to give a chance of life to millions on the verge of extinction.

The real hero of the American contribution was not even among the public figures or church leaders at the forefront of the struggle. He was the ordinary American citizen, the millions of John Does scattered throughout the fifty States whom the professional manipulators of power in government would so dearly love to be able to forget. They refused to be forgotten. On one day the State Department received 25,000 letters about Biafra and the officials were worried sick. It is to these millions of unnamed Americans who kept yelling when their masters wished they would shut up, along with others in Germany, Holland, Norway, Britain, Switzerland, Sweden, Canada, Denmark and Ireland, that the credit must go for the biggest humanitarian relief operation in modern history.

12. The Peace Conferences

THE eighteen months of the war between July 1967 and December 1968 were punctuated by three peace conferences, all of them abortive. Their failure surprised no one, least of all those on the Biafran side. The prerequisite of any peace conference, if it is to be successful, is that both parties must *ipso facto* be persuaded that the conflict in progress is no longer susceptible to a military solution within their grasp, and that a negotiated solution is not only desirable but in the long run inevitable.

Those on the outside of the conflict, wishing to see the conference successful, must, if their role is to be anything other than a sophistry, do all in their power to bring both parties to that persuasion. For any power outside the conflict to profess a desire to see a peaceful and negotiated solution on the one hand while providing one of the partners with a reason for failing to come to share that view is hypocrisy.

In the case of the three conferences between Nigerians and Biafrans, Britain and America acted diplomatically, and Britain practically, to keep Nigeria locked in her original conviction, which was that a total military solution was feasible and within her grasp, while a negotiated solution was by no means inevitable in the long run. As a result the Nigerians showed within a few hours of each conference opening that the presence of their delegation was solely in order to discuss the terms of the Biafran surrender. Failing acceptance of this basis for negotiation, the war must inevitably go on. Which it did. Part of the responsibility for this must rest with the two Powers, and with the supineness of the African states who allowed themselves to be persuaded into a 'hands-off' policy towards a matter which had already become a slur on the whole continent.

The first conference resulted from some diplomatic activity by the Commonwealth Secretary, Mr Arnold Smith, an amiable Canadian possessed of much goodwill and little astuteness. After contacting Lagos several times in the early spring of 1968 he finally told the Biafrans that the former were willing to talk peace. As this development had been the Biafran desire for the length of the war, they agreed, and an arrangement was made for preliminary talks at Marlborough House, London, to discuss the formula for the conference.

At the time Nigeria was under pressure. Repeated attempts to take the major Biafran city of Port Harcourt from the seaward side had failed, and the commander of the Third Division had promised he could take the city by the end of May.

While the Third Division continued its cumbersome progress across the marshlands towards Port Harcourt, the situation changed alarmingly on the diplomatic side. On 13 April Tanzania recognized Biafra as a sovereign state. This heartened the Biafrans as much as it demoralized the Nigerians, even down to the level of the infantry. It was at this juncture, with Ivory Coast and Gabon thinking of following Tanzania's example, that the Nigerians intimated to Mr Smith that they were willing to talk. On the Biafran side it was immediately expected that 'stall' was a more appropriate expression, for the fall of Port Harcourt would probably swing diplomatic tendencies in Africa the other way again. And so it proved.

The preliminary talks began in London on 2 May with the Biafran Chief Justice Sir Louis Mbanefo leading for one side and Chief Anthony Enahoro heading the Nigerian delegation. The points to be discussed were the venue for the conference, the chairman and international observers (if any) and the agenda. Biafran suspicions that the talks were a stalling manoeuvre were strengthened from the outset. Sir Louis told Mr Smith that he was persuaded the talks could not succeed. For one reason the British had refused to suspend arms shipments to Lagos even while the talks were in progress, a gesture not misinterpreted by the Nigerians; for another because of the composition of the Nigerian delegation.

Apart from Chief Enahoro they included Alhaji Amino Kano, a Northerner but definitely not of the Northern Establishment, and who could not speak for Northern Nigeria, and three Biafran collaborators, Asika the Lagos-nominated Ibo charged with administering the Ibo heartland, Brigadier

George Kurubo, a renegade Rivers man renounced by his own people, who had once been a Brigadier in the Biafran Army before defecting to Lagos when offered the Nigerian Ambassadorship in Moscow, and Mr Ikpeme, a Calabar Efik, who had represented Lagos in Calabar while the reprisals against the Efiks were in progress in late November and December.

It was rather like the South Vietnamese delegation turning up in Paris with three Vietcong defectors as their spokesmen; the reaction of the Vietcong and North Vietnamese delegations can be imagined.

But although he was aware that this group of men could under no circumstances be regarded as competent to speak for the people of Nigeria, Sir Louis carried on. As a venue the Biafrans asked for Dakar, which was refused by Enahoro who offered no alternative site. After three days' delay Sir Louis asked Enahoro to submit a list of places suitable to Lagos, adding that the Nigerian hope for London being chosen was out so long as Britain continued to supply arms to Nigeria.

Enahoro submitted a list of seventeen capitals in the Commonwealth, out of which Sir Louis proposed Kampala, which had been his own second proposal. But he had kept it up his sleeve. Discomfited but cornered, Enahoro agreed to Kampala, capital of Uganda. Biafra wanted a talks chairman and three independent international observers, aware after Aburi of the necessity of witnesses to such meetings. Enahoro wanted neither, and suggested this matter be settled at Kampala. Sir Louis agreed. After further delays, the agenda came to be discussed.

Sir Louis wanted a two-point agenda: agreement on a ceasefire, and more prolonged talks on the terms of the future nature of association between the two parties, that is, the political solution. Enahoro countered with a seven point agenda which amounted to discussing the ways and means of organizing Biafra's total and unconditional surrender. Sir Louis protested that a ceasefire was the main aim of the talks, and that without a ceasefire the talks would in any case be bound to founder. Besides, he pointed out, the original offer brought back by Smith had been for talks on a ceasefire, without preconditions. The two-point agenda was eventually accepted.

The main conference opened in Kampala on Thursday 23 May 1968. By this date the Nigerian advance patrols had entered Port Harcourt and the conference became an academic exercise. It took two days to agree that there should be no chairman, but one observer. The Biafrans asked for President Milton Obote, their host, putting the Nigerians in the position of either ceding the point or snubbing their host. They agreed, and Dr Obote named his Foreign Minister Simon Odaka to sit in. On the Saturday the Nigerians complained that one of their secretaries, Mr Johnson Banjo, was missing, and they could not resume until the errant stenographer was found.

By this time the talks were looking like comic opera, while in Umuahia Colonel Ojukwu angrily described them as 'a grisly farce'. Enahoro could not resume the talks on Sunday morning because of going to church, and made two more excuses for Sunday afternoon and evening. He asked to see President Obote, and then sought private talks with Sir Louis. These led nowhere. On Tuesday he put forward a twelve-point proposal discussing in detail the surrender of Biafra, disarmament of her armed forces, administration of the territory by the Nigerians and the fate of the Biafran leadership. Sir Louis reminded him they were in Kampala to discuss a ceasefire, the first item on the agenda, and the political solution after that. Enahoro stuck to his proposals, which effectively reversed the order of the agenda. By this time the details of the capture of Port Harcourt were through, and hopes for any conversion of Lagos Government thinking to a peace policy were finished.

While the London and Kampala talks had been going on three more countries had recognized Biafra, Ivory Coast on 8 May, Gabon on 14 May and Zambia on 20 May. But the news of Port Harcourt, reaching Kampala between 23 and 27 May, swept away any chance of these recognitions having the effect of changing Nigerian policy.

It was at that time generally believed that the loss of Port Harcourt airport, which fell several days after the city, would cut Biafra off from the outside world and from her arms sup-

244

plies. In that case it was presumed the Biafran resistance could not last longer than a fortnight.

But the recognition, if underrated by the exuberant Nigerians, disturbed the British and American Governments. Intense diplomatic activity behind the scenes was undertaken by both parties to dissuade any other tempted nations to follow suit. Mr Alfred Palmer, U.S. Under-Secretary of State for African Affairs, a former Ambassador to Nigeria, made a tour of West African countries coming out strongly in private and public against Biafra and for Nigeria. The joint action was not without its effect; the rash of recognitions stopped, and three other African countries which had privately informed Colonel Ojukwu that they were considering recognizing Biafra, but whose economies were somewhat dependent on dollar aid, decided to hold their horses.

On Friday 31 May Sir Louis told Dr Obote first and then the press that his country was of the view Nigeria was totally convinced that there was a military solution, that he was wasting his time, and intended to withdraw. To judge from what they wrote most of the international correspondents had already come to the same view.

Disappointed but still hopeful, Sir Louis returned not to Biafra but to London, where after spending seven days with British officials he finally applied to see Mr Harold Wilson. Instead he got a call from an official suggesting he see the Minister of State at the Commonwealth Office, Lord Shepherd. Sir Louis agreed and they met at Mr Arnold Smith's house. Lord Shepherd opened the discussion with a massive solecism.

He made plain that up till that moment he had thought the Biafrans an obscure tribe of a few thousands living somewhere in the bush. Even case-hardened veterans like Sir Morrice James, Permanent Under-Secretary, were reduced to staring uncomfortably out of the window. It was the first appearance of Lord Shepherd on the diplomatic scene.

The two had three meetings, during which Lord Shepherd stressed the British Government's desire to see a ceasefire and more peace talks. He asked if Biafra would accept British mediation. Perplexed that Shepherd had not grasped the situation yet, Sir Louis replied it was his government's view British mediation was out of the question while Britain supplied more arms to Lagos. Press reports at the time indicated those shipments were escalating. The viewpoint appeared to surprise the noble Lord.

However Lord Shepherd produced a plan for a ceasefire, which Sir Louis asked be put in writing, which it was. When viewed beside the Biafran plan, no major points of difference in principle emerged. The ceasefire, the need for an international peace-keeping force, the subsequent negotiations for the political solution – all tallied. Lord Shepherd appeared pleased and said he would go to Lagos to try for agreement there on the basic formula already agreeable to the British and Biafrans. He asked Sir Louis to remain in London till he got back from Lagos, but the latter preferred to fly back to Biafra, promising to return to London if Lord Shepherd's mission proved fruitful. The latter flew off on 13 June, and Sir Louis the next day.

What followed stunned the observers. Lord Shepherd's plan, if it was ever broached in Lagos, was turned down flat. For Lagos the political solution, in the form of the Biafran surrender, must be a pre-condition of a ceasefire. Undaunted, Lord Shepherd flew off to Calabar, which was now in Nigerian hands. Here he behaved in an extraordinary manner for a putative mediator, making speeches and asides that showed he had become within a few days a total devotee of Nigeria and its cause.

Confronted by two *News of the World* correspondents, Mr Noyes Thomas and Mr Graham Stanford, who related to him with passion the sights of human misery and degradation they had witnessed in Nigerian-occupied Ibibio territory, notably at Ikot Ekpene, Lord Shepherd manifested some surprise and shock. But within a short time, again the centre of attraction, he was delightedly waving to the crowd (Biafran agents in the town later reported many were Yoruba soldiers in mufti) and even got himself into a situation where he was observed greeting a choir which had been enjoined to serenade him with the psalm 'The Lord is my Shepherd'. Comparisons with Lord Runciman's mission to Czechoslovakia in 1938 and that ridiculous earl's performance at Petrovice were unavoidable.

In Lagos he made more statements of a strongly pro-Nigeria flavour and departed with any chances of a negotiated settlement through his mediation in shreds and tatters.

The effectiveness of British diplomacy in the issue was at an end, and despite subsequent claims of great victories won in the corridors of Lagos, of concessions, of tentative agreements and lots more besides, the British Government has subsequently been able to affect by not one jot or tittle the chances of peace in Nigeria, except perhaps that her continued policy has moved them even farther away. Yet observers were left wondering why Britain of all countries, with a fund of fine diplomats of the calibre of Sir Humphrey Trevelyan who acted so shrewdly over Aden, felt itself obliged when confronted with a situation of the utmost delicacy like the Nigeria–Biafra war to confine her efforts to using the services of Lord Shepherd who is not a professional diplomat.

The next move came from Africa. Emperor Haile Selassie of Ethiopia had for months headed the six-nation Committee on Nigeria of the Organization of African Unity, a committee which had remained mute since the previous winter when it had been warned off visiting Biafra by General Gowon and had meekly succumbed. After contacting the other five heads of state, those of Liberia, Congo Kinshasa, Cameroon, Ghana and Niger Republic, the Emperor convened a conference in the capital of the last named country, Niamey. The host was the President of Niger, Hamani Diori. The meeting was opened on Monday 15 July, and was attended by General Gowon on the following day. Hardly had he flown home in the afternoon, than the committee issued an invitation to Colonel Ojukwu to come and present his case.

The news reached Biafra first by radio, but the official invitation took longer, being delivered through the offices of President Bongo of Gabon that night. The next day, Wednesday, Colonel Ojukwu held a long-scheduled press conference at Aba, during which he proposed two means of getting food into Biafra to alleviate the human suffering. One was via a sea and river route up the Niger River to the port of Oguta, still firmly in Biafran hands. The other was for the internationalization of Port Harcourt under neutral control, and for a ten-mile-wide corridor from there up to the front-line positions north of the town where the Biafran Red Cross would take over. He was asked at the same conference if he would go to Niamey, but he ruefully shook his head and replied that though he would like to he felt the military situation would not allow it.

Later that evening he had cause to change his mind. A message arrived outlining the availability of speedy transport, and after a hurried meeting with the Executive Council, he and a small group of delegates left shortly after midnight on the morning of 18 July. They landed at Libreville before dawn, were spotted by Mr Bruce Oudes, a knowing Canadian correspondent on African affairs who had got a tip-off, and the story broke. After breakfast with President Bongo, Colonel Ojukwu flew north in the private jet of President Houphouet-Boigny of the Ivory Coast, who had laid the aircraft at his disposal.

Addressing the committee, Colonel Ojukwu brought the full force of his advocacy and personality into play. The proposals for one or two mercy corridors by land or sea were reiterated. The Biafran case was stated. The committee, three of whose members represented governments previously hostile to Biafra, indicated their assent, which somewhat dismayed the Nigerian delegation.

On the Friday Colonel Ojukwu left Niamey and flew to Abidjan to see President Houphouet-Boigny and they had talks in private. On Saturday he returned to Biafra, having left Professor Eni Njoku in Niamey to head the Biafran delegation. On the Sunday he held another press conference, this time a relaxed affair in a garden in Owerri, during which he expressed cautious optimism that the forthcoming peace conference at Addis Ababa, Ethiopia, the most important outcome of his Niamey visit, might produce results.

Meanwhile at Niamey the two delegations discussed relief aid, since the beginning of July a subject of growing concern to the world at large. Various criteria for a relief corridor were agreed upon, but when these criteria came to be applied to the various proposals so far made, it became clear that the Biafran proposal for a river-route was more feasible, cheaper, could carry more bulk in less time, and contained less strategic disadvantage to either side and a greater variety of safeguards against abuse than the Nigerian proposal for a land corridor in the north from Enugu to Awgu. When this became apparent the Nigerian delegation backtracked fast, and it was while explaining why suddenly all the agreed criteria were unacceptable that the Nigerian leader Allison Ayida produced his viewpoint on starving children quoted in the next chapter: 'Starvation is a legitimate weapon of war, and we have every intention of using it on the rebels.'

From that point Nigeria went steadily backwards on the question of the permissibility of relief aid reaching Biafra, and subsequent minor concessions had to be wrung out, not by British Government pressure or advocacy, but by a growing wave of hostile world opinion stemming from the people in the streets. Nevertheless, an agenda for Addis Ababa was agreed, the order this time being reversed to suit the Nigerians: political settlement first, ceasefire second.

The Addis Ababa conference convened on Monday 29 July. Colonel Ojukwu had left Biafra the previous night and flown straight to the Ethiopian capital, this time with a bigger delegation and in a bigger jet, also provided by the President of the Ivory Coast. Predictably General Gowon refused to attend, or was prevented by advisers aware the contrast could hardly be flattering.

The first meeting, to hear the opening addresses by the two delegate leaders, was an open one, with representatives of every African head of state, and some of the heads themselves, the whole diplomatic corps of Addis Ababa, scores of observers and a host of pressmen present. Chief Enahoro sought to have the press excluded, particularly the television cameras. The move failed, and he contented himself with a twelve-minute speech.

Colonel Ojukwu rose. He began by what sounded like a plea for the Biafran people on humanitarian grounds After four paragraphs he revealed that he was quoting direct from the speech Haile Selassie had made to the League of Nations in 1936 over the rape of Abyssinia by the Fascists. The point was not lost. He continued to speak for one hour and ten minutes, describing the history of the Biafran people from its earliest days, the persecution, rejection, separation and subsequent suffering. When he sat down, he became one of the few men in the world to receive from a predominantly diplomatic gathering a standing ovation. In seventy minutes Biafra had ceased to belong to Nigeria, or Africa, or the British or the Commonwealth. It had become a world issue. Colonel Ojukwu at thirty-four had become a world figure, an accolade translated into press terms twenty-four days later when his face featured on the cover of *Time* magazine.

But the Addis Ababa conference got bogged down after the glitter of publicity had died away. Like its predecessors it became lost in a quagmire of delays, stalling, intransigence and ill-will. In all it sat for over five weeks, but world attention, the only thing that might have given it stimulus, swung away to the Russian invasion of Czechoslovakia.

The Nigerian delegation again had an aim in stalling. Ceasefire was no longer a live issue as on 17 August the Nigerian Third Division crossed the Imo River and threatened Aba, the largest city remaining to the Biafrans. By this time the attitude of the American gun-runner Wharton appeared to have changed. South of Aba Biafran soldiers defended on two bullets per man per day, attacked on five. The ammunition planes broke down, turned back, jettisoned their cargoes over the sea. Despite terrible Nigerian casualties Aba fell on 4 September 1968.

Soon all eyes were on the Heads of State conference of the Organization of African Unity scheduled for 14 September in Algiers. From Lagos frantic messages went out to the commander of the Third Division that Owerri must fall by then, or Uli airport. African states friendly to Biafra let her know that in preparation for Algiers British and American diplomacy was working overtime behind the scenes to persuade Africa that Biafra was finished. Considerable pressure, not excluding financial inducements, was repeatedly brought to bear. It worked.

The agenda committee of the Summit Conference, meeting in Algiers as from 8 September, left Nigeria–Biafra off the agenda. The conférence met on 14 September. After an abortive effort to take Uli airport, the Third Division launched an attack towards Owerri on 12 September. Still short of arms and ammunition (the American gun-runner had been fired, but an alternative route had not been completely set up) the Biafrans fought with their usual handful of bullets against a spearhead of British Saladin armoured cars. Owerri fell on 16 September. On the following day the Algiers meeting passed by thirty-two votes to four a hastily-appended resolution calling on the Biafrans to cooperate with the Nigerians in restoring the territorial integrity of the Federation: in other words to surrender.

In doing so the organization that prides itself on being the repository of the conscience of Africa washed its hands of the biggest conscientious issue in the continent. It was the nadir of Biafra's fortunes, military and diplomatic. At that time and for the succeeding weeks it was hard to find a single voice prepared to say Biafra was not completely finished. It took a hundred days before the world realized Biafra was still alive, still fighting.

By that time the situation had changed in most of its aspects. In Biafra there had been a re-surge of morale, of confidence, an increase in the amount of aid coming in or expected. Biafran troops were counter-attacking heavily for the first time in the war. Several nations, by-passing Britain, had declared that they intended actively to seek a means of bringing peace. In Nigeria an agreement with Russia had been signed that opened the door wide to Soviet infiltration of all walks of Nigerian life. In the North there were growing rumbles of discontent from the Emirs, dissatisfied with the government by minority-tribe civil servants who could not fulfil their promises. In the West there had been riots, shootings, mass arrests. In America Mr Nixon had been elected.

The failure of the diplomacy was the failure not so much of the Nigerian front-men whose concern with preserving their own careers was predictable, but the failure of those able to bring pressure to bear to do so. Never once did the Nigerian delegations give an indication that their basic conviction, that a solution through war was feasible and attainable, had been shaken, nor did their supporters once seek to persuade them away from that conviction. The chance was there and it was thrown away.

The year 1969 was no more successful in bringing about a negotiated peace than 1968 had been, and still largely for the reasons already stated. Apart from numerous unofficial contacts between diplomats of various countries with the Biafran and Nigerian régimes, there was only one full-scale peace conference during 1969. It took place at Monrovia, Liberia, on 18 and 19 April, and turned out to be as big a farce as its three predecessors of 1968.

The first step was early in April when the Biafran Government received a letter from President William Tubman of Liberia, inviting Biafra to send a peace delegation to Monrovia to discuss peace without pre-conditions. A delegation was composed of Sir Louis Mbanefo, Mr Christopher Mojekwu, the Home Affairs Commissioner, Chief E. Bassey, the Commissioner for Lands and Survey, Mr Ignatius Kogbara, Biafran Special Representative in London, and two officials. They left Biafra on 14 April and arrived in the Liberian capital on the 16th, where they were well and courteously received.

The talks were to take the form of an attempt by the Organization of African Unity Committee of Six to bring about an agreement for peace between the two sides. The six O.A.U. mediators were President Tubman, the host, Emperor Haile Selassie of Ethiopia, President Hamani Diori of the Niger Republic, President Ahmadu Ahidjo of Cameroun, President Joseph Mobutu of the Congo Kinshasa, and for Ghana Mr Charles Harley, Deputy Chairman of the National Liberation Council. The Nigerian delegation was led by the Commissioner of Works, Mr Femi Okunu, and Mr Allison Ayida.

The keynote speech was made by President Tubman, who was followed by the Emperor of Ethiopia. After that the conference went into session. It was the evening of 18 April.

The conduct of the conference was unusual. First the 'panel' called the Nigerian delegation and sat in closed session with them for forty-five minutes. Then the Biafran delegation was sent for. Sir Louis addressed the Six with a prepared statement, and intimated he had certain proposals he wished to make regarding a ceasefire. These he duly made. One of the Six asked if Biafra was prepared to accept a supervisory force between

252

the two combatants. He replied in the affirmative providing that there was a truce or ceasefire to supervise.

Later in the evening he was asked to meet two of the Six in closed session. The two turned out to be President Tubman and President Diori. They asked Sir Louis to state the Biafran position, which he did. He explained that Biafra's primordial concern was her security, and that of her citizens' lives and property. The Biafrans were prepared to discuss 'One Nigeria', but wanted to know precisely what that phrase meant first.

Both listening presidents appeared to show understanding of Biafra's position. President Diori proposed a formula as a basis for peace talks, which included internal and external security for Biafra with an international presence on the spot to guarantee this. The proposal was made verbally in French, and Sir Louis asked for the proposal in writing in English. President Diori agreed and asked the Secretary General of the O.A.U., Mr Diallo Telli, who was sitting by his side, to withdraw and prepare what he had said on paper and in English.

Mr Telli went out, but within five minutes was back, speaking in rapid French to the Niger President. Hamani Diori repeated to him two or three times the French phrase 'securité interne et externe'. Telli left again, but seemingly did not carry out the Niger President's bidding, for ten minutes later he was back to say the two O.A.U. presidents were wanted by their colleagues. They were away for forty minutes, and on their return President Diori produced a document in English which spoke only about discussion of peace on the basis of One Nigeria. There was no mention in it of Biafra's internal and external security.

Sir Louis replied again that he was prepared to discuss One Nigeria but not on the prior condition of his acceptance of a still unexplained One Nigeria. He said he would accept the document if they would delete the three words that implied Biafran prior acceptance of One Nigeria as a pre-condition. With that the night's parley broke up.

The following morning President Tubman asked Sir Louis if he had seen the *New York Times*. The Biafran chief delegate said he had not. Tubman said it contained a report from

Lagos to the effect that General Gowon had said if the Biafrans would accept the principle of One Nigeria, everything else would be negotiable. President Tubman thought this might provide the answer. Sir Louis replied that he knew the reporter in question, that Gowon's statement was nothing new, and that he could hardly envisage major diplomatic initiatives being launched on the basis of a newspaper report.

The day passed with more fruitless talk, the two delegations still separated, and Mr Telli using his offices as a messenger between the conference rooms. Sir Louis finished the day with the distinct impression that Mr Telli was a strong supporter of the Federal cause. That evening both delegations were finally summoned to a plenary meeting of the Six. Emperor Haile Selassie handed over to Sir Louis a document in English, already cleared with the Nigerian delegation, which he begged the Biafrans to accept.

To Sir Louis's concern it was even worse than the document produced by Mr Telli the previous evening. It made quite clear that any future talks would be on the basis of the Biafran prior acceptance of the phrase One Nigeria, and that alone. Sir Louis rejected the document and explained yet again why. He had been invited to Monrovia, he said, to discuss peace without pre-conditions. He and his colleagues had found that the same Nigerian pre-conditions existed as before, and were apparently supported by the putative peacemakers.

At a later press conference the Biafran Chief Justice expressed his view that the O.A.U. had neither the will nor the ability to make a breakthrough in the present deadlock. No serious attempt was made later to bring the two sides together.

On 31 July, however, the Pope made a four-day visit to Kampala, Uganda, to canonize posthumously a number of Ugandan martyrs to Christianity. It was hoped that the Pontiff's presence in the continent might provide the occasion for renewed efforts for peace. General Ojukwu proposed a truce for the duration of the Pontiff's stay on African soil, but this was rejected from Lagos. Although Pope Paul held separate meetings with representatives of both Biafran and Nigerian régimes while at Kampala, nothing came of the meetings.

Towards the end of 1969 observers were again entertaining

faint hopes that with the lassitude towards the war present in both armies, and civilian disturbances mounting in Western Nigeria against the war, the New Year might bring some fresh and more meaningful initiative for peace.

Two things, however, militated against such a breakthrough. One was the lack of a mediator who combined the respect of both sides for his strength and the acceptance of both sides for his integrity. The other factor was the Federal régime's determination to cling to its original belief that a total and decisive solution to the Nigeria–Biafra problem could be achieved by continuing hostilities. In this its mainstay and support remained the British Government, whose ministerial statements in the closing months of 1969 made clear to observers that the official view in London remained that of sustaining and supporting Lagos for a complete victory over Biafra, to be attained if necessary by starvation in the absence of a victory by force of arms.

13. The Question of Genocide

GENOCIDE is an ugly word. It is the name given to the biggest crime man is capable of. What constitutes genocide in the modern world? What degree of violence offered towards a people justifies the use of the word? What degree of intent is necessary to justify the description? After years of study, some of the world's best legal brains assisted in drawing up the definition written into the United Nations Convention on Genocide adopted on 9 December 1948. Article Two specifies:

> In the present Convention genocide means any of the following acts committed with intent to destroy, in whole or in part, a national, ethnical, racial or religious group, as such:
>   a. Killing of members of the group;
>   b. Causing serious bodily or mental harm to members of the group;
>   c. Deliberately inflicting on the group conditions of life calculated to bring about its physical destruction in whole or in part;
>   d. Imposing measures intended to prevent births within the group;
>   e. Forcibly transferring children of the group to another group.

Article One states that genocide, whether committed in time of peace *or war*, is a crime under international law, and Article Four makes plain that constitutional rulers, public officials or private individuals may be held responsible.

Obviously, in time of war men get killed, and as they belong to a national, ethnical, racial or religious group this paragraph is perhaps too wide to be practicable. It is the use of the phrase 'with intent' that separates the usual casualties inflicted during war from the crime of genocide. The killing party must be shown to have had, or to have developed, intent to destroy, and the victims must be a national, ethnical, racial or religious group.

There are two other points about genocide that have become habitually accepted in law: one is that intent on behalf

256

of the Head of State of the inflicting party need not be proved. An individual general can direct his troops to commit genocide, and the Supreme Commander is held responsible if he cannot control his armed forces. Secondly, the deliberate decimation of the leadership cadres of a racial group, calculated to leave that group without the cream of its educated manpower, can constitute genocide even if the majority of the population is left alive as a helpless mass of semi-literate peasantry. The society may then be presumed to have been emasculated as a group.

The Biafran charges against the Nigerian Government and armed forces rest on their behaviour in five fields: the pogroms of the North, the West and Lagos in 1966; the behaviour of the Nigerian Army towards the civilian population they encountered during the course of the war; the behaviour of the Nigerian Air Force in selection of its targets; the selective killings in various captured areas of chiefs, leaders, administrators, teachers, technicians; and the allegedly deliberate imposition of famine, which was predicted in advance by foreign experts and which during 1968 carried away an estimated 500,000 children between the ages of one and ten years.

About the massacres of 1966 enough has been said. It is generally admitted that the size and scope of the killings gave them 'genocidal proportions' and there exists ample evidence to show that they were planned, directed and organized by men who knew what they were about; that no inquiry was ever instituted by the central government, nor any punishments, compensations or restitutions exacted, which may in law be taken to presume condonement.

The widespread killing of Biafran civilians and of Ibo inhabitants of the Midwest State is equally incontrovertible. After the withdrawal of the Biafran forces from the Midwest in late September 1967 after a six-week occupation, a series of massacres started against Ibo residents. The explanation that it was difficult to differentiate between soldiers and civilians cannot hold water, for as has been explained the armed forces were withdrawn in almost every case before the Second Division of the Federal Army came within firing range. These massacres were witnessed by numerous foreign residents of the various

Midwestern towns concerned, and widely reported in the international press. Some examples will suffice:

New York Review, 21 December 1967: 'In some areas outside the East which were temporarily held by Biafran forces, as at Benin and the Midwestern Region, Ibos were killed by local people with at least the acquiescence of the Federal forces. About 1,000 Ibo civilians perished at Benin in this way.'

Washington Morning Post, 27 September 1967: 'But after the Federal takeover of Benin Northern troops killed about 500 Ibo civilians in Benin after a house-to-house search.'

London *Observer*, 21 January 1968: 'The greatest single massacre occurred in the Ibo town of Asaba where 700 Ibo males were lined up and shot.'

New York Times 10 January 1968: 'The code [Gowon's Code of Conduct] has all but vanished except from Federal propaganda. In clearing the Midwest State of Biafra forces Federal troops were reported to have killed, or stood by while mobs killed, more than 5,000 Ibos in Benin, Warri, Sapele, Agbor and Asaba.'

Asaba, referred to above in the *Observer*'s report, lies on the western bank of the River Niger, and was a wholly Ibo township. Here the massacre occurred after the Biafran troops had crossed the bridge back into Biafra. Later Monsignor Georges Rocheau, sent down on a fact-finding mission by His Holiness the Pope, visited both Biafra and Nigeria. At Asaba, by then in Nigerian hands, he talked with priests who had been there at the time. On 5 April 1968 he was interviewed by the French evening newspaper *Le Monde,* to whom he said: 'There has been genocide, for example on the occasion of the 1966 massacres. ... Two areas have suffered badly [from the fighting]. Firstly the region between the towns of Benin and Asaba where only widows and orphans remain, Federal troops having for unknown reasons massacred all the men.'

According to eyewitnesses of that massacre the Nigerian commander ordered the execution of every Ibo male over the age of ten years.

The Midwest killings had nothing to do with the prosecution of the Nigerian war effort, and for the Biafrans they represented what was widely interpreted as a taste of things to come.

The fact that the overwhelming majority of the Ibo population of the Midwest stayed behind after the withdrawal of the
Biafran troops under Banjo's orders indicated that they were
confident neither they nor their fellow-Ibos from across the
Niger had done anything to warrant reprisals. If they had
taken advantage of the armed Biafran presence to inflict suffering on their non-Ibo fellow Regionals, they would have fled
helter-skelter with the retreating Biafrans.

Later, at Calabar in Biafra, more massacres took place. Mr
Alfred Friendly reported in the *New York Times* of 18
January: 'Recently in Calabar, a port in the secessionist region
captured by Federal forces, soldiers were said to have shot at
least 1,000 and perhaps 2,000 Ibos, most of them civilians. ...
Some killings have included the members of the Efik tribe, one
of the minority groups whose allegiance, Lagos maintains, is
to federalism, not secession.'

These reports merely skim the surface of what happened. I
have deliberately confined them to foreign correspondents, but
the testimony of the refugees now runs to thousands of transcript pages. Since the autumn of 1967 the Ibo population of
the Midwest has been drastically reduced. Calabar marked the
last town in which the Ibos stayed behind, believing they
would come to no harm. Since then all have fled, almost without exception, some few returning timorously months later.
But all the towns of Biafra now in Nigerian hands, even the
very first to be captured, have remained ghost towns in comparison to their former selves.

One could go on to quote many newspaper reporters'
accounts of what they saw or were told, but it would serve no
purpose. In forays behind the Nigerian lines with the Biafran
Commandos I have seen the hinterland of desolated villages,
wrecked farms, sacked and looted buildings, burned habita-
tions and by the wayside the executed bodies of peasants
foolish enough or slow enough to be caught in the open by the
Federal Army. The killings of civilians have not been confined to Ibo land; the Efiks, Calabars, Ibibios and Ogonis have
suffered heavily as the reports of their emissaries to Colonel
Ojukwu describe. Nor was the killing process a flash in the
pan, the first reaction of an army in the grip of the heady

elation of victory or the vengeful gloom of defeat. The practice has been too standardized, too methodical for that.

It continued after the troops of the Third Nigerian Division of Colonel 'Shoot anything that moves' Adekunle crossed the Imo and started to move through the river basin. At Akwa, accompanying Biafran reconnoitre scouts, I saw the corpses of the occupants of the refugee camp at that place, about 500 wasted forms who in life had already fled once from further south. They had been caught by surprise and exterminated. South of Aba, in the villages of Ubute and Ozata, moving with a small group of shock troops, we came across two more examples of communities caught before they had time to flee. The menfolk had had their hands tied before shooting; to judge from appearances the women had been subjected to appalling mutilations either before or after death. The bullet-broken bodies of the children lay scattered like dolls in the long grass.

At Onitsha in March 1968, I was present with the Biafran 29th Battalion when it pursued the Second Division spearhead down the main road into the city. There 300 members of the Apostolic Church who had stayed behind while others fled to pray for deliverance, had been dragged from the church and executed. One woman survived by feigning death; she was later treated by another Englishman, Dr Ian Hyde.

In war there are bound to be innocent victims, occasional excesses, here and there a wanton brutality conducted by soldiers of a low level. But seldom has such a remarkable pattern of bestiality been established over such a wide territory by such diverse army units.

The evidence of the Biafran survivors continues to mount, and to be discounted outside Biafra as forming part of the all-purpose evil, the Ojukwu propaganda machine. A group of foreign observers, put together at the suggestion of the British Government, has accompanied Federal soldiers in various sectors and produced a report saying that they had found no evidence of genocide. The initiative was a white-washing operation and it worked, for their findings were widely published and have since become the basis for several complacent statements in the British House of Commons.

But the mission was also irrelevant. Failure to find evidence of a crime, when one is being conducted to the site by the alleged perpetrators, is a practice hardly likely to convince even a police cadet. In terms of evidence in court, when a man is accused of murder it is no use for the defence to produce witnesses who said they did not see anything, particularly when they were guided by the accused. The evidence of those who did see something is still being largely disregarded by a world that would prefer not to know.

The testimony of the Ibos, Efiks, Calabars who saw and survived cannot be so easily discounted. The evidence that hanged the Nazi war criminals did not come from a few observers accompanying the Wehrmacht; ninety per cent of it came from the survivors among the victims, Jews, Russians, Poles and so forth. Their evidence was not discounted at Nuremberg as Jewish propaganda. Of the remainder about nine per cent came from Nazi documentation, and barely one per cent from confession from the German side.

In a country like the Midwest and Biafra, quite thickly populated with Europeans engaged on various projects, it would be unlikely for much to occur without their being aware of it. It may then be wondered why, apart from some doctors and priests, few have spoken out. The answer would appear to be the same as in all cases where witnesses are hard to come by, a situation often experienced by police officers in all countries. There is a strong tendency not to want to get involved, least of all when such involvement might bring sanctions. Broadly speaking the European population of both areas falls into three categories.

Businessmen are often prepared to say over a private drink what they saw in their own area, but then hastily add 'Not for publication, old boy. My firm would be right in the mire if that ever got out.' Most businessmen in both areas are employed by firms with other interests elsewhere in Nigeria, and fear reprisals if their employees start leaping into print with tales injurious to the Federal Army or Government.

Civil servants are usually very much in touch with events in their area of service, and little escapes them. They too tend to shyness, for being men of few means they count on their pension in retirement and would hardly welcome expulsion in mid-career and termination of contract for a few denunciatory paragraphs in a newspaper.

The third group is the priesthood. These men probably know their parishes as well as anyone, and even after they have fled their parishioners still seek them out to report what has been going on in the newly overrun area. Inside Biafra they are outspoken in private, but seldom prepared to go into print. A priest's instinct is to protect, but then he has to think: what would happen to the flock if he were expelled? What is his real duty, to his parishioners or to the dead? By speaking out he may endanger his own Order by provoking their expulsion, and he possibly comes to the view that he serves the parishioners best by staying on, even though he knows this means he must keep silent.

Even those in Biafra have in their possession letters from other priests continuing a precarious missionary existence under Nigerian Army control, asking them not to be too outspoken. The priesthood, and notably the Catholics, forms a nation-wide network of men who know what goes on. The attitude of the Vatican has surprised and pained the Nigerian Government, which has apparently failed to realize that the Vatican now possesses the best-documented history of what has gone on in the captured areas of Biafra.

It may be as well at this point to touch on the counter-allegations. As various areas of the minority people fell to the Nigerian Army individuals were found to come forward and claim the Ibos had conducted atrocious pogroms against the minorities. These accounts caused some flutter in the Western world, and caused delight to the extremist supporters of the Federal Government. There were tales of several hundreds being lined up and forced to dig their own graves before being shot down, rather the pattern established by the Nazi *Einsatzgruppen* in Eastern Europe. The Roman Catholic (European) parish priests of some of the parishes where these massacres were alleged to have taken place are now in unoccupied Biafra. One of them told me: 'I was there at the time. It would have been absolutely impossible for such a thing to have happened without the whole parish being aware. I would certainly have known about it. To my certain knowledge nothing of the kind occurred.'

A senior priest in the same Order added: 'In this country nothing can happen without the parish priests being aware very quickly. We go out to hear confessions in the remotest areas daily, and hear all the local gossip as well. Not only the parish priest but the whole Order would soon know every detail. If anything like that happened I would be up to see Colonel Ojukwu like a shot.'

It is difficult to see why two middle-aged Irishmen should bother to cover up such a thing, had it occurred, unless they feared reprisals; and those who know Colonel Ojukwu and Biafra are aware that the Biafran leader is not a tyrant who takes reprisals on priests, and that any attempt to penalize the Roman Catholic Church in Biafra would be the end of the despot.

Of the selective killing of community leaders, the evidence to date stems exclusively from Biafran witnesses. These report executions of teachers, chiefs and elders in a wide variety of locations, but predominantly in the minority areas, partly because these form the bulk of the overrun territories, partly because the Ibos no longer stay behind expecting mercy. Reports of this emasculation of the civilian communities have come from Ikot Ekpene, Uyo and Annang (Ibibio areas); Degema, Brass and Bonny (Rivers areas; the Kings of Bonny, Opobo and Kalabari are now refugees with Colonel Ojukwu); Calabar (Efik and Calabar areas); Ugep, Itigide and Ndiba (Ekoi, Igbo and South Ogoja areas); and Ogoni and Ikwerra, in the areas inhabited by people of the same name. In many cases these executions were alleged to have been public, the villagers being herded into the main square to watch. Significantly most of the refugees from the minority areas slipped through the lines into unoccupied Biafra *after* several days or weeks of occupation.

The air war is bound to remain controversial. Civilians have always been casualties of bombers and fighters used against ground targets. From Guernica onwards the world has come to accept punitive raids by bombers on civilian targets. In the Second World War bombers of the two opposing sides pulverized each others' cities by day and night, though these cities were usually industrial centres as well. Bombing cannot be accurate to the nearest street, even when Pathfinders are used. But the behaviour of the Nigerian Air Force, equipped by Russia and often manned by Egyptians, has managed to throw overboard any few rules remaining. Very rarely have aircraft been used in conjunction with ground forces, or against Biafran ground forces. When they have, the bombers have preferred to fly very high out of small-arms range and drop their bombs at random, which means that they usually fall in the bush. Similarly, defended targets in Biafra of a strategic nature – bridges, rail yards, barracks – have seldom been hit, or seriously aimed at, for they usually have a Bofors or a heavy machine gun in the vicinity.

Most of the air war has been conducted against the civilian population. Far too many times have the bombers and fighters roared in low to plump their cargoes right in among packed groups of people for any excuse of accident or mistake to be viable. Highly prized targets appear to be hospitals (or anything marked with a Red Cross like the Relief Airport at Obilagu), close-packed townships, churches on Sunday and market places at midday. The latter are known in Africa to be largely the preserve of women, with their babies strapped to their back. At Awgu market on 17 February 1968 a bomber managed to kill 103 people in less than a minute, and at Aguleri market in October 510 people lost their lives. The actual number of different raids is now countless, but the death toll has topped 5,000 with several thousand more maimed for life.

Repeated pledges by General Gowon that only military targets were being selected has shown that he has no more control over his air force than over his army. Despite periodic pauses in intensity, the raids have continued throughout the war. As this book was being written in Umuahia, MiG 17s and Ilyushin 28s paid six visits in Christmas week in breach of a truce offered by General Gowon, killing over 100 people and wounding another 300 with bombs, rockets and cannon fire.

But whether the use of aircraft and high explosives against helpless civilians, to extract casualties, cram the hospitals and inspire stark terror, can be counted as forming a part of genocide is something that legal brains are still arguing.

'Some may say it [mass starvation] is a legitimate aspect of war', stated the Nigerian Commissioner for Information, Chief Anthony Enahoro, usually regarded as the top-ranking politician in Lagos, at a press conference in New York in July 1968. At the peace talks at Niamey, Republic of Niger, two weeks later the head of the Nigerian delegation refused to consider further the feasibility criteria for a food corridor with the words, 'Starvation is a legitimate weapon of war, and we have every intention of using it against the rebels.'

These two assertions, coming from some of the highest men in the land, may be taken as representing Nigerian Government policy. The latter one forms a statement of philosophy and of intent. What happened afterwards cannot be explained away as a regretted but inevitable by-product of war. What happened was that despite the presence close to Biafra of adequate food supplies, the availability of means of transport to bring them to the needy people, five hundred thousand children, pregnant women and nursing mothers died of malnutrition, starvation and their attendant diseases. These have been described in another chapter.

But there was no doubt of the technical ease of bringing food to those areas well behind the Federal advance points. The international agencies made available ships, planes, helicopters, trucks, vans and technical personnel. Within a short while the latter were complaining bitterly of the inability to work in face of the Nigerian Army attitude. A ship was commandeered, a plane requisitioned, relief foods off-loaded to make way for arms, men and ammunition. Sacks of relief foods ended up in Federal Army trenches or sold on the black market. Some of the relief personnel resigned in protest.

Ironically, in the last week of October 1968, when the airlift by night to the Biafran-held areas, still technically illegal, had at last brought the malnutrition problem under control and had saved, for a while at least, the remaining child population, Mr Harold Wilson admitted that the difficulty of getting relief supplies by road even to the Nigerian-held areas was due to Federal obstructionism.

As regards the rest of the phrases in the United Nations Convention on Genocide, one refers to a 'national ethnical, racial or religious group'. There can be little doubt that the Biafrans, either regarded as a nation, or as separate racial groups, come under this heading. With regard to the 'intent' mentioned in Article Two the position is more complex. Intent is not easy to prove, since it concerns what happens inside the human mind, unless it is written down on paper.

Nevertheless, intent may be shown by default of any other plausible explanation. A judge may tell a prisoner about to be sentenced: 'I cannot believe that you were unaware ... there is ample evidence to suggest that you knew what the consequence of your actions would be ... despite repeated warnings you did nothing to prevent or arrest ... etc.' Such phrases are often used in courts, and intent in law may be proved in such a way. It is no defence for an arsonist, having wilfully set fire to a structure and having killed those inside, to claim he did not mean the occupants any harm. This is somewhat the case of General Gowon, who claims he has nothing against the Ibos, either the leadership or the rank and file, yet who has apparently been able to take no meaningful steps to prevent a course of conduct by his armed forces that has shocked much of the world.

Occasionally, however, evidence of intent does come to light, not from individual firebrands but from senior politicians, officials or government-controlled propaganda media on the Federal side.

Dr Conor Cruise O'Brien, 21 December 1967: 'Unfortunately this [Gowon's] enlightenment at the top level does not penetrate very deep: a Lagos police officer was quoted last month as saying that "the Ibos must be considerably reduced in number".'*

George T. Orick in *The World Game of Patronization*: 'Biafran civilians are aware that upwards of 10,000 non-combatants have recently been slaughtered by Federal troops in the combat areas: they experience little confusion therefore when they compare federal broadcasts from Lagos promising safety to the somewhat more realistic broadcasts from

* *New York Review*

Radio Kaduna in the Northern capital, discussing the final solution of the Ibo problem and dolefully listing names of Ibo leaders marked for execution. If the truculent Biafrans show no signs of giving up it is because they at least know they are literally fighting for their lives.'

The theme-song of Radio Kaduna, government-controlled, is a chant in Hausa, which when translated reads: 'Let us go and crush them. We will pillage their property, rape their women-folk, kill off their menfolk and leave them uselessly weeping. We will complete the pogrom of 1966.'

Edmund C. Schwarzenbach, *Swiss Review of Africa*, February 1968:

A conversation with one of the most impressive ministers provided significant insight into the political aims of the Federal Government. . . . The Minister discussed the question of the reintegration of the Ibos in the future state. . . . The War aim, and solution properly speaking of the entire problem, he said, was 'to discriminate against the Ibos in the future in their own interest'. Such discrimination would include above all the detachment of those oil-rich territories in the Eastern Region which were not inhabited by Ibos at the start of the colonial period (1900), on the lines of the projected twelve-state plan. In addition the Ibos' freedom of movement would be restricted, to prevent their renewed penetration into other parts of the country. . . . Leaving any access to the sea to the Ibos, the Minister declared, was quite out of the question.

Reference to 'the *projected* twelve-state plan' indicates that this interview must have taken place before the East broke away from Nigeria. Since the start of the war a senior Canadian correspondent told the author: 'I was having a talk to Enahoro the other week and asked him whether Ibos would ever be allowed to move around Nigeria after the war. He replied, "Well the army boys tell me they do not intend to let more than 50,000 Ibos live outside the East Central State ever again".'

An interesting comparison may be made with the Germans' treatment of the Jews during the Hitler period. The Nazi plan for the Jews of Germany was not a single-stage plan but three-fold: first, discriminatory legislation, denial of job opportunity and civic rights, accompanied by wide-scale harassment, pillage and brutalization; second, the uprooting of the ghettoes and all Jewish communities and the transference of those communities for resettlement in the eastern areas of the Reich; third, the Final Solution through forced labour for those capable, and extinction for those not.

In the Biafran experience the first two stages of this kind of plan have already been completed, the eastern resettlement area being in effect the homeland of the Ibos and their associated fellow-Easterners. The difference from their point of view is that they then imported arms and started to defend themselves, to the manifest outrage of their persecutors. But even the most sober and disinterested foreigners inside Biafra have long since lost any doubts about their chances of survival as a distinct ethnic group under Nigerian military occupation.

It would be presumptuous for a writer to arrogate to himself the functions either of an inquiry or of a court. The evidence quoted above, indeed all the evidence available, is still only the tip of the iceberg. Before any complete picture could emerge it would need the efforts of a professional team of fact-finders in the framework of an independent tribunal of inquiry; this mass of documentation would then have to be studied by a panel of legal experts before a worthwhile judgement could be pronounced, and even that might only establish the existence of a *prima facie* case.

But even at this stage certain points can be made with absolute certainty. First, whatever has been done, the Nigerian Military Government and its Head, the Supreme Commander, cannot escape responsibility in law.

Second, *prima facie* cases already exist against individual Nigerian Army commanders for instigation of, or responsibility for, distinct and numerous cases of mass murder over and above the requirements of war.

Third, the charge of genocide is too big for the world authority vested by the signatories of the Convention in the United Nations to be required to wait for a *post factum* inquiry, or none at all. If the Convention is to rate as anything other than a useless piece of paper, a reasonable suspicion of genocide must suffice to bring investigation. This reasonable suspicion has been established months ago; and the United Nations is in breach of its own sworn word, embodied in Article One, so long as it continues to refuse to investigate.

Lastly, whatever the Nigerians have done, the British Government of Mr Harold Wilson has voluntarily made itself a total accomplice. As of December 1968 there can be no further question of neutrality, or active neutrality, or ignorance, or a helping hand to a friendly government. The involvement is absolute.

The *Spectator* magazine, not normally given to wild hyperbole, said in an editorial on 31 May 1968: 'For the first time in our history Britain has become an active accomplice in the deliberate slaughter of hundreds of thousands of men, women and children, whose only crime is that of belonging to a proscribed nation: in short, an accomplice in genocide. And the British people, together with a supine Opposition, have averted their eyes and let the Government pursue its shameful way without hindrance.'

14. The Role of the Press

By and large the press of the world has given fair coverage to the Nigeria–Biafra war. It took some time for the story, in journalistic terms, to get off the ground.

At the start of the war there was a brisk flurry of activity, with journalists hopping into Biafra for a week. But at that time it was regarded as a one-week story. Besides, African wars are not easy subjects to 'sell' to a Foreign Editor, for these men know that by and large their readership has become satiated with violence in Africa. The overwhelming majority of the world's mass communication media are dominated by the white races; they produce the bulk of the newspapers, the magazines, the radio shows and the television programmes, and they are largely produced for the consumption of the white races.

The press in Asia and Southern America is still parochial, relying for the comparatively little foreign news it carries on the international news agencies. In Africa newspapers as Europe and North America know them hardly exist, and dissemination of news depends largely on radio, with the big transmitters of Britain, America, Egypt, Russia and China dominating the ether, and each of them producing their own Government's version of events.

In the spring of 1968 the war was still to most people in Western Europe and North America a forgotten affair. There had been some articles, very few assessments in depth, and the occasional running of the story for a week in a single publication, a sure sign that the newspaper had a correspondent there for a week and did not wish to waste his fare. But the story had certainly not hit any national consciousness nor stirred any popular reaction outside Nigeria.

Then in mid-April four reporters from Britain's top newspapers came on a visit. They were William Norris of *The Times*, Walter Partington of the *Daily Express*, Richard Hall of the *Guardian* and Norman Kirkham of the *Daily Telegraph*.

They were present at the bombing of Aba by an Ilyushin 28 of the Nigerian Air Force, a raid in which over eighty people were killed and nearly a hundred wounded. The sudden, savage violence in the hot and peaceful lunch hour, the sight of an ordinary street turned into a charnel house within seconds, the prospect of shattered bodies, affected the reporters deeply. All four wrote extremely graphic accounts of the raid, and two left no doubt through the tone of their dispatches what they thought about it. In Britain these accounts were responsible for the first wave of public consciousness.

In mid-May an article by myself appeared in the *Sunday Times* and caused some small interest. It was the result of ten weeks spent with the Biafran Army, often the Commando units who probed behind the Nigerian lines on hit-and-run raids, and the experience had given me the opportunity of seeing at first hand what kind of treatment was being accorded to the Ibo civilian population by the Nigerian Army. The description of what I had seen was subsequently and bitterly denied in Lagos by General Gowon, but has since become only one of several eye-witness accounts by foreigners of what goes on.

The big break came in June. In that month the Commonwealth correspondent of the *Sun*, Mr Michael Leapman, was touring Biafra, and the first signs of starvation and malnutrition among the child population were becoming noticeable in large numbers. Mr Leapman spotted the story, and the *Sun* blew it across several pages for quite a few days in succession. Biafra was on the headlines at last. The rest followed. Suddenly Biafrans lobbying for support in London for the Biafran cause were being listened to. More insistent questions were raised in Parliament, not only about the possibility of relief aid to Biafra, but about British arms shipments to Nigeria.

The wind blew a gale. Journalists started flocking into Biafra, partly to report the plight of the children, partly to scout for other 'angles'. What they wrote shook the conscience of the world. Western Europe became interested about two months after Britain. Protests were raised by most major opinion-forming organs from the Iron Curtain to Galway Bay.

By the autumn thousands of Britons and Europeans were working for Biafra, a country they had never seen and whose people they had in all probability never met. They collected money, demonstrated, paraded, performed hunger strikes, paid for full-page newspaper advertisements, toured, lectured, appealed, lobbied parliamentarians, called for action.

The British Government was forced to answer more and more hostile questions, twice to debate the issue before the House, issue denials, promises, explanations, donations. Despite assurances first that in the event of another major attack or more 'unnecessary deaths' in Biafra Britain would be forced to 'more than reconsider her policy' and later more assurances that it was really in the Biafrans' interest to be the victims of a 'quick kill' policy after all, Parliament remained unconvinced.

Elsewhere Czechoslovakia, Belgium, Holland announced they would send no more arms to Nigeria, and cancelled existing orders. Italy slipped out quietly without a word. America said it had never sent any at all (which was not true) and France and West Germany said neither had they (which was true).

In Basle, Switzerland, anti-British-Government protests forced cancellation of British Week, in Downing Street windows were broken in protest. Still the press coverage flowed in, and still it was lapped up. Looking back it is odd to think that despite the efforts of the Biafran publicists and lobbyists on their own behalf, this translation of the Biafra affair from a forgotten bush-war into an international issue was basically caused by a typewriter and a strip of celluloid, used many times over. It showed the enormous power of the press to influence opinion when its organs are used in concert. The coverage was largely fair. Some was over-effusive, some inaccurate on questions of fact, some slushy, some vituperative. Mostly the reporters stated the facts and let the editorial writers pound out the superlatives, which is the way it should be.

The radio networks covering Africa, mostly owned by governments and dedicated to the task of putting forward that government's viewpoint, tended to orient their news coverage towards Nigeria. Strangely, the 'experts' on West Africa turned out to be wrong; the best coverage came from the ordinary reporters who described what they saw. Most of the senior veterans of the West African circuit plumped in the beginning

272

for a quick victory for Lagos, and were hopelessly misled. Reading back through the files of these correspondents' dispatches can be amusing. In the early days the few, very few, who suggested the Nigeria–Biafra war was likely to be long and bloody, finally inconclusive and fraught with the most dangerous perspectives of international intervention and subsequent escalation, were loftily regarded as naïve fools or in love with the Ibos.

In subsequent months the West Africa veterans sometimes came near to gymnastics trying to explain away Nigeria's failure to achieve a quick victory. Animus began to enter into the dispatches of the most sober writers, inevitably aimed against the presumptuous people who continued to resist the fate decided for them.

The reason is that senior correspondents of the Establishment-oriented press tend to be too closely allied to the powers-that-be, from whom they get most of their information on the old-boy network. The Establishment of London and Lagos backed Nigeria heavily. The correspondents, circulating between Commonwealth Office and the right parties on one side, and between Chief Anthony Enahoro's office and the cocktail bar of the Ikoyi Hotel further south, tended to believe what they were told rather than do a bit of leg-work in order to find out for themselves what was happening. Being constitutionally creatures of the *status quo* and not wishing to vacate their cosy existence on the fringes of the diplomatic galaxy, these gentlemen have given themselves to reports so one-sided as to suggest they sought rather self-justification than a realistic appraisal of the situation. Two notable exceptions are Mr Walter Schwarz, the West Africa correspondent of the *Guardian*, and Mr Michael Leapman, Commonwealth correspondent of the *Sun*. Both correspondents showed that it was possible to write balanced and objective reports, and although neither came out wholly on one side or the other, both said things which, although no doubt their sincerely held view, could not have been pleasing to both sides simultaneously. Ironically, in view of the partisanship of others, both these correspondents are still *persona grata* in both countries.

One organ that has put up a remarkable record has been the

External Service of the B.B.C., notably the Africa Service. Throughout the whole war listeners and some contributors to the Africa Service were astounded by the number and variety of the misrepresentations of the situation presented by these programmes. Editorial-type comments were liberally mixed with what were supposed to be factual news reports from Lagos, and within a short time most, white and black, living in Biafra and tuning in nightly to the B.B.C., became convinced there existed a strong pro-Nigerian bias in the coverage of the story.

Graphic accounts were related of things alleged to have happened in the heart of Biafra which had not happened, towns were described as having fallen to Nigerian troops long before the Nigerian soldiers actually entered them, and some far-fetched speculation was attempted apparently on the basis of little more than gossip or the over-optimistic hopes of the Nigerian authorities. For example, there was speculation after Colonel Ojukwu (a devout Roman Catholic) had gone into a week's Lenten retreat in 1968 that he had fled the country or been the victim of a coup; and on another occasion an alleged popular demonstration in Umuahia in favour of Chou En-lai was described. Neither had a vestige of truth.

The overall effect appeared to indicate to an uninformed listener that the Nigerian case was wholly right, while that of Biafra was wholly wrong, and more misleadingly for a listener elsewhere, that Biafra was permanently on the verge of imminent collapse Throughout this time the reportage of the External Services fell consistently far short of the standard of journalism expected of the B.B.C. and which indeed the B.B.C. claims to be its own.

The effect was to cause widespread disgust among the Biafrans and equal disenchantment among the British living in the country. For the former at any rate the editorial attitude at Bush House towards Biafra was explained by the fact that the annual budget of the B.B.C. External Services was not met by the British licence-payer, but by an ex gratia payment from the Treasury through the Foreign and Commonwealth Office.

One notable exception was the file of dispatches sent from Nigeria by Mr John Osman, the B.B.C. Commonwealth Correspondent; a skilled and conscientious reporter, Mr Osman gave objective and balanced reports, and was subsequently expelled from Port Harcourt by Colonel Adekunle in a remarkable display of the latter's violent temperament.

Of all British newspapers, indeed probably of all newspapers anywhere, the most consistent, fullest, fairest and most balanced coverage of both sides of the war came from *The Times* of London. It was the only newspaper that managed to keep up a consistently high reporting standard of factual news wherever and whenever it was possible to get it, and supplemented this by commissioning some very full and informative feature articles. One of *The Times* staff reporters, Mr Michael Wolfers, seriously showed up by contrast the inability of some of his colleagues to file dispatches out of Lagos without becoming the mouthpiece of any Nigerian or British High Commission spokesman with something crass to say. Confining his reports to factual information about what was happening under his eyes in the Nigerian capital, and eschewing speculative guesses as to what might be happening four hundred miles away, Mr Wolfers turned in a file of copy during his sojourns in Lagos during 1969 that was *in toto* an object lesson of how foreign reporting should be done.

During February and March there was another of the periodic upsurges of parliamentary, public and press interest in Biafra from London, and this time the direct cause was a series of reports and articles commissioned by *The Times* from Mr Winston Churchill.

Armed with this commission, Mr Churchill went first to Nigeria, then Biafra. After returning from both visits, he told the author that after visiting Nigeria he had returned to London wholly convinced that Biafran civilian centres were not being bombed, and that the famine victim figures were being grossly exaggerated. These convictions, he said, had been primarily induced by assurances from the British High Commissioner in Lagos, Sir David Hunt, and the British Military Attaché, Colonel Bob Scott. A few days in Biafra came as a jolt.

Mr Churchill, after witnessing the full extent of the famine caused by the blockade and seeing at first hand the terror tactics of the Nigerian Air Force, came to the view that nobody in official British circles had much idea of what was really going on. He was the first journalist to have the courage to say (in his first news report) that he was 'ashamed' to admit that he had fallen for the misinformation fed to him in Lagos.

Although there was nothing substantially new in Mr Churchill's articles – the starvation and the terror bombing had been going on unremarked or disbelieved for months past – they nevertheless sparked off a spate of articles, letters and public concern in London, and gave added credence to the view hitherto held by a small handful of journalists in beleaguered isolation that warfare was not a feasible solution to the Nigeria–Biafra problem. They also triggered the first counter-attack from Fleet Street to the smearing by the British High Commission in Lagos and the Foreign and Commonwealth Office in London of individual journalists who had reported from Biafra what they saw and the conclusions they, and others from different countries, had reached.

In the wake of Mr Churchill's articles, the same tactics were tried against him. In an editorial on 12 March, *The Times* complained of a 'niggling campaign' against Mr Churchill and concluded by condemning 'an attempt to cover over the facts of starvation, bombing and death by resorting to personalities'.

The following day, in a letter to the editor of *The Times*, Mr Michael Leapman related how a Commonwealth Office official had taken the liberty of ringing the assistant editor of a provincial newspaper to warn him against believing what Mr Leapman, after three visits to Biafra and one to Nigeria, had got to say. Mr Leapman further intimated that he had heard the suggestion which had been put about that he had taken money from Ojukwu to write as he did.

After this point, character assassination of pressmen seems to have been dropped by the officials previously responsible, and the British Press was left alone to continue reporting the Nigeria–Biafra story as it saw fit – which by and large was factually.

On 28 June *The Times* published an editorial entitled 'A Policy of Famine'. It was a strongly worded, closely argued but unreserved condemnation of the whole British Government policy towards the conflict. It went unanswered by any Government spokesman, and was indeed unanswerable. By the end of the year every major British newspaper with the sole exception of the *Daily Telegraph* had come out against British Government policy of sending arms to Lagos and thus assisting in the continuance of the war. But the weight of British Press opinion had no more effect on Mr Wilson and Mr Stewart than had the weight of Church opinion or the Labour Party Conference. Nevertheless it can fairly be said that whatever odium may have accrued to Britain through this policy, it was not the fault of the British Press, which had done its job, and all else it could do.

15. Conclusion

AT long last the scale and the outlook of the Nigeria–Biafra war have aroused the disquiet not only of the humanitarian groups but of powerful governments who belatedly see the dangerous perspective ahead. They are coming to realize that the situation contains elements of peril not only for Biafra, but just as much for Nigeria and for the rest of West Africa.

Now the talk is all of a search for a peaceful solution, and those who in their time did their utmost to support the idea of a purely military solution are unconvincingly protesting they have been in favour of a negotiated peace all along.

So far as Biafra is concerned, their position is not complex. They have said since the start of the war that they viewed the problem as being a human one, and consequently not susceptible to a military solution but to a political one. Their offers of a ceasefire have been unrelenting, possibly because they have largely been on the receiving end of the war. But whatever their motivations, they are in favour of an end to hostilities and a negotiated peace.

It is in the mood of the Biafran people that one comes up against the main difficulty on that side. They left Nigeria possessed by three sentiments: a feeling of rejection, of mistrust of the Lagos Government, and of fear of extermination. To this has now been added a fourth emotion, more intractable, more profound, and consequently more dangerous. It is the emotion of hate, pure, keen and vengeful.

Some of those now talking of peace, notably in Whitehall, seem under the impression that nothing has changed over the previous eighteen months. On the contrary, everything has changed. It is not a question of the growth of the 'army of penpushers' into a redoubtable military machine, nor the recent access to larger quantities of arms. It is the mood of the people who have watched their entire country shattered and despoiled, their children waste away and die, their young men cut down in thousands. Concessions one could have had at the

278

start of the war, had a firm stand been taken and mediation offered, are no longer available. It is possible that in midsummer 1967 one could have saved at least a Confederation of Nigeria with enough economic cooperation between the consenting partners to have offered all the economic advantages of the Federation. It is doubtful if this is now possible, at least in the short term. It is useless for men in charcoal-grey suits to talk of the benefits of a single, united, harmonious Nigeria, and to express mystification that the Biafrans do not want it. Too much blood has flowed, too much misery has been caused and felt, too many lives have been thrown uselessly away, too many tears have been shed and too much bitterness engendered.

No one in Biafra now has any illusions about the behaviour of Biafrans if they ever again came to have military sway over any of their present persecutors. Nor does anyone believe that a Nigerian will be able to walk unarmed and unescorted among Biafrans for a very long time to come. The only possible consequence of a militarily enforced 'unity' now would be total military occupation apparently in perpetuity, with its own inevitable outcome of revolt and reprisal, bloodshed, flight into the bush, and famine. The incompatibility of the two peoples is now complete.

The voice of the Biafran people is the Consultative Assembly and the Advisory Council of Chiefs and Elders, and they are unanimous on that. Colonel Ojukwu cannot go against their wishes – or on that topic their demands – no matter how much vituperation is thrown at him for intransigence, obduracy and stubbornness.

On the Nigerian side the position is more complex. For the Nigerian people have no voice. Their newspapers, radios and television stations are either Government-controlled or edited by men who know that outspoken criticism of Government policy is not the best way to health. Dissenting intellectuals like Pete Enahoro and Tais Solarin are either in exile or, like Wole Soyinka, in prison. The Chiefs, usually the best spokesmen of grass roots opinion, are not consulted.

It is interesting to speculate what would happen if General Gowon were obliged to follow the counsels on his war policy of a Consultative Assembly which included strong representation of the farming community, the academic community, the trade unions, the commercial interests and the womenfolk; for all these groups are presently showing increasing restiveness at the war policy. But General Gowon can dispense with consultation; recently he felt able to use firearms against demonstrating cocoa farmers at Ibadan.

The result is that the people of Nigeria are muted, and their real views cannot be known to the peacemakers, who must be content to talk with a small régime of men who are more interested in their personal careers than in the welfare of their people. The recent open invitation to the Russians to play a big role in the future of Nigeria indicates that this may well be so.

So far this régime has maintained its position that a military solution is not only feasible but imminent, and that a return to normality would be just around the corner after final victory. But the record of Enugu, captured over a year ago and still a smashed ghost town, does not give credence to this theory. On this position the Nigerian Government has stipulated that any termination of hostilities must be dependent on a number of conditions to be agreed by the Biafrans as a basis for negotiations. But the conditions themselves are so sweeping that they represent in fact all the points that the negotiations would have to be about, i.e., future nature of Biafra, terms of association with Nigeria, permissibility of a potential for self-defence, etc.

The terms of their ceasefire are effectively the total and unconditional surrender of Biafra, to be delivered bound hand and foot into the hands of the Nigerian Government to do with as it wishes. It must be presumed that the Gowon régime has not abandoned its policy of believing a totally military solution can offer the final answer.

But in the face of this the danger grows. None of the policies hitherto adopted by the governments of the Western world has been successful in promoting peace. Most governments appear to have accepted British requests for a 'hands off' attitude, reminders that the Commonwealth is habitually Britain's sphere of influence, and assurances that it would all soon be over.

The British Government's policies are in ruins; all the explanations and the justifications have been proved to have been based on false premisses. Even the assurance that these policies would bring to Britain great influence with the Nigerian Government, which could then be used to bring peace, has fallen on its face. Far from having gained in influence Britain, once a powerful adviser in Nigerian affairs, has been shown to be now quite impotent. Ironically the war hawks whom British arms made powerful now feel strong enough to seek new friends while the Wilson Government, unwilling to admit this, has the courage neither to do something positive itself nor to withdraw its caveat to the other major Powers.

Only the Russians have gained from the present mess, being now in a position to move ever more strongly into Nigerian life. It cannot be presumed that they have the interests of the people of Nigeria at heart, for a continuation of the war is in their interest, putting the Nigerian régime ever more deeply in their debt.

In essence, nothing is likely to break the present stalemate until the Nigerian Government has been brought to the view that its own personal interests and those of an undelayed ceasefire have become synonymous. This conversion of view can only be brought about by the sort of diplomatic initiatives that alone the Big Powers can make effective.

In the event of the desire for an early ceasefire becoming mutual, it would probably be necessary for the ceasefire to be supervised by a peace-keeping force, either a body of international composition, or preferably that of a Protecting Power agreeable to both sides. On this basis alone can humanitarian aid of sufficient scope to even dent the problem have a chance of success.

Once a return to normality had begun, protracted negotiations would be necessary to find a formula capable of bringing lasting peace. At present it appears impossible that any such formula could have a chance of success that is not based on the will of the people. This presumes some form of a plebiscite, at least among the minority groups, whose destiny has become one of the key features in the present war.

Few seriously think that a Biafran state confined to the Iboland now called by Nigeria the East Central State, cut off from the sea and surrounded on all sides by Nigeria, could have much chance of viability. And the Nigerians have made one of the pillars of their case the supposition that the non-Ibo groups, inhabiting what Nigeria now calls the Southeastern and the Rivers States, were dragged into partition against their will by the Ibos. The issue having become so crucial, it must be tested.

So far it is General Gowon alone who declines to put the matter to the test, though it should be admitted that circumstances at present are hardly apposite to the holding of a plebiscite. Yet if one were held now, the advantage would lie with Nigeria, for her army occupies the area, and millions of minority people supporting Biafra have become refugees in the unoccupied zone. All the same, conditions for a plebiscite would have to be created before it could be conducted in a manner other than one calculated to bring protests from one side or the other. Ideally such an operation would be supervised by the Protecting Power, with Federal Army garrisons quarantined in their barracks for the hours necessary.

Whatever the permutations and combinations, they are at the moment purely speculative and must remain so pending a ceasefire. But it is no speculation to assert that the way things stand at the end of 1968 the degree of incompatibility between the peoples east and west of the Niger has become so absolute that for the immediate future at least some form of partition will be necessary to prevent further bloodshed.

The longer this is delayed the worse becomes the situation, the deeper the hate, the more intractable the tempers and the darker the portents.

Epilogue

THE preceding chapter, the Conclusion, alone dates back to January 1969. All the other chapters in the second part have been brought up to December of that year.

It was allowed to stand because even in December, with no end to the war, the points it made remained valid in part. By late December the Nigerians' fourth 'final assault' had made little headway. Lord Carrington, the British Conservative (Opposition) spokesman on defence matters, had spent a week inside Biafra, the first Conservative factfinder to be sent there in two and a half years. On his return on 22 December he said no end to the war was in sight.

Then in the second week of January 1970 Biafra collapsed. It came quite suddenly. A unit on the southern front, exhausted beyond caring and out of ammunition, quietly stripped off its uniforms and faded into the bush. There was no response from the Nigerians, and the rot could have been stopped by a competent commander. The Biafran officer concerned was incompetent and failed to notice the gap in his line. Units on either side of the missing men took fright and followed suit. Soon a gaping hole ran along the entire defence line from Aba city to Okpuala Bridge.

A Nigerian armoured-car patrol, probing north, met no opposition and rolled forward. Within a day the front was breached. The remainder of the Twelfth Division ran off into the bush. Between Okpuala Bridge and the River Niger to the west, the Fourteenth Division was outflanked. Here too, exhausted troops faded into the bush. Colonel Obasanjo's Third Nigerian Division rolled forward into the heart of the Biafran enclave, heading for the airstrip at Uli.

There was no opposition; men who had not eaten for weeks had no strength left to go on fighting.

In a last cabinet meeting on 10 January, General Ojukwu (he had been elevated in rank during 1969) listened to his advisers for the last time. Their advice was almost unanimous. To stay and die would be futile; to stay and be hunted through the bush would bring further misery to the entire population.

That evening, after darkness had fallen, he drove to Uli as the Nigerian guns rumbled on the southern front. With a small group of colleagues he boarded the Biafran Super Constellation, the Grey Ghost, and flew out into a lonely exile. Brigadier-General Effiong, taking over as acting head of state, sought surrender terms twenty-four hours later. The long struggle was over.

East of the Niger the former Eastern Region, Biafra, was split into three states in accordance with Gowon's decree of May 1967 which had triggered the secession in the first place. In the south the Rivers State was formed under a military governor called Diete-Spiff. In the extreme south-east the South-Eastern state came into being under a certain Colonel Essuene. The Ibos, the predominant force of Biafra, were allocated their postage-stamp-sized East Central State. Here Ibo Ukpabi Asika stayed on as governor, to run an administration that became a byword for corruption. He was finally removed and required to hold himself available for public inquiry in August 1975.

Following the war, Nigeria seemed to prosper, at least on the surface. The oil revenues increased year by year, then in 1973 the world price for oil doubled, and doubled again as the Organization of Petroleum Exporting Countries (O.P.E.C.) struck at the oil-consuming West. The fact of the Nigerian régime's oil production, and the vast amounts it was spending in Britain, made it very popular in London. The British Press, eternally following London's Establishment thinking, almost elevated Yakubu Gowon to sainthood. Not a contrary word could be said or written about him or Nigeria.

Towards the end of Gowon's reign the mismanagement finally came home to roost. The Port of Lagos was jammed with over 400 ships unable to discharge; the telephones ceased to function; the public services were in chaos; the roads had not been maintained in years; communications became almost im~ ssible. Eventually even the British Press began to publish
~ critical of the Gowon régime.

9 July 1975, nine years to the day after he came to

power over Ironsi's body, Gowon was attending the summit of the Organization of African Unity in Kampala, Uganda, when he was toppled. The man who took over, with a pledge to eradicate corruption, was General Murtala Mohammed, who sacked all twelve State governors and appointed new ones. Gowon went into exile in Britain and soon joined the pupils at Warwick University, announcing that he intended to study politics because he felt it was time to learn something about them.

In early February 1976 a junior officer walked calmly up to General Mohammed's car as it sat in a traffic jam and emptied two magazines of sub-machine carbine ammunition into it. Mohammed died instantly. The attempted coup aborted, nevertheless, and General Obasanjo, formerly commander in succession to Adekunle of the Nigerian Third Division in the war, took over.

Meanwhile General Emeka Ojukwu remained in exile in the Ivory Coast. He had arrived there with precisely one 100-dollar bill in his possession.

He was perhaps the only man who ever held power in West Africa who came out without a private nest-egg of money embezzled from public funds. Not only had he not milked the till, he had spent every penny of his private fortune on his people. He was penniless.

Starting from scratch and with a small loan from a friend, he began a transport company with two lorries. By late 1975 he had built up a chain of companies in transport, construction, gravel quarrying and distribution franchises ...

Throughout these six years, endless delegations of Ibos and others slipped across the borders from Nigeria to visit him. In East Central State the Gowon régime had tried desperately to find an Ibo who could break the charisma exercised by Ojukwu over his own people. They failed dismally. In fact the opposite occurred. Compared with the public corruption they saw all around them, the integrity of the Ojukwu régime began to appear more and more remarkable to the Nigerians, and not merely the Ibos. Delegations of Yoruba and Tiv began to ask to come and visit him in exile.

It took years for the Ivorians, and the French civil servants and businessmen who abound in the Ivory Coast, to come to believe that he had not a secret hoard of Biafran public money stashed away in Switzerland. When they did believe it, some thought it admirable, others madness.

Back in the heart of Iboland, some of the cream of the educated Ibos, perhaps 10,000 in all, went to work for the Nigerians. For the masses of the Ibos, farmers and small traders, artisans and clerks, the road was hard. But they got by, working all hours of the day and half the night, building up a sort of life again. They silently rejected the Lagos Ibos proposed to them by the Gowon government. They scrawled on walls and the sides of lorries the words, 'Akareja ['he who has gone away'] must return'.

Whether he will return to Nigeria one day is in the lap of the gods. But the Ibos have a saying, 'No human condition in this world is permanent.' Perhaps it will be realized that the events of the past should be set aside, the more so now that Gowon has gone from Lagos, and that Ojukwu should be allowed to return to Nigeria.

He was and is a remarkable man. He could have had everything, if he bowed the knee to Gowon. Instead he lost many things, his fortune, his homeland, his passport. But he never lost the loyalty of his people; and he never lost any man's respect. Even his worst enemies respect him. Knowing him, he would say that he had still had the best of the bargain.

Ireland, February 1976